How to Rule the World
Yes We Can

By Paul E. Troutman, Jr.

How to Rule the World: Yes We Can was printed in the United States of America. Copyright © 2016 by Paul E. Troutman, Jr. Permission is hereby given to anyone to copy any and all parts of this book.

ISBN 978-0692654996

This book is dedicated to the God we are, the ruler of the Universe.

Contents

Forward 1
Introduction 7
Principles 15
   Principle 1 – We are all One. 15
   Principle 2 – We are Divine. 25
   Principle 3 – We each have free will to live our lives as we please. 31
   Principle 4 – Our purpose is to produce the greatest imaginable life we can conceive. 35
   Principle 5 – Everything in this Universe is an illusion. 36
   Principle 6 – Love. 39
   Principle 7 – There is no right or wrong. 44
   Principle 8 – Everyone acts appropriately based on their model of how the world works. 46
   Principle 9 – When helping anyone, work for their Independence. 47
   Principle 10 – We are each the Savior of the world. 48
   Principle 11 – It is appropriate to solve all disputes peacefully. 49
   Principle 12 – True wealth is spiritual, not material. 51
   Principle 13 – We create everything in this world 52
   Principle 14 – Everything in the Universe is for our benefit. 58
   Principle 15 – Truth is what works to get us to where we want to go. 62
   Principle 16 – Life is all about change. 64
   Principle 17 – Forgiveness will transform the world. 69
   Principle 18 – Transparency and honesty go hand in hand to demonstrate our unity. 72
   Principle 19 – Tolerance is the way to peace by accepting and respecting everyone regardless of their beliefs or who or what they are. 79
World Peace 83
   Solutions 83
   Inner Peace 94
   Violence 97
   Three Steps 100

- Final Thoughts 101
Sex, Marriage, and Nudity 105
- Sex 107
- Marriage 112
- Nudity.. 118
- Summary... 119
Religion and Spirituality... 123
- The Problem with Religion 125
- Civil and Moral Codes... 132
- Deciding on the Truth.. 132
- God's Requirements 146
- God... 149
- Changing Our Beliefs 152
- Things to Consider as Truth 157
Science, Technology, Health, and Medicine 165
- Science and Technology.. 166
- Health and Medicine.. 182
- Final Thoughts 189
Politics... 191
- Governments and Beliefs... 191
- Governments and Peace 194
- The Application of Government 200
- Summery.. 203
Law and the Penal System 207
- Morals 208
- Functionality.. 210
- The Ten Commandments 212
- The Will of God and Death 216
- The Basis of Law 219
- Ending Crime 223
- Dealing with Offences Against the Law 225
- Other Thoughts 229
Economics and World Hunger 233
- The Problem 234
- Solutions.. 239
- Summary.. 255
Education and Raising Our Young 257
- Critical Thinking.. 259

Creativity and Core Concepts 261
Teaching Principles 265
Teachers 269
Summary 275
Earth and the Environment 277
The Problem 278
The System 281
Solutions 288
Summery 293
The Future and Implementation 297
Changing Our Beliefs 298
Unity 301
Solutions 306
World Peace 334
Sex, Marriage, and Nudity 336
Religion and Spirituality 341
Science, Technology, Health, and Medicine 344
Politics 349
Law and the Penal System 354
Economics and World Hunger 359
Education and Raising Our Youth 364
Earth and the Environment 370
The Next 50 Years 373
The Following 400 Years 374
The Following 1000 Years 376
The Far Future 377
How to Rule Now 377
References 381
Acknowledgments 385

Forward

William Shakespeare said in *Hamlet*, "There are more things in heaven and earth, Horatio, than are dreamt of in your philosophy." And so it is. God is unlimited, and there are more things going on in life than we imagine.

This is a spiritual book about spiritual writings. Spirituality is life as it is, and everything is a part of life. Therefore, spiritual writings are about life. The spiritual writings referenced in this book include some texts referred to as "sacred." Not all spiritual writings are connected to a religion, but sacred texts are.

The texts excerpted in this book compare life as it has been lived with life as it could be lived. Based on these comparisons, there is much room to evolve.

This is not a comprehensive survey of all spiritual writings. Being a slow reader, there are far too many for me to read in a lifetime. My own personal biases have influenced my selections of the included writings and these are my interpretations of the writings. This is my truth. Your truth could be different. I could be wrong about my interpretations, conclusions, and future speculations. These are my ideas about what the spiritual writings say and not necessarily what God may have intended. Organized religions would do well to realize their doctrines fall into this same category, as usually many people over an extended period studied each religion's scriptures and then produced the doctrines. They may or may not be the truth of

God. No book, including this one, is worthy of trust unless it has been closely examined and compared with our inner knowing of what is true.

Most people accept what they are told to be true, but for our own benefit, we should decide for ourselves what is true and correct. This is a God-given right and should not be abdicated to anyone else. Ultimately, we are each responsible for what we believe, and what we believe will affect how we experience life. Be wise and carefully choose what to believe as truth.

This book is based on the nineteen principles listed in the chapter titled "Principles." There is a lot of repetition of ideas because many spiritual writers from different times and places had similar ideas. The repetition of ideas adds credence to the validity of the ideas.

How helpful are spiritual writings? Can they be trusted to provide good advice on how to rule the world? All spiritual writings were true and perfect for the writer when they were written, but that was then, and this is now. Everything changes over time, and what was written then may not be true and perfect now. Wouldn't it be prudent to sift through all this material and decide for ourselves what is true and perfect? In the end, we ultimately decide what is true and correct whether we critically examine each truth for ourselves, or just accept someone's word. These beliefs then affect our experience of life, and how we live our lives.

Our ability to understand truth is dependent on the context we have to understand it. We are evolving beings and our ability to understand anything improves over time. We are better able to understand truth today than yesterday, or a year ago, or two thousand years ago. There are truths we will understand in the future, but if we were told them today, we would only hear gibberish. We don't have the context to understand them now. It is inevitable we will be exposed to new truths as time goes by. If we close our minds to new ideas, we may miss a great idea that would change everything as we know it for the better. History has shown us the progression of new ideas changing the world over time. History has also shown we tend to oppose new ideas, even though it is in our best interest to keep an open mind and test new ideas as they appear. If they work, we should implement them, and if they don't, we should discard them.

Truth can be confusing. There is the truth of this World, and there is the truth of the Absolute World. The Absolute World is the Spirit World or Real World. The truths of these two Worlds can become confused. The truth of this world is not the same as the truth of the Absolute World. As an example, change is true of this world, and truth changes over time. For example, at one time the Earth was thought to be the center of the Universe and was thought to be flat. Neither is thought to be true today. There is no change in the Absolute World, truth or otherwise, because It is eternal.

Everything in this world is an illusion. Birth is an illusion because we existed before we were born. Death is an illusion because we are eternal and never die. Time is an illusion because everything is happening concurrently. Distance is an illusion because we are everywhere. Our name and body are illusions because we are not our body and have used many names over many lifetimes. Everything associated with a body is an illusion. We are not a male or female, but both. We are not a particular race, but all races. We are not members of a particular religion but are members of all religions, and no religion. We are not a resident of a single country but are residents of all countries. What we are is all-inclusive. One of the greatest illusions is we are all separate individuals with no connections to each other. This is an illusion because we are all part of One Thing. Everything in our world is made up by us.

We are eternal, but everything born in time, is not, and will eventually end in time.

Because everything in this world is an illusion, it's easy for us to change our beliefs, our political structures, our school systems, our economic architectures, our social systems, our legal organization, our religious institutions, and our military arrangements. It's easy to change all of these if we choose to change and if we can agree on the change. Agreeing is the hard part.

This book is about making changes as suggested in spiritual writings. We don't have a good track record implementing spiritual recommendations from sacred texts. We still kill each other even when told not to. But I'm optimistic. I believe someday we will have peace on Earth, and we will love our fellow man and woman, as ourselves. When we see the benefit of loving others as ourselves, we will make the changes necessary to produce a Heaven here on Earth.

The central theme of this book is there is only One Organism, and we are all a part of it. This one thought, "We are All One," is the basis for all my speculations for how we might live differently. These are not the definitive solutions to all our problems, but just a starting point for us as humans to start the process of changing how we live in important ways. I'm sure other solutions are available for us.

This Organism that includes everything, has been called many things including The All, The Universal Energy, The Unmoved Mover, Isis, Zeus, Goddess, Master of Life, Yahweh, Lord, Jehovah, Allah, Brahma, Krishna, The Source, I Am, Supreme Being, You, and Me. I will call this Organism God. Of course, this Organism is unlike anything we are familiar with in this world and cannot be fully described. When you see the word "God" in this book, think of unlimited, all-inclusive, formless energy, and lacking description. If we all act as if we were a part of this Organism, life as we know it would change dramatically for the better. An example of this in action would be to do to others as we would like them to do to us if it's agreeable to the others. This works well if we love ourselves. It sounds counter-intuitive to help others. After all, if we give something to someone we're minus the gift. So what good did it do us? If we believe we are all part of One Organism, when we give something to someone we are giving it to ourselves. The gift is for us. When we send some love into the life of someone, we will notice we feel better. This is just the down payment with other rewards to follow.

There are no shoulds or should nots in God's World. This means we have free will and the freedom to do anything we wish without any fear of being punished or condemned by God. But to create the world we want, there are certain things we should do or not do to reach our goals. If we want world peace we should live our lives as if we are all One Thing, and we should not live our lives as if we are all separate individuals. In general, we now live our lives as if we are all separate individuals fighting each other for what we consider to be scarce resources. Notice we don't have world peace. Whatever we do will have consequences. Any shoulds or should nots in this book are in the context of not being requirements, but as suggested ways to get to a goal.

This book is not about salvation because we don't need to be saved from sin as is commonly understood. But then again, it is about salvation because it offers solutions to the living hell we have created for ourselves. An actual Hell doesn't exist, but we have become quite good at creating hellish conditions here on Earth. We created our hell and we can uncreate it. We are that powerful. All we have to do, is decide on the heaven we want.

Introduction

Imagine a world of peace where love is shared to the fullest, and each person's cup is full of joy.

Imagine a world of wealth where each person can live a life of abundance.

Imagine a world where everyone is free to live their life fully, if it doesn't infringe on the freedom of others.

Imagine a world where service to our fellow humans is the highest service and rewarded with the highest recognition.

Imagine a world where words like war, poverty, lack, pollution, crime, ignorance, and illness do not exist.

This is not the world we live in. Our world is upside down because we base our beliefs on fallacies. This is not a condemnation. It is a statement of fact. If our beliefs were based on the truth, we would have a totally different experience.

In 2004, the High Level Threat Panel of the United Nations identified the ten most important threats facing the world today. We can look at them as the most important problems needing solutions. They are in order of importance:

1. Poverty
2. Infectious Disease
3. Environmental Degradation
4. Inter-State Conflict
5. Civil War
6. Genocide
7. Other Atrocities
8. Weapons of Mass Destruction

9. Terrorism
10. Transnational Crime

How do we deal with these problems? What is the best way to rule the world? Is the way we live now the best we can do? At each stage of our evolution, we think we have eclipsed past civilizations and we have evolved to the pinnacle, the best there is, but eventually, we discovered newer and better ways to live. There is nothing "wrong" with the way we live now, we are just at this stage in evolution, and we will evolve to higher states of being.

Can we have world peace, universal health care, universal education, enough food, clothing, and shelter for all, tolerance for all, and unlimited opportunities for all? Do we even consider these possibilities?

Our potentials, both individually and collectively, are unlimited. The only things preventing us from reaching fantastic possibilities are our beliefs.

We create our experience of reality in this world by what we imagine the reality to be, by what we believe it can be, and by what we say it is. What we create may or may not serve us well. Does our concoction of reality work, can it adapt, and is it sustainable?

The reality we are creating is based on the purpose of this world. We create relationships with people, places, and things to experience who we are, and to experience our attributes such as love, compassion, and appreciation. We use these people, places, and things to experience success in overcoming obstacles and challenges. When the people, places, and things have served their purposes, we can change the cast of characters, locations, and props in our play and move onto new adventures. In our creation of our reality, there is only One Thing morphing into all these people, places, and things, including us.

Life is not what it appears to be. There is more going on than we imagine. Life can be likened to a computer game, a game to end all games. We start our game at birth, and the game ends at death. But we may play many games. We existed before birth, and we will live forever after death. We each have a fantastic interface device called our body, but we are not our bodies. Our bodies allow us to control the game and receive feedback from the game. Like all games, we cannot be hurt by the game although our avatars, our bodies, can be injured, become sick, and die. We write the script for the game, and we decide what we want to experience. We each have our own customized version of the game. We can and do sabotage our lives by producing different crises, such as failing health, physical and mental disabilities, lack of a job, or a relationship problem. This is all to experience the thrill of overcoming the challenge. In our simulation, some of us play the parts of "bad" guys, doing something we are not. Someone must act the part of an antagonist to produce the drama we desire. We get to choose the type of game we play, along with our sex, sexual orientation, our parents, life goals, life challenges, people we meet, and whom we marry, before we are born, when we write the script for our lives. Although we write the script for the computer game before the game starts (birth), we can change the script as the game progresses. When our avatar dies, we may choose to start another game, or stay in the Real World (not the physical world) and move onto other things. Death is also reversible, so we may choose to go back to the game and rewrite the script, so we don't die and continue on with life.

We are beings with unlimited potential, and so our experiences can be unlimited. We can experience the whole spectrum of emotions from fear and anger to gratitude and love. We are here to experience everything, and it takes many lives to accomplish this. We may start one experience in one lifetime, but finally, complete it in another. There is only success. We may choose to be a doctor, lawyer, or Indian chief, and we will need a supporting cast for the full experience. A doctor needs patients, a lawyer needs clients, and an Indian chief needs tribe members. We all need a context for our experience, and we all supply it for each other.

The Earth is a special place in the Universe. Life is different here than anywhere else. We are all volunteers to facilitate the evolution of the Universe. We all have lived lives at other places in the Universe and have come here to accelerate our own evolution. Our memories are erased before we are born, so we remember none of this. We don't remember who we are or why we are here. Beings in the rest of the Universe know everything.

The world is working perfectly just the way we constructed it to create the outcomes we are receiving. It may not be a perfect utopia, but it is perfect to provide us with the experiences we wish to experience. We may choose to live totally different. Every area of human endeavor can be changed. The areas of economics, politics, education, how we treat the environment, religion, and social interactions are all areas we can change. Peace on Earth has eluded us so far, but it is attainable. Our cities have turned into battlegrounds, not just in other parts of the world, but here in the United States. The world we have created is not taking us where we say we want to go. It's time we moved forward and created another, more advanced world. Life could be so different. We could move through life experiencing ecstasy. I don't mean high on drugs. I mean high on life.

Based on the beliefs of each person, no one does anything inappropriately. What a person believes, guides this person to do what he or she does. The murderer in their own mind was justified in killing the person. The thief in their own mind was justified in stealing. The nation in the minds of the leaders was justified in going to war. To change these behaviors, we must change our beliefs.

Because of our beliefs, we have made life more difficult than necessary. As we believe, so is our experience. Our beliefs condition us to expect certain outcomes limiting how we experience life. We limit our lifespans by thinking humans can only live to be seventy to a hundred years of age. We think we are restricted to enjoying a certain level of wealth when we can live life abundantly, not just some, but all of us can. Half the population is treated as inferior when in fact women are equal to men. Most religions think of themselves as the one true religion and all others are inferior, when in fact each has something to offer. Violence is thought of as appropriate for countries and people to use to settle differences when it is not. People think there are not enough food and other goods to go around when there are plenty of resources for all. And the list could go on.

The United States has long thought itself to be a nation "under God, indivisible, with liberty and justice for all." This kind of thinking has led it to become the most prosperous nation in the world. The phrase "under God, indivisible," means just that, a Universal Truth of Unity and Oneness. Anything built on unity is difficult to destroy. But this unity has been weakened.

Religious freedom has disintegrated into religious righteousness very close to religious intolerance.

Individual freedom has diminished as individual responsibility has disappeared. Individual responsibility now means "every man for himself," imagining the early American rugged individualism. The early American vision was based on the concept of Brotherly Love, and as America progressed, every person accepted individual responsibility for the survival of all. At one time, America would help the hungry, the needy, the weary and the homeless, and would share its abundance with everyone.

Then America became greedier as Americans wanted more and more even if it meant others had less and less. As greed increased, compassion for those with less decreased. Those with less were told America was the Land of Opportunity and if those with less lacked, it was their own fault, even though those doing the telling knew opportunity in America was limited, institutionally, to the "haves." Unfortunately, the "haves" do not include many minorities.

America's generosity increasingly became an extension of her vested interests. America helped others when it served America's richest elite, and its military machine. America changed from the ideal of Brotherly Love and now looked out for its own self-interest.

We must be responsible for ourselves, but we must also be responsible for us as a whole.

The old way of living is collapsing in on itself. We think we are separate individuals and make decisions based on this belief when we are all One. These decisions don't work because they're based on a fallacy. The collapse of our present-day institutions will allow for changes to be made. A new and different system can arise from the ashes of the old. We're living in a critical period of time. We have the technology to destroy ourselves from off the face of the earth in many different ways, and we are just now maturing spiritually to be able to take effective steps to prevent it. The time is right to grow up spiritually. If we don't, we could create the worst hell imaginable here on Earth.

We all have a golden opportunity to change our lives to produce a Heaven here on Earth. This is a very challenging time to live. We were born into this time of our own choosing. Let's seize the moment and do monumental things. Let future generations rise up and call us blessed for giving them a wonderful world.

Each person should be allowed to participate fully in any society at the highest degree possible regardless of any aspect of the person, including race, gender, nationality, religious affiliation, or sexual orientation.

The suggestions listed in this book are just suggestions, and possibilities, of how we can live our lives if we choose. They are based on spiritual writings, wisdom from the past, to help guide us into the future. We have an infinite number of possibilities available for us to choose from. We are very creative, and I'm sure with billions of us contributing creativity to the project, better solutions will emerge. We are One and we must do this together. The process will involve trial and error, but each error is just one more step closer to the world of our dreams. We must decide what we want, and although the choice is ours, the problem will be agreeing on the world of the future.

Baha'u'llah, founder of the Bahá'í faith, said, each period of time has problems unique to itself with each person having their own aspirations. We would do well to concentrate on the problems we face now. The future will take care of itself.

What is best for us? We must decide the answer to this question. Each era has problems to solve only those living at the time can solve. We have ours, and they are many, and there are enough of them to keep us busy for a lifetime. The possibilities may appear impossible to achieve, but nothing is impossible.

Practically, we will reach our ultimate goals step by step and not all at once. Our level of human consciousness will restrict the possible solutions. We can't go from killing each other in the streets to loving all our fellow humans overnight. Make no mistake about it; we will reach these utopian goals.

Our perspective affects how change occurs because it will affect how we want to live. It all comes down to what we believe. If we believed Everything was One Thing, our politics, economics, relationships, parenting, sexuality, conflict resolution, careers, and ideas about the purpose of all of Life would change.

We the people of the world have all the power. No government can rule unless we give it the power to rule. No church can dictate beliefs unless we are willing to believe their doctrines. No school can educate unless we allow the education to take place. There can be no war unless we the people allow it. There can be no starvation unless we the people allow it. No institution, no social structure, no corporation, or no government has any power over us unless we grant it. We are all powerful!

This is a compilation of ideas from many sources with the creative power of God behind them. If these ideas are implemented, we will change civilization as we know it, and this is a good thing. There are many ways, and together we can find the best way for us all.

This is only a starting place. We have unlimited potential. We can and will do great things. This is not us versus them. This is us with us. We need to change our view of life from each person in competition with everyone else to a view of life where we act in concert with everyone to produce the best life for all. We are all part of Everything There Is, so it only makes sense to work together.

Principles

The solutions to lead us to the world of our dreams are based on nineteen principles. The governments of the world, institutions, businesses, societies, and people, in general, have largely ignored the following nineteen principles allowing the world of our nightmares to persist.

These principles are:

Principle 1 – We are all One.

A study of sacred scriptures will show all souls are part of One Soul. There is no place where one person ends, and another starts. It is impossible to be separated.

Following are quotes from major sacred texts verifying our unity:

"In the beginning, my dear, there was that only which is, one, without a second" (Chandogya Upanishad 6.2.1).

"Where one sees nothing else, hears nothing else, understands nothing else - that is a Plenum. But where one sees something else - that is small. Verily, the Plenum is the same as the immortal; but the small is the same as the mortal" (Chandogya Upanishad 7.24).

"Understand all things rest in me [Krishna]" (Bhagavad Gita 9:6).

"There is nothing moveable or immovable which can exist without me [Krishna]" (Bhagavad Gita 10.39).

"The things which from of old have got the One (the Tao) are--
Heaven which by it is bright and pure;
Earth rendered thereby firm and sure;
Spirits with powers by it supplied;
Valleys kept full throughout their void
All creatures which through it do live
Princes and kings who from it get
The model which to all they give.
All these are the results of the One (Tao)" (Tao Te Ching 39).

Seeing the unity of all things by seeing and hearing nothing allows for the understanding of the infinite. Being spiritual beings and united, we are infinite. By seeing and hearing division allows a person to discern only the finite. The infinite is immortal while the finite ends in death. Our bodies being born in time and appearing to be separate, die. We are not our bodies.

"'For when there is as it were duality, then one sees the other, one smells the other, one tastes the other, one salutes the other, one hears the other, one perceives the other, one touches the other, one knows the other; but when the Self only is all this, how should he see another, how should he smell another, how should he taste another, how should he salute another, how should he hear another, how should he touch another, how should he know another? How should he know Him by whom he knows all this? (Brihadaranyaka Upanishad 4.6.15). We live in a world where there is the illusion of duality. In our illusion, we perceive others separate from us when in reality, we are all part of One Thing.

"The Master said, 'Sin, my doctrine is that of an all-pervading unity'" (Confucian Analects Book IV.XV.1).

"Unto thee it was shewed, that thou mightest know that the Lord he is God; there is none else beside him" (Deuteronomy 4:35).

"The LORD he is God in heaven above, and upon the earth beneath: there is none else" (Deuteronomy 4:39).

"Hear, O Israel: The LORD our God is one LORD" (Deuteronomy 6:4).

"for he [God] is thy life" (Deuteronomy 30:20).

"Behold, how good and how pleasant it is for brethren to dwell together in unity" (Psalms 133:1)!

"Whither shall I go from thy spirit? or whither shall I flee from thy presence?

If I ascend up into heaven, thou art there: if I make my bed in hell, behold, thou art there.

If I take the wings of the morning, and dwell in the uttermost parts of the sea;

Even there shall thy hand lead me, and thy right hand shall hold me" (Psalms 139:7-10).

"Man's goings are of the LORD; how can a man then understand his own way" (Proverbs 20:24).

"I am the Lord, and there is none else, there is no God beside me: I girded thee, though thou hast not known me: That they may know from the rising of the sun, and from the west, that there is none beside me. I am the LORD, and there is none else" (Isaiah 45:5-6).

"For I am God, and there is none else" (Isaiah 45:22).

"He that receiveth you receiveth me [Jesus], and he that receiveth me receiveth him [God] that sent me" (Matthew 10:40).

"And whoso shall receive one such little child in my name receiveth me" (Matthew 18:5).

"And the King shall answer and say unto them, Veryly I say unto you, Inasmuch as ye have done it unto one of the least of these my breathren, ye have done it unto me" (Matthew 25:40).

"Then shall he answer them, saying Veryly I say unto you, Inasmuch as ye did it not to one of the least of These, ye did it not to me" (Matthew 25:45).

"The kingdom of God is within you" (Luke 17:21).

"Believest thou not that I am in the Father, and the Father is in me" (John 14:10)?

"Believe me that I am in the Father, and the Father in me" (John 14:11):

"At that day ye shall know that I am in my Father and ye in me, and I in you" (John 14:20).

"And the glory which thou gavest me I have given them; that they may be one, even as we are one: I in them, and thou in me, that they may be made perfect in one; and that the world may know that thou hast sent me, and hast loved them, as thou hast loved me" (John 17:22-23).

"For in him [God] we live, and move, and have our being; as certain also of your own poets have said, For we are also his offspring" (Acts 17:28).

"For I am persuaded, that neither death, nor life, nor angels, nor principalities, nor powers, nor things present, nor things to come, nor height, nor depth, nor any other creature, shall be able to separate us from the love of God, which is in Christ Jesus our Lord" (Romans 8:38-39).

"So we being many, are one body in Christ, and every one members one of another" (Romans 12:5).

"Know ye not that ye are the temple of God, and that the Spirit of God dwelleth in you" (1Corinthians 3:16)?

"For as the body is one, and hath many members, and all the members of that one body, being many, are one body: so also is Christ. For by one Spirit are we all baptized into one body, whether we be Jews or Gentiles, whether we be bond or free; and have been all made to drink into one Spirit. For the body is not one member, but many. If the foot shall say, Because I am not the hand, I am not of the body; is it therefore not of the body? And if the ear shall say, Because I am not the eye, I am not of the body; is it therefore not of the body? If the whole body were an eye, where were the hearing? If the whole were hearing, where were the smelling? But now hath God set the members every one of them in the body, as it hath pleased him. And if they were all one member, where were the body? But now are they many members, yet but one body. And the eye cannot say unto the hand, I have no need of thee: nor again the head to the feet, I have no need of you. Nay, much more those members of the body, which seem to be more feeble, are necessary: And those members of the body, which we think to be less honourable, upon these we bestow more abundant honour; and our uncomely parts have more abundant comeliness. For our comely parts have no need: but God hath tempered the body together, having given more abundant honour to that part which lacked: That there should be no schism in the body; but that the members should have the same care one for another. And whether one member suffer, all the members suffer with it; or one member be honoured, all the members rejoice with it. Now ye are the body of Christ, and members in particular" (1 Corinthians 12:12-27).

"There is neither Jew nor Greek, there is neither bond nor free, there is neither male nor female: for ye are all one in Christ Jesus" (Galatians 3:28).

"There is one body, and one Spirit, even as ye are called in one hope of your calling. One Lord, one faith, one baptism. One God and Father of all, who is above all, and through all, and in you all" (Ephesians 4:4-6).

"Where there is neither Greek nor Jew, circumcision nor uncircumcision, Barbarian, Scythian, bond nor free: but Christ is all, and in all" (Colossians 3:11).

"God is love; and he that dwelleth in love dwelleth in God, and God in him" (1 John 4:16).

"Mankind was but one people" (Sura 2:209).

"All that is in the Heavens and all that is on the Earth is God's: and God encompasseth all things" (Sura 3:126)?

There is only One Thing. Nothing is outside of God. We are all within God. There is no space or distance separating us from each other or God. God is omnipresent in all things including each of us with no space between us. Each one of us is God's eternal Son. We are a part of the body of God. We are never separated from anyone, including those who have died. God is everything seen or unseen. Being a part of Everything, we are a part of God. All of life is united in oneness. Each of us is in, around, and through all of life. This includes dust, rocks, minerals, plants, and animals, and occurs at all times and places.

Separation does not exist. We are all joined together and cannot be separated. We are married to each other, and divorce is not possible. We were present with all the prophets and great masters of the past. We were with Krishna when he restored Dharma. We received the Ten Commandments with Moses. We experienced Nirvana with the Buddha. We walked on water with Jesus. We received the Koran with Mohammad. We translated the golden pages with Joseph Smith. We were in prison with Bahá'u'lláh. These great persons are always with us. We will do great things in the future through other great persons.

Only One Consciousness exists. Everything is part of One Soul. We are all members of this Universal Matrix of Energy. God fills all space, and there is no empty space. There is no past or future. There is only the present. There is no need to hurry because there is only the present. We have all the time in the world. This is summed up by saying God is the Alpha and Omega, and this Spirit unites Everything in oneness and unity.

Because of this unity, all thoughts and intentions are conveyed to all the members. When this is realized, communications will be instantaneous, the future will be revealed, empathy will be realized, and loneliness will cease.

We can operate from one of two perspectives: either we are one or we are separate. Most of humans believes in the separation paradigm. We have been indoctrinated to believe God is separate from us. This is not true. If we think of life as composed of parts or pieces, we tend to be obsessed with what is ours and we oppose what we perceive to be the other fragments. There is a feeling of inadequacy and fear when striving for external power. Any external power is borrowed or counterfeited, and this acquired power produces a need to have more without a limit. There is never a feeling of completeness. The need for more produces a life of reaction rather than an embracing of Life.

If we think of Life as One, totally unified, proactive behavior results. This is based on the true power originating in the heart and its connection to God, the source of all creation. Choices made from the heart are fulfilling and sustain Life. If we were to act as one, we would heal our world. This is the answer to our problems. With unity comes power with, not power over, and in unity is inner strength, true power. This power will allow us to do, be, and have anything both as individuals and a society. This power allows creation. Inner strength does not come from separateness. The idea of separation causes all the dysfunction and suffering in the world. It produces all the class, race, and gender power struggles, and it produces war.

Unity leads to improving world conditions. Division leads to deteriorating world conditions. Unity is constantly evolving into greater potential with God as the source. Division retards growth, uses judgment and conflict to retard unity from improving conditions.

Societies move from separateness to unity. Viewing the world as composed of separate things is the bottom of evolution. Viewing the world as One Thing is at the top of evolution. Anything viewed as separate is an illusion. All things viewed as One is the truth.

Society is constructed with a hierarchy. All structures and institutions in our society have a hierarchy be they social, economic, political, military, legal, educational, or religious, but instead of creating unity, this hierarchy creates separation. The power at the top oppresses those at the bottom. To protect the power at the top, rules and regulations are enacted. Choosing independence over unity allows for the manipulation of most of the population for the benefit of those in power. Many can be sacrificed to allow the system to continue leading to prejudice, a struggle for power, war, and abusive relationships. Is this natural? Is there a possibility of living in unity? Could we live cooperatively? God does not relate as a hierarchy but as a unity. A Mayan greeting says, "I am another yourself."

As we believe, so is it to us. What we believe to be so is real to us. Nothing has any value except the value we give it. Correct perception is to see each person met not as a body, but as One with us and as the Son of God.

Life is Oneness with Everything. Expressing unity is expressing joy. The inability to express unity because it is limited or prohibited by any condition creates the feeling of sadness.

It is impossible to be alone, but it is possible to experience aloneness when nothing or no one else is around, and the feeling is devastating. However, when we are by ourselves, we may connect with God within and experience joy. We bring joy to God, and God brings joy to us, the perfect picture of love.

One of the greatest fallacies about Life is we are separate from one another. But all things visible and invisible are One with God. The belief we are separate from God has created the illusion of sin, sickness, poverty, and death. However, knowing we are One with God allows us to become whole in body and Spirit. We are aware of our diversity, but we perceived our diversity to be separation. The great challenge for each of us is to elevate our perception to see us all as One. When we realize we are One with Everything and God, we will realize we are in God's Kingdom, and experience Heaven, now, here on Earth. We are One, One Mind, One Body, and One Spirit. This is something the mystics have said for ages.

God dwells within everything, including the air, water, plants, trees, animals, humans, rocks and minerals. God comprises everything. A golden light extends to infinity in all directions enclosing all of us, and we are all One in this light. The light contains everything lacking a limit without a break in continuity. Nothing is outside this light for the light is everywhere. God is Everything, and therefore God is united with Everything. God has everything; therefore, God needs nothing. We are all One even though we appear to be in different forms. Individuality does not exclude us from Oneness, and this individuality need not lead to divisions and conflicts. Our individual body parts are all part of one body, even though they all look different. The mere act of experiencing an increase in our sense of unity will cause a decrease in the amount of pain and disappointment.

Gottfried Müller said, "There in the eyes of a cat or dog, in the eyes of a fly or fish, in the eyes of a friend or enemy, you are looking into the eyes of God."

From our view of separate things, we imagine our part of separateness is the best. I, our family, our town, our county, our state, our nation, our planet, our solar system, our galaxy, or our Universe is the best there is. This thinking is demonstrated in our decisions affecting our societies, governments, religions, economies, education, and relationships with other people and God. In imaging being separate from God, we believe God does not speak to us, denying our own experience.

Jesus said He is in God and We are in Him, making Us in God. Since God is immortal, we are immortal.

The idea of the Golden Rule is found in every major religion. This rule works because we are all One. What we do **to** other humans, animals, plants, or the environment, we do **to** ourselves. What we fail to do **for** other humans, animals, plants, or the environment, we fail to do **for** ourselves. There is the natural law of cause and effect. What we cause someone else to experience we will eventually experience ourselves because we are all One. As they say, "What goes around comes around."

Do unto others as we would have it done unto us. Because we are all One, what we do to another, we do to ourselves. If we do something for ourselves, we're doing it for others. If we do something for someone else, we're doing it for ourselves. We would be wise to send blessings into the lives of others because we'll receive the blessings back. Sending harm into the lives of others sends harm into our lives. This works best if we love ourselves. Giving and receiving is the same thing.

Louis Hay, an American motivational speaker and founder of Hay House publishing company, said, "What we give, we get. Our thoughts and words create our world."

"The sage does not accumulate (for himself). The more that he expends for others, the more does he possess of his own; the more that he gives to others, the more does he have himself" (Tao Te Ching 81).

"Cast thy bread upon the waters: for thou shalt find it after many days" (Ecclesiastes 11:1).

"For the day of the LORD is near upon all the heathen: as thou hast done, it shall be done unto thee: thy reward shall return upon thine own head" (Obadiah 1:15).

"Therefore all things whatsoever ye would that men should do to you, do ye even so to them: for this is the law and the prophets" (Matthew 7:12).

"But I say unto you which hear, Love your enemies, do good to them which hate you, Bless them that curse you, and pray for them which despitefully use you. And unto him that smiteth thee on the one cheek offer also the other; and him that taketh away thy cloak forbid not to take thy coat also. Give to every man that asketh of thee; and of him that taketh away thy goods ask them not again. And as ye would that men should do to you, do ye also to them likewise" (Luke 6:27-31).

"Give, and it shall be given unto you; good measure, pressed down, and shaken together, and running over, shall men give into your bosom. For with the same measure that ye mete withal it shall be measured to you again" (Luke 6:38).

"Bear ye one another's burdens, and so fulfil the law of Christ" (Galatians 6:2).

"Whatsoever a man soweth, that shall he also reap" (Galatians 6:7).

"And let us not be weary in well doing for in due season we shall reap, if we faint not. As we have therefore opportunity, let us do good unto all men" (Galatians 6:9-10.

Everything is One Thing, One Unit. This thing is not a union of diverse subunits and cannot be separated from the whole. All parts of the One Thing are interrelated. On Earth, all living things are mutually dependent upon one another. If we killed all plants, we would in effect kill ourselves. It is helpful if we conduct our lives in a manner of respect for other parts of Ourselves. We are talking quality of life here for everyone in the world because our quality of life is diminished if anyone's quality of life is diminished. Since we are all One, it makes sense we provide for the welfare of everyone. We should share all the resources of the world. Each should be guaranteed good health care, adequate shelter, clothing, and nourishment, all the education a person wants, and the opportunity to express their life as they wish if it doesn't impinge on the freedom of others. We should be guaranteed the opportunity for diversity.

The principle of unity is the most important principle. It forms the foundation for all the others. There is only one problem, imagined separation, and there is only one solution, knowing our true unity. The answer to all questions can be found inside from God.

In summary, what does it mean to be One, and what are the implications? If you and I are One, then you are I having a different experience from me, and I am you having a different experience from you. If I execute you, I am executing a part of me. If I put you in jail, I am putting a part of myself in jail. If I allow you to starve, I am allowing a part of me to starve. If I fail to educate you, I am failing to educate a part of me. If I restrict your freedom, I am restricting my freedom. If I fail to love you, I am failing to love myself. If I give you a gift, I am giving a gift to myself. If I love you, I love myself.

This applies to the Earth and everything in and on it as well as to other people. If I pollute the Earth, I am polluting myself. For example, if I burn something, sooner or later I will breathe some of the molecules vented from the combustion.

Principle 2 – We are Divine.

The world is very much interested in the concept of the self. Who and what are we? When we were born, our parents assigned a name to us, and so the concept of our self began. As time passed, we explored our bodies and its abilities and further expanded this concept. We were told what others thought we were, and much of the time we accepted these definitions as an expansion of this concept. We made choices, entered relationships, acted on our wishes and thoughts and continued to color this concept. Mostly we thought of ourselves as an individual body, separated from other bodies, with special characteristics setting us apart from others. We developed a set of beliefs different from all others. We thought of ourselves as unique. This and much more all go into our concept of who we are. But is this correct?

We are not our bodies. As a spirit without a body, we have no race, culture, religion, beliefs, sex, sexual orientation, job, family, country, or any physical traits. When we experience life without a body, we'll know how huge, powerful, and all-encompassing we are. Even without a body, we will still exist, not reduced in any way, but greater, intense, expansive, magnificent, and eternal, without beginning or end. We are all spiritual beings. We don't have to try to be spiritual because we are spiritual. We are God's perfect beautiful children. We deserve unconditional love because we are love.

We are equal to God and each other. All of us are of equal specialness. No one from history, who lives today, or who will live in the future is superior to anyone. We are all equal. Moses, Jesus, Muhammad, nor Siddhartha Gautama are superior to any of us. All their followers try to emulate them. This means they try to equal or exceed them. These masters encouraged all of us, as examples, to follow them.

Because there is only One Thing, there can be no superiority. All of us are magnificent, each in our own way, but all lack superiority. Knowing our greatness and our unity will transform our politics, economics, social interactions, and our educational systems. Conversely, inferiority is also an illusion. We are greater than we think.

Because there is only One Thing, God, composed of everything, we are a part of God. In Psalms, it says we are Gods, and this is quoted by Jesus in the New Testament. The Hebrew word translated as gods is *Elohim*. It is a plural word translated as God in about 2,200 other verses. We might think the reason it is plural is for God the Father, God the Son, and God the Holy Spirit. But since God is Everything, including us, the plural includes us. Psalms and John make it clear it's about us.

"I have said, Ye are gods; and all of you are children of the most High" (Psalms 82:6).

"Jesus answered them, Is it not written in your law, I said, Ye are gods? If he called them gods, unto whom the word of God came, and the scripture cannot be broken" (John 10:34-35).

The Koran uses the word "We" meaning God, frequently.

Other sacred scriptures describe us as:

"Now, the light which shines higher than this heaven, on the backs of all, on the backs of everything, in the highest worlds, than which there are no higher - verily, that is the same as this light which is here within a person." (Chandogya Upanishad 3.13.7).

"The man who believeth that it is the soul which killeth, and he who thinketh that the soul may be destroyed, are both alike deceived; for it neither killeth, nor is it killed. It is born, nor does it ever die, nor having existed before, does it exist no more; it is ancient, constant, and eternal, and is not to be destroyed in this its mortal frame. How can the man, who believeth that this thing is incorruptible eternal, inexhaustible, and without birth, think that he can either kill or cause it to be killed? As a man throweth away old garments, and putteth on new, even so the soul, having quitted its old mortal frames, entereth into others which are new. The weapon divideth it not, the fire burneth it not, the water corrupteth it not, the wind drieth it not; It is indivisible, inconsumable, incorruptible, and is not to be dried away: it is invisible, inconceivable, and unalterable; therefore, believing it to be thus, thou shouldest not grieve" (Bhagavad Gita 2:19-25).

"The kingdom of God is within you" (Luke 17:21).

"Know ye not that ye are the temple of God, and that the Spirit of God dwelleth in you" (1Corinthians 3:16).

Everyone in the world is more than we appear to be. Since we are all part of God, we are all wonderful, all-powerful creatures. We are unlimited, and the soul rebels at limitation. We can be, have, or do anything. We have unlimited potential, and we have God's greatest gift - unconditional love. We are not limited by our bodies. We are love. We are not limited by anyone or anything unless we give it the power to limit us. We are totally free with unlimited possibilities, and we exist in every dimension, seen and unseen. By removing our judgment and our limiting beliefs, we remove restrictions on our body as well. Our true being is infinite. The soul will exhibit the attributes of God, including loving-kindness and wealth. God cannot be damaged, hurt, or injured in any way, and therefore will harm no one. God will not condemn nor punish anyone. Because we are all a part of God, we cannot be damaged or harmed in any way. We only think we can.

It is true the soul after it separates from the body will progress into God's presence. Nothing can prevent or alter this, and the soul will endure forever. It is joyful to be living with a body, and it is joyful to be living without a body. Nothing in this world will last forever; therefore, nothing in this world is real. Only eternal things are real.

We are evolving. In each moment, decision by decision, we define who we are. If our choice serves our purpose, we will continue living in this way. If our choice no longer serves our purpose, and purposes change, we will decide differently.

What are we trying to be at any moment of time is the most important question. Right now, is this who we choose to be? Do we choose to be a warring people, or do we choose to be a loving people? Do we choose to eat healthy foods? All decisions are important because all decisions define who we are.

We are the expression of God. Each second, God is expressing Itself in, as, and through us. We get to pick how we will express God in each second. In this way, we are creating God second by second. The reason we are here is to experience the greatest feeling of love we can imagine. Another way of saying this is we trying to experience the greatest version of God we can imagine. What version of God do we want to create in each moment of time?

In each second, we get to choose our next idea about whom we are, and we may choose the lowest idea or the highest idea about ourselves. Only by choosing the highest, can we lift ourselves from the lowest. The world will follow our choice. There is no escape from this. Our lives are holy. What we do is holy. Who we are, God is. We define God. God created us to re-create It. We and God, Us, are doing this holy work together, Our greatest joy. It is the very reason for Our being.

We are good, compassionate, wise, infinite in potential, and God. All this we deny.

God requires only what is within the Everything God is. We being made in the likeness of God need only what is within us. We need nothing to be perfectly happy. What we have cannot be destroyed or lost. Our bliss is within. Nothing outside can compare.

Life as we have constructed it is hard. When we live a life based on whom we are, life becomes easy. We are pure, unlimited, and unconditional love. When we live open, transparent lives, releasing others to live their lives as they please, and granting ourselves the same, life becomes easy and peaceful.

There is nothing we need to do to survive. We are eternal, immortal, and death is only a doorway. This is a reality and not just a hope. We can relax and enjoy life. We don't have to struggle to survive. No roads lead away from God because there is no place to go. We are found only where God is. All roads lead to God. We are all messengers of God. We are all saviors. We are all holy. Everyone who is aware of us is impacted by our lives.

Jesus came to Earth to remind us of how life works. His message was He and all of Us are the Christ, and We can do even greater works than He did (John 14:12). God is the Creator of All and is The All.

Jesus is one of us, demonstrating what we all can do. Jesus, the personality, should not be idealized, but the Spirit or God, who energizes the personality and body of Jesus should be.

We are not our physical bodies. We are infinite. Our body is a machine our soul uses to navigate this world. We breathe life into our body. The body can be damaged, but we cannot. The body can die, but we cannot. Our souls encase our bodies. We are the energy configuration of the Universal Spirit, God. We are a force field, a radiating, pulsating energy package. We are an energy field without end. We mingle with all other energy fields. Our energy has no limit in time and space. There is only One Soul, One Energy – God expressed locally as individuals. This Energy has intelligence and is the repository and source of all knowledge, awareness, data, information, understanding, and experience. This Energy is the All in All. We are One with this Energy, and this Energy forms our world. What is good for one of us is good for all of us.

The wisdom, love, and truth of God are found in each soul, expressing our bodies through consciousness. We have all the answers to all the questions. We know how to solve and deal with all our problems. The biggest problems of all will be to have the *will* to solve them and agreeing on the best course of action. What we hold in our minds, is created in our world. If we believe we are separate from Spirit, our bodies will age and die. If we believe we are One with Spirit, then we will know Spirit produces Spirit, and we are all immortal. We are as we were created, perfect beings. Being perfect beings allows us to communicate with God. Communicating with God allows us to know we are perfect beings. Being born again is remembering we are perfect beings. This allows us to be free from commercial bondage and materialism.

We are limited or unlimited, slaves or free depending on what we believe. As we think, so it is. All people are created equal, each able to do the mighty works of God. We are the Mind, and self-consciousness of the Universe. This Intelligence is everywhere from a single cell in our bodies to great geniuses. This great Intelligence called God is united with us and working in harmony with us. If we are One, who could be the victim or the villain, or the victor or the loser, or the attacker or the attacked, or the murderer or the murdered, or the predator or the prey?

It is insane to believe is possible. Because of this fear, we devise all kinds of protection including heavy armaments, legal definitions, legal codes, ethics, passwords, firewalls, locks, complicated defense structures, medicine, life-protecting aids, beauty products, and walls. Building defenses produce attacks. When we are defenseless, we are at our strongest.

We will always succeed. Failure is an illusion. What we think of as a failure is an aspect of success. Since we are all part of God, "failures" are just aspects of God manifesting.

Life has no meaning except the meaning we give it. We define ourselves based on the meaning we give to life experiences. To take charge of our lives, we must define the meaning of life for ourselves, and in the process define ourselves in relation to the events.

We are all powerful, and we can to anything! We are all the rulers of our world. We are the kings and queens of our lives. Unfortunately, most of us don't know this. Those who knew this we have called Jesus, and Buddha, and they lived their lives as the rulers of their lives.

Our basic nature is fairness, love, and Oneness. Otherwise, no one would jump instinctively to save another. Our basic nature loves. When we act mean, it's because of what we believe. We are not evil at our core, and we are not contaminated from birth with original sin.

Everyone who enters our lives is an angel. They all appear in our lives to allow us to experience who we are. When someone is messing up our lives, they are just actors in our play to allow us to experience ourselves as the next greatest version of God we can imagine.

We are all eternal, unlimited, and totally free. If we imagine ourselves less than this, we go against our very nature. Life as we construct it should be based on this truth. We are all worthy of all love. God knows so.

Principle 3 – We each have free will to live our lives as we please.

There are no rules. We have free will. We are free to create our lives any way we wish. If we like fear, starvation, and war, we need do nothing differently. And the paradox is we enforce the laws we inflict on ourselves now. If we want love, joy, peace, and freedom, change must be made to the way we see ourselves, and the way we interact with each other. While we have free will, we should not impinge upon the free will of another. The basis of all freedom is the free will granted by God to each person. We each have the right to our own beliefs. Each should be free to live the life of his or her dreams if it doesn't limit the freedom of others. We are freedom itself. The best form of government allows the most freedom. The best economic system is the freest. The best educational system allows the most freedom for the students. The best institutions allow their members the most freedom. Controlling others is impossible and attempting to control someone else only lessens our conscious control of our own lives. We are unlimited, eternal, and free.

If God gave us free will, and God did, then who are we to deny others the freedom to express their lives as they wish? Anything reducing, restricting, impinging upon, or eliminating freedom is working against life.

No one knows what is best for another. No one knows how another can best express himself or herself. It's inappropriate to force someone to think and believe according to any religion or doctrine. We could say don't try to force someone to think or believe anything. Period. When we suppress any individual's ability to express their greater ability, we are ethically depleted.

Love is free and so are we.

Love commands matter, and so we command our lives.

Love is the master of conditions, and so we are no man's slaves.

The greatest gift we can give someone is self-realization. Self-realization is God's will for each person. It's called free will. Be love and we will act appropriately.

Humans should be allowed to change viewpoints, mind, or heart. Legal documents, agreements, and loyalty should not be used to maintain conformity. Such restrictions restrict creation. The place of least restriction is love. Freedom is what humans are, and this freedom should not be restricted.

The Universe always agrees with itself. If we attempt to kill a mosquito, both the mosquito and us will agree on whether the mosquito seems to die or not because the mosquito cannot die in any event, but it can change shape giving the appearance of death. It is impossible to do anything to a mosquito or to someone without their permission.

Everything happening is the will of God. Nothing can happen against the will of God. Everything happening is our will since we are One with God. Everything happening is happening perfectly. No one can decide an event for someone else without their permission. No one is murdered without their consent. We are free to wage war against anyone, or kill anyone, or love anyone. Because we are all One, any event is a co-created event with the co-operation and consent of all involved. Only if we are separate from each other could one individual affect another without their consent.

Anything we do is acceptable to God. If God required certain behavior, it would not be free will. Therefore, God accepts everything. Free will would be nonexistent if we were punished for making a wrong choice. God has no preference about what we choose. God is on the side of everyone. There is no evil in God's World, only what we define as evil. We are totally free to do, be, and have whatever we want. We are under no obligations, restrictions, limitations, or rules. There are no "Laws of God" leading to any punishments. Judgment day does not exist. Condemnation and punishment are only done by us to us. God does not judge, condemn, or punish.

This freedom applies to all of life, not just our relationship with God. We are under no obligation to our fellow woman or man. There is only opportunity. The opportunity is to express our highest ideal of us. Is it possible for us to express ourselves as God would? The answer is yes. And God is not an angry judgmental God, but a God of unconditional love.

Greatest freedom produces the greatest growth. God doesn't want obedience. God is all about growth.

It is difficult to keep promises for the following three reasons. First, most people don't know what they are doing in any situation, and it is difficult to act consistently in all situations. To complicate things more, life is constantly changing. Second, most people can't predict the future so a promise cannot be made truthfully. Third, a person's truth evolves and changes over time eventually producing a conflict between what was promised and what the person's current truth is. Therefore, when confronted with whether to keep a promise or not, remember the highest betrayal is a betrayal of ourselves even if it is an effort to prevent the betraying of another.

People are constantly changing. No one should expect anyone to keep a promise. No one should be forced to keep their word because they didn't want to or felt they couldn't. Forcing anyone to do something they don't want to do is an aberration of free will.

Forcing others to keep a promise inflects injury both ways. People doing what they felt they were forced to do, does more damage than people freely living their lives. Granting freedom to others removes danger. Granting others freedom grants us freedom. Acceptance is important here.

What we do, we do in concert with everyone. We co-create everything together. There are no victims or villains. We have all decided together what will be expressed in life.

As a society, we have said it's OK to kill someone against their will such as in war or as an execution for a crime. But it's not OK to assist someone who wants to die. This is hypocritical.

We are deciding what is good and bad, what is OK and not OK as we go along. It has to be this way, or we wouldn't be able to make any progress. This allows for change and allows us to replace old values with new ones.

The most harmful decision we have ever made about ourselves is the decision to believe we have been born in sin and we are basically evil. Because we create our reality, we have created a world where laws are required to protect us from each other. If we believed we were basically good, few laws would be required. Our present society is freedom limiting. If we restructured our society to believe we are good, our new society would be freedom giving.

To fully love, we must love our selves. To do this, we must believe and behave as if we are basically good. To fully love, we must be totally free. Limited freedom produces limited joy and limited love. The solution to getting to totally loving is to allow everyone to be anything.

Life as we have constructed it is hard. When we live open, transparent lives, releasing others to live their lives as they please, and granting ourselves the same, life becomes easy and peaceful.

By totally accepting and totally loving everyone, we become a total blessing to everyone including ourselves, making everyone including us totally joyful.

All roads lead to God. No path to God is better than any other. This makes no religion better than any other. Also, there is no race, nation, philosophy, political party, or economic system better than others. There are many ways to Heaven, and everyone should be allowed to take their own path.

We are constantly recreating life as we wish with God's permission or it wouldn't happen. We may recreate life in the most hideous and grotesque forms, and we have, or we may choose the most glorious and heavenly. God gives us free will to do either.

How does someone decide what to do? We have studied the sacred scriptures to determine God's will in matters of killing another to making promises. No matter what we determine God's will to be, we haven't implemented it. We have tried the system of rewards and punishments for millennium without success. The truth is our will is united with God's will. God has no preference except ours. This is free will.

So how do we decide what to do? What is good and what is bad? What is the best of all the possibilities? Given this freedom, we never have to worry about rewards or punishments from God. In all matters, we are free to decide what we want. To decide, we should go within and allow our hearts, our passions, and our joy to guide us.

We are all brothers and sisters, and not enemies. It is possible for each to have a different perspective. Different views do not mean those different from us should perish. Interfering with the free will of another to choose a different perspective retards our development and isolates us. This is self-defeating. We can do the Godly thing and allow others to live freely.

Principle 4 – Our purpose is to produce the greatest imaginable life we can conceive.

Shakespeare said, "To be, or not to be? That is the question." Is our life here on Earth to continue as it is, or are we as a species to become extinct? We seal our fate by our decisions. Our lives are a series of decisions; the sum decides how our lives, collectively and individually, turn out. Do we choose life, or do we choose death? Do we go to war, or do we work together for compromise, for forgiveness, for trust, and for peace? Do we continue to believe in doctrines that are killing us, or do we choose life? "To be, or not to be? That is the question."

We have some great models to emulate such as Jesus and the Buddha. We are here to experience who we are, and who we are is God. So, by extension we allow God to experience Itself through us.

In order to experience who we are, we need the negative to contrast the positive we are. We do not need to experience the negative as we have done in the past, but only know it exists somewhere. This is the "knowledge of the fruit of the Tree of Good and Evil" and it is the original blessing as Matthew Fox said, who was a Dominican friar and later Episcopal priest.

The purpose of life is to create ourselves. Each decision defines Who We Are.

In all matters, we are free to decide what we want. But in the deciding, we demonstrate who we are. We are also announcing who God is because we are all One with each other and with God. The purpose of life is for us to decide who we are and then to experience our decisions. The outcome is unlimited. We can experience the greatest feeling of love imaginable.

Principle 5 – Everything in this Universe is an illusion.

Everything we see, hear, touch, taste, or experience in life is an illusion. Our whole world is a grand illusion. Nothing in this world will last forever. Only eternal things are real. Therefore, nothing in this world is real. Our true nature is spiritual, not material. Only love exists.

The first and greatest illusion is separation. Our bodies foster this belief. It appears we are separate because we each have our own separate body. If we were One, instead of separate individuals, how could someone attack and who would be attacked? Could there be a victor? Could there be a prey? Could there be a victim? Could there be a murderer? Bodies are illusions. Our bodies are vehicles for moving around in this world.

Death is the second greatest illusion. It appears life stops with death, but we all live forever. Our delusion of mortality is a result of thinking our identity is our bodies. All variants of death such as sadness, fear, anxiety, doubt, anger, faithlessness, distrust, health and safety concerns for the body, envy, and all desires to be other than the Son of God we are, do not exist. Our perspective on life has a profound impact on our experience of life. If we see death as an illusion instead of the end of our lives, we profoundly change everything. We can decide what death, ours or someone else's, means to us. We are limitless and eternal and cannot die. Nothing can harm us.

The third greatest illusion is birth providing the appearance life starts with birth. Both are doorways leading in and out of our experience of this world. We existed before birth, and we will continue to exist after death. We are not our bodies.

Scarcity is an illusion. There is enough of what it takes to make everyone in the world happy. There is enough food. There is enough medical care. There is enough education. There are enough opportunities for all. We need not compete against each other for anything. The Universe grants every request, so there is no competition.

Ignorance is an illusion. It doesn't exist. Before we were born, our memory of everything was erased. We only have to remember what we forgot.

And time is an illusion. Everything that has happened in the past, or will happen in the future, is happening now. There is only now. All solutions, answers, experiences, and understandings are happening now. Everything created is created now. Anything we wish for is present now. There is no time. Everything happens at once. There is no past or future, only now.

Superiority does not exist. We are all equal. Women are not better than men. Homosexuals are not better than heterosexuals. Negroes are not better than Caucasians. Older humans are not better than younger humans. Shorter humans are not better than taller humans. There are no chosen people because all are chosen. There is no human who has lived in the past, who lives now, or who will live in the future who is better than any other human. No religion is better than another. No nation is better than another. Only difference exists. Superiority is a judgment humans have made having no basis in fact.

We have created the illusion saying we need money to buy food to prevent starvation. We have created the illusion saying we need pills or antibiotic injections to provide us with good health. We have created the illusion saying we are alone if no other body is present with us. Our religions have created illusions separating us from God. Sin is an illusion. There is no way we can offend God. Anything not unlimited, eternal, or free is false. God includes all. God loves everyone. Everyone is included in God's Kingdom.

Forgiveness knows the illusion of an offense by someone did not happen.

We will always succeed. Failure is an illusion. What we think of as a failure is an aspect of success. Since we are all part of God, "failures" are just aspects of God manifesting.

Ownership is an illusion. No one owns any physical object. We are only stewards of things under our control. When our bodies die, all we thought we owned passes on to someone else.

"Moreover it is required in stewards, that a man be found faithful" (1 Corinthians 4:2).

"For we brought nothing into this world, and it is certain we can carry nothing out" (1 Timothy 6:7).

To experience our Oneness, a world of illusions was created where it appears we are separate. It's an upside-down world where things are not what they seem to be and seem to be what they are not. Knowing the purpose of the illusion allows us to experience the illusion, making it real to ourselves, or we may choose to experience True Reality at any moment. This world provides us all with a grand opportunity to declare our truth and announce to the world Who we really are.

Sacred scriptures say this:

"Look upon the world as a bubble, look upon it as a mirage" (Dhammapada 4).

"All beings are bewildered in this world by the delusion caused by the pairs of opposites, arising from desire and aversion" (Bhagavad Gita 7:27).

"All is vanity" (Ecclesiastes 1:2).

"For now we see through a glass, darkly; but then face to face: now I know in part; but then shall I know even as also I am known" (I Corinthians 13:12).

"Through faith we understand that the worlds were framed by the word of God, so the things which are seen were not made of things which do appear" (Hebrews 11:3).

"The life in this world is but a play and a pastime" (Sura 6:33).

In William Shakespeare's *As You Like It,* Jaques says,
"All the world's a stage,
And all the men and women merely players.
They have their exits and their entrances,
And one man in his time plays many parts"

Just as a play is an illusion, so is everything in our world. Some of us are playing the parts of the "good" guys, and some of us are playing the parts of the "bad" guys. As in a play, in our world, whether we play the part of a "bad" guy or play the part of a "good" guy, all of us are really, really "good" guys regardless of the parts we play. Murderers, rapists, and terrorists are all "good" guys playing the parts of "bad" guys. And as in a play, where all the props belong to the production company, all the props in our world belong to God. We are just stewards of what we possess and use the props for the grand production of Life. Births and deaths are only entrances and exits. And each one of us plays many parts over many lifetimes.

Jesus throughout his life proved many things we thought were true are only illusions. He walked on water, caused food to multiply, changed water into wine, healed the sick, raised the dead back to life, moved through walls, levitated, and rose from the dead himself. Likewise, other spiritual leaders have done similar things. Life is not what it appears to be.

Principle 6 – Love.

Love is the place to be because love is who we are. Love ourselves and others by doing what is best for all of us, and what is best for one of us is best for each of us. We should enlarge our concept of who we are to include everyone but always include ourselves. Do to and for others as we would do to and for ourselves if the others desire our gift. For our gift is for ourselves. Love everyone in our lives, friend and foe alike, and defiantly love ourselves.

Love is free and so are we. Love commands matter, and so we command our lives. Love is the master of conditions, and so we are no man's slave. Love is the law, and so for a law to be valid, it must be rooted in love. Jesus left only two commandments: love God with all our heart, and our neighbor as ourselves. We have a sacred right to be the love we are, and to be unconditional love.

Love has no conditions, limitations, or needs. Lacking conditions, love asks nothing to be expressed. Nothing is required in return. Love takes back nothing to retaliate. Lacking limitations, none are placed on another. Love is infinite, having no end, boundary, or barrier. Lacking need, love wants only what is freely given. Love holds only what desires to be held and gives only what is desired. Love is free. Freedom is God, and love is God expressed. It is possible to experience love all the time with everyone we meet. The greatest gift love can give is to allow the object of the love to be whoever they choose to be.

Institutions like governments, religions, and schools, in general, foster separation and control agendas, reducing the effects of love. Unity increases the effects of love.

Every time we send love, kindness, or service into the life of someone, even if no one is aware of it, the world changes.

Choose love in making every decision. Then we will live a grand life, and experience Who we are, Love. Only love exists, and everything else is an illusion.

The love, compassion, wisdom, intention, and purpose of All That Is are big enough to encompass the most heinous crimes and criminals. Forgiveness is human, unconditional love is Divine.

Love is expressed by God. Unfortunately, we have incorrectly decided our God is jealous, needy, and possessed of great expectations for us. Any of these traits kills love, the antithesis of God. These beliefs have prevented us from experiencing true love. A true picture of love would be of us loving everyone without limitation all the time. This is what it is like to realize our Oneness.

We believe in a God who trades Heaven for our love. So we live our lives imitating this God we have constructed and we have made love conditional.

All sexual experiences of love in life are temporary and intermittent. A wiser understanding of dealing with love for another is to apply maximum love to the object of love at the time of love. Expanded, applying maximum love to all of life in every moment is total love, loving without limit or condition. This loving is called Godliness.

God is love. Love is eternal, limitless, changeless, extending beyond vision into forever. Love reveals the Christ within each of us. Love heals humanity, harmonizing nations, and producing peace and prosperity in the world.

Expressing the love in our hearts causes us to give, and by giving we receive. If we give without expecting anything in return, we will receive abundantly. When we experience unity with Life, Love, and Wisdom, we are in conscious contact with God, and receiving abundance.

Safety can be found in truth and love. If we know we are love, we will know we are safe.

Our basic nature loves. When we act mean, it's because of what we believe. Our basic instincts are fairness, Oneness, and love.

Sacred scriptures have this to say:

"Thou shalt love thy neighbour as thyself" (Leviticus 19:18).

"And thou shalt love the Lord thy God with all thine heart, and with all thy soul and with all thy might" (Deuteronomy 6:5).

"Love the Lord your God with all your heart, and with all your soul and with all your mind. This is the first and greatest Commandment. And the second is like unto it: Love your neighbor as yourself" (Matthew 22: 37-39). For this to work, we must love ourselves. Loving ourselves, loving our neighbors, and loving God are the same thing, because we are all One with God and One with each other. When we love the One we love the All.

"And thou shalt love the Lord thy God with all thy heart, and with all thy soul, and with all thy mind, and with all thy strength: this is the first commandment. And the second is like, namely this, Thou shalt love thy neighbor as thyself. There is none other commandment greater than these" (Mark 12:30-31).

"But I say unto you which hear, Love your enemies, do good to them which hate you, Bless them that curse you, and pray for them which despitefully use you" (Luke 6:27-28).

"And he answering said, Thou shalt love the Lord thy God with all thy heart, and with all thy soul, and with all thy strength, and with all thy mind; and thy neighbour as thyself" (Luke 10:27).

"A new commandment I give unto you, That ye love one another; as I have loved you, that ye also love one another" (John 13:34).

"This is my commandment, that ye love one another, as I have loved you" (John 15:12).

"Thou shalt love thy neighbour as thyself" (Romans 13:9).

"Though I speak with the tongues of men and of angels, and have not charity, I am become as sounding brass, or a tinkling cymbal. And though I have the gift of prophecy, and understand all mysteries, and all knowledge; and though I have all faith, so that I could remove mountains, and have not charity, I am nothing. And though I bestow all my goods to feed the poor, and though I give my body to be burned, and have not charity, it profiteth me nothing. Charity suffereth long, [and] is kind; charity envieth not; charity vaunteth not itself, is not puffed up, Doth not behave itself unseemly, seeketh not her own, is not easily provoked, thinketh no evil; Rejoiceth not in iniquity, but rejoiceth in the truth; Beareth all things, believeth all things, hopeth all things, endureth all things. Charity never faileth: but whether there be prophecies, they shall fail; whether there be tongues, they shall cease; whether there be knowledge, it shall vanish away. For we know in part, and we prophesy in part. But when that which is perfect is come, then that which is in part shall be done away. When I was a child, I spake as a child, I understood as a child, I thought as a child: but when I became a man, I put away childish things. For now we see through a glass, darkly; but then face to face: now I know in part; but then shall I know even as also I am known. And now abideth faith, hope, charity, these three; but the greatest of these is charity" (1 Corinthians 13). Charity is love.

"For all the law is fulfilled in one word, even in this; Thou shalt love thy neighbour as thyself" (Galatians 5:14).

"And above all these things put on charity, which is the bond of perfectness" (Colossians 3:14).

"If ye fulfil the royal law according to the scripture, Thou shalt love thy neighbour as thyself, ye do well" (James 2:8).

"Beloved, let us love one another: for love is of God" (1 John 4:7).

"God is love" (I John 4:8).

"Beloved, if God so loved us, we ought also to love one another" (I John 4:11).

"And we have known and believed the love that God hast to us. God is love; and he that dwelleth in love dwelleth in God, and God in him" (I John 4:16).

"There is no fear in love; but perfect love casteth out fear" (1 John 4:18).

"If any man say, I love God, and hateth his brother, he is a liar" (I John 4:20). God and our brother are One. It is impossible to love one without the other. We can't love God more than our fellow human. And we can't love our fellow human more than we love ourselves.

"Woe to those who STINT the measure: Who when they take by measure from others, exact the full; But when they mete to them or weigh to them, minish" (Sura 83:1-3).

"The sage has no invariable mind of his own; he makes the mind of the people his mind. To those who are good (to me), I am good; and to those who are not good (to me), I am also good;--and thus (all) get to be good. To those who are sincere (with me), I am sincere; and to those who are not sincere (with me), I am also sincere;--and thus (all) get to be sincere" (Tao Te Ching 49).

"Select for your neighbor what you select for yourself" (Epistle to the Son of the Wolf 30).

"Now the man of perfect virtue, wishing to be established himself, seeks also to establish others; wishing to be enlarged himself, he seeks also to enlarge others" (Confucius, *Analects* 6:28).

"Tsze-Kung ask, 'Is there one word which may serve as a rule of practice for all one's life?' The Master said, 'Is not reciprocity such a word? What you do not want done to yourself, do not do to others.'" (Confucius, *Analects 15:23*).

"The bottom line of our responsibility to our fellow human is to never do anything to others that would bring pain to us" (The Mahabharata, 5:1517).

Love is who we are. It is natural for us to love everyone we meet. But we have established rules and regulations, conditions, laws, restrictions, customs, and taboos limiting who, how, and when we may express love. To make matters worse, we pass onto our children biases, and prejudices affecting how they practice love as adults. This restricted prejudiced love is not love because love is unlimited and unconditional.

Principle 7 – There is no right or wrong.

Right and wrong, and good and evil do not exist in God's world. In our world, they exist as illusions. Again, these are subjective judgments humans have made having no basis in fact. However, we only exist as we relate to something else. Therefore, we must define evil, so we will know when we are good. When we define evil, we define ourselves.

Definitions of right and wrong are necessary to define who we are. Notice we keep changing these definitions as we redefine ourselves. These definitions change from time to time, culture to culture, religion to religion, place to place, and person to person. What is right or wrong depends on where we are in time and space.

No one is evil. They just have a different perspective. Based on their perspective, they do no wrong, as do we all.

Our values of right and wrong are decisions we as individuals and as a society make, and then change as what we want changes. What is right and wrong is fickle as it changes over time.

Our values change and change all the time. When we change what we want to be, do, or have, our values will change. As our perceptions, desires, and wants change, our values change. If we want something badly enough, we will justify obtaining it. There is no absolute right or wrong.

What we believe is good today, will change over time depending on circumstances. It has been this way down through history. There are no ends to revelations. New information will constantly be streaming to us. Some things once thought good, are now thought evil. Some things thought evil, are now thought good. We each determine what good and evil are, and what we determine changes over time. And when we don't agree, arguments, fights, and war can result.

We need problems to solve or there would be nothing to do. We need "wrongs" to right. We could choose to end starvation. We can make this grand decision and change the world. But we haven't.

God accepts everything. There is no evil in God's World, only what we define as evil. Ultimately there is no evil. There are only events and experiences. Evil is a judgment we have made about these events and experiences.

In terms we can't understand, evil does not exist, even though it appears to exist in our experiences. Good and evil are part of the greater good. Even so, the end does not justify the means. If we believe in good and evil, it's always appropriate to choose good.

Doing something wrong will not produce eternal punishment. However, what we cause others to experience, we will experience at some point. The admonition by Jesus to do unto others as we would have done unto us is excellent advice if we choose to have pleasant experiences in our lives.

The old belief of separation where we have right and wrong, good and bad, crime and punishment, and everlasting rewards and everlasting damnation has not solved our problems. Changing our beliefs to "We are All One" will change the world to end suffering, torture, and killing.

Wrong can be used in two different ways. It can mean mistaken or immoral. Being mistaken means not achieving the desired or predicted goal. Immoral means breaking a man-made or Deity-made law. The problem with morals is they change over time and from place to place, and they are subjective.

In some societies, a mistake can be equated with being immoral instead of just an operational failure. The mistake can then become a sin, and the mistake can then be equated with an offense against God, with severe consequences. If we disagree with these standards, we may be labeled an apostate and killed. This situation creates all the ingredients necessary for war. We would now be defending the faith if another group disagreed with our laws. Thus, this holy war would be authorized by and required by God, and this kind of behavior has been happening for hundreds and thousands of years. This can be changed by removing God from this mess by separating morals and mistakes.

In life, there is no evil, only good.

Principle 8 – Everyone acts appropriately based on their model of how the world works.

No one does anything inappropriate given her or his model of how life works. To change the world, we must change the beliefs these models are based on. This means we must change ourselves. One person changing himself or herself will have a minor effect on the world, but when groups change, there will be major world changes. The solutions are spiritual solutions, and the changes must come at the level of belief.

We, humans, have made great strides in our technology, but few advances in our thinking. Our model of the world is primitive, and our actions would be inappropriate in enlightened civilizations.

An attacker sees their attack as a defense. We have only defenders, no attackers. We can then say we were forced to kill them because we were only defending ourselves. This is the way attackers see their situation. This applies to all situations of conflict including war, encounters in bedrooms, and discussions in boardrooms.

Principle 9 – When helping anyone, work for their Independence.

When helping someone, allow him or her to become independent. Keeping anyone dependent does not help her or him.

The greatest gift we can give someone is self-realization. Self-realization is God's will for each person. It's called free will. It is inappropriate to try to coerce anyone to believe as we do. We have no control over others, and it is foolhardy to try to control others. Help others by helping them to help themselves.

To support others and the world, we need to give without wanting anything in return, allow others to be themselves, and see each person as perfect, whole and complete just as they are, and just as we all are.

There are no accidents or coincidences because all is perfect. Observe others as they make choices, and allow them their freedom, but don't question, interfere, or condemn. Assist as best as possible to help others make a higher choice. Each choice is perfect at the time it is made. Allow all to follow their own path. We may not understand the perfection, but it exists.

The most important help to be given to anyone is to let them know we are all the Son of God. Sometimes it's best to just leave them alone and empower them to help themselves.

The worst help is help where dependence is continued instead of rapid independence. Don't allow anyone to continue dependence in the name of compassion. This is compulsion. It would be taking responsibility for a person instead of building up their self-worth.

The goal is to make a person needing help stronger, empowered, and self-sufficient. Many government programs, in order to justify their existence and perpetuate themselves, often make their clients weaker rather than stronger. A solution would be to put a limit on assistance. This provides help when needed, but prevents addiction and dependence while promoting self-reliance. Governments know help is power. By helping many people, governments get support from many people.

We can never help another by disempowering them. Anything producing dependency is disempowering. Providing too little help disempowers. Offer the help we can provide and let them decide what they want. Maybe they'll want nothing. Ignoring the genuine plight of others is not the answer. It is impossible to help anyone who refuses to help themselves. Each person has their own path to walk, and they have the free will to decide how to walk it themselves.

In providing the Earth's inhabitants with equality, equality of opportunity is what should be provided and not equality in fact. To provide an equal opportunity each person would be provided with the basic needs and the opportunity for advancement.

Presently, our social, religious, political, and economic systems are primitive. We consider them the best, because we don't know of, nor can we think of better systems. We resist change or improvements involving any loss of power or wealth even if these would help the vast part of the world's population, and result in a huge change in consciousness, awareness, and respect for all of life, and a greater understanding of the unity of Everything.

Principle 10 – We are each the Savior of the world.

Each one of us is the Savior of the world, and if we don't do it, it won't get done.

Divinity lies within each of us. We are all messengers of God. We are all saviors. We are all holy. All we must do is follow the God found within.

All of us are of equal specialness. No one from history, who lives today, or who will live in the future is superior to anyone. We are all equal. Every one of us is a messenger. Our lives as we live them demonstrate to the world Who we are every second of every day. Everyone who is aware of us is impacted by our lives. Jesus, Muhammad, and Siddhartha Gautama are not superior to any of us. We are all equal. All their followers try to emulate them. This means they try to equal or exceed what they did. These masters encouraged all of us, as examples, to follow them. What they did, we can do.

We were holy and perfect from before time was created, but we feel we are lacking and need a savior. We are our own savior who will teach us we are already saved. If asked if Jesus is our personal savior, we can say "yes" because Jesus and we are One. Jesus said he would be with us up to the end of the world, and in truth there is no way he can be separated from us. We are all the holy Child of God. Jesus and God are One, just like we and God are One. We as the energy of Life are God expressing Love.

Sacred scriptures say:

"Verily, verily, I say unto you, He that believeth on me (Jesus), the works that I do shall he do also; and greater works than these shall he do; because I go unto my Father" (John 14:12).

"But Christ is all, and in all" (Colossians 3:11).

"And we have seen and do testify that the Father sent the Son *to be* the Saviour of the world" (1 John 4:14).

Messiah and Christ mean the same thing, savior. We are all One and therefore we are all the Christ and Messiah. We are also the Son of God. There is no one else to be the savior. There is no one outside us. We are our own personal savior.

Principle 11 – It is appropriate to solve all disputes peacefully.

Sacred scriptures have declared:
"Seek peace and pursue it" (Psalm 34:14).
"Behold, how good and how pleasant is it for brethren to dwell together in unity" (Psalm 133:1)!
"It is an honour for a man to cease from strife" (Proverbs 20:3).

"They shall beat their swords into plowshares, and their spears into pruninghooks: nation shall not lift up sword against nation, neither shall they learn war any more" (Isaiah 2:4).

"Love the truth and peace" (Zechariah 8:19).

"Blessed are the peacemakers: for they shall be called the children of God" (Matthew 5:9).

"Have peace one with another" (Mark 9:50).

"Glory to God in the highest, and on earth peace, good will toward men" (Luke 2:14).

"If it be possible, as much as lieth in you, live peaceably with all men" (Romans 12:18).

"Let us therefore follow after the things which make for peace, and things wherewith one may edify another" (Romans 14:19).

"Be perfect, be of good comfort, be of one mind, live in peace" (2 Corinthians 13:11).

"Endeavouring to keep the unity of the Spirit in the bond of peace" (Ephesians 4:3).

"And let the peace of God rule in your hearts, to the which also ye are called in one body; and be ye thankful" (Colossians 3:15).

"Be at peace among yourselves" (1Thessalonians 5:13).

"Follow peace with all men" (Hebrews 2:22).

"Seek peace, and ensure it" (1 Peter 3:11).

"And the servants of the God of Mercy are they who walk upon the Earth softly; and when the ignorant address them, they reply, 'Peace!'" (Sura 25:64).

"And when they hear light discourse they withdraw from it and say, 'Our works for us and your works for you! Peace be on you! We are not in quest of fools!'" (Sura 28:55).

"For hatred does not cease by hatred at any time: hatred ceases by love, this is an old rule" (Dhammapada 5).

"An attitude of being friendly with those who are happy, of being compassionate toward the unhappy, of joy for the virtuous, and of disregard for the wicked, will produce calmness in the mind" (Patanjali Yoga Sutras Book I verse 33).

"When harmony prevails, there will be no scarcity of people" (Confucius, Analects 16.1).

Principle 12 – True wealth is spiritual, not material.

True wealth is not the material things we possess. The world and everything in it, including everything most people consider wealth, such as land, gold, diamonds, and automobiles, are all illusions. True wealth is spiritual in nature: Love, Joy, Peace, and Freedom. The true measurement of wealth is how much joy we experience.

Cultivate an understanding of truth, the abilities of creativity and intuition, the emotions of love, and joy, and the mastery of accomplishments such as playing musical instruments, painting works of art, or understanding mathematics. These are the only true realities.

Our definitions of "life" and "better" need reconsidering. Is it better having a bigger house, or a bigger car, or having more money, more power, more sex, or more stuff? Because life is not the period between birth and death, a corrected definition of better is a grander experience and a greater expression of our state of being. A corrected definition of life is an eternal, sustained, never-ending process of being.

A better life is not collecting as much stuff as possible. The person with the most stuff at death is not the winner. Yet collecting stuff is what drives most people. If we don't care for things, it's easy to let them go.

There are pleasures of the body and there are pleasures of the spirit. The pleasures of the spirit are the greatest.

Some people fight for survival each day. Some have the basics of survival and try just to get ahead. These two groups make up most of the people on Earth. Another much smaller group has all it could ever ask for, and yet many in this group ask for more and hold tightly to what they have. Then there is the last and smallest group of all. The members of this group don't need material things. For them, spiritual truth, reality, and experience are most important. Their goal is to know God, fulfill self, and express truth, a process of self-discovery, of growth, and of being. Instead of concerns of the body, their concerns are of the soul. For them, greatness is measured by spiritual progress. For them, the definition of success is not coveting, acquiring, protecting, and increasing in worldly possessions, but in developing their spirituality.

Sacred scriptures of old have said:

"A little that a righteous man hath is better than the riches of many wicked" (Psalms 37:16).

"There is that maketh himself rich, yet hath nothing: there is that maketh himself poor, yet hath great riches" (Proverbs 13:7).

"As he came forth of his mother's womb, naked shall he return to go as he came, and shall take nothing of his labour, which he may carry away in his hand" (Ecclesiastes 5:15).

"Lay not up for yourselves treasures upon earth, where moth and rust doth corrupt, and where thieves break through and steal: But lay up for yourselves treasures in heaven, where neither moth nor rust doth corrupt, and where thieves do not break through nor steal: For where your treasure is, there will your heart be also" (Matthew 6:19-21).

"Beware of covetousness: for a man's life consisteth not in the abundance of the things which he possesseth" (Luke 12:15).

Principle 13 – We create everything in this world.

We create the world and everything in it, and we are responsible for everything. Life is not happening to us. We are creating it. It is being produced by us. If what we've created doesn't serve our agenda, we have the power to create something matching our agenda. We are masters of our own fate and can do, be, or have anything. We are unlimited, and any limits we experience are placed on us by ourselves. Everything in our world and everything coming into our world was, is, and will be created by our thoughts. All things are possible, and since we create our world, any villains, or victims have been created by us for our benefit, thus making the terms villains and victims meaningless. There are only outcomes of our desires. The Universe always agrees with Itself. Nothing happens by accident and all involved agree with what happens, a result of our unity. Perfect Souls forget who they are to come to Earth to experience life. It may appear they do imperfect things, but everything is done for a reason.

All events are miracles providing us with the context to experience life and to announce to the world Who we are. Nothing happens against God's will. Therefore, condemnation is inappropriate.

What we think not only affects our lives today but also our lives in the future. This applies to us individually, and collectively. If we think thoughts of compassion, love, empathy, patience, and forgiveness the future is much different than if we think thoughts of malice, hate, jealousy, greed, and covetousness. Earthquakes, Tornadoes, floods, Hurricanes, and epidemics are the result of thoughts and intentions.

How we think, and act produces our world. At one end of the spectrum, we can produce earthquakes, famines, floods, and disease. At the other, we can produce happiness, joy, harmony, prosperity, and peace. Only we can decide what we want to create. When we are compassionate, loving, gentle, kind, and considerate, we produce the positive end of possible outcomes. When we are rude, inconsiderate, thoughtless, unkind, and belligerent, we produce the negative end of possible outcomes.

Our thoughts are creative, and if our thoughts are constantly on the starvation, floods, and earthquakes of the moment, they will tend to persist. If we are visionary and think about a world without starvation, floods, and earthquakes, they will diminish in our experience. We should give our attention to what we choose, not to what we don't want in our experience. We can feel our way to our desired goals with feelings of joy, knowledge, freedom, love, appreciation, passion, enthusiasm, eagerness, happiness, positive expectation, belief, optimism, and hopefulness.

There is nothing we cannot be, do, or have, so let us welcome and bless everything in life, and whatever fails to serve us, release it, and send it on its way with our blessing.

Since we each create our lives, we are each responsible for everything showing up in our lives. We are not victims. Look for solutions not for blame. This leads to happiness. We are creating our experience of life. If we don't like our creation, accept it as our creation and choose something else. Don't judge or condemn anything. Change or support a change of those things not reflecting who we are.

We should examine our souls for our needs, passions, and desires, and seek to manifest these in our lives to produce happiness. This is our unique happiness. Seek this and not what someone else says will make us happy.

Everything in life happens just as we planned it. Nothing happens by accident. We have created it all for our own personal growth, and we can create anything we can imagine. What we fear is attracted to our experience. This creative process is magnified when groups of people have similar imaginings and fears. The more people involved, the greater the creative forces.

The world as we know it was created by the combined consciousness of everyone on Earth. If we are satisfied with it, we need do nothing. If we are not satisfied, we must change our conscious desires, starting with the individual and moving from smaller groups all the way up to all of humanity. Changing the consciousness of others is best done by our example, and our example is magnified by joining with other like-minded individuals. Everything starts with us. If we don't do it, it won't happen.

We are literally just One Big Thing. We could say we create our lives, or God creates our lives or God and we create our lives because we are all One. So, God creates all the pain, suffering, and death in our world. But it's all an illusion because it never happens. All events in our lives are for our benefit including pain, suffering, and death. It's all part of the play, or video game, or whatever we call life in this world. If God wanted to prevent something, say starvation, it wouldn't happen, but then we wouldn't have free will. But we do have the power to end starvation if we choose. We haven't made that choice, so we still have starvation. Free will allows us to make this grand choice. All of life is there for us to experience what we choose to experience. Do we want to experience compassion? There is the starving, those injured by storms or earthquakes, and the ill. If life were perfect, how could we experience compassion? The problems of the world are there for us to conquer and experience what we choose to experience.

Our will is God's Will or Joint Will. The Joint Will produces our world and our experiences.

God causes us to do everything. All things done are done by God through us. God is Life. God is the life force in us and everything, seen and unseen. Nothing is dead for God or Life is in everything. The Universe is part of the body of God, and all Intelligence comes from the mind of God, all Love comes from the Heart of God, and all Power comes from the Will of God. God creates all things and lives in all things. God lives in the hearts of humans, the hearts of animals, the hearts of trees, and the hearts of stones, producing the humans, the animals, the trees, and the stones in the world as God wishes to produce them.

The illusion of separation is made by our own personality or our ego. Eventually, all will come to know our unity, and all personality will be replaced by God's Impersonality.

Some believe one thing, and others may believe just the opposite. This demonstrates the power of thought. Through thought, we produce our bodies, personalities, characters, the environment, and the world in our present experience of them. In the next moment, we can change our thoughts and produce something different. We have the power to change them to whatever we choose. Everything appearing outside of ourselves is an illusion. The truth is found within. If we think something outside cause's discomfort, just decide it doesn't. We can change our mind about it.

Each one of us pleases God because everything we do is caused by God for God's purpose, even though at times it appears contrary to our perception of God's purpose and wish. God gives each of our minds the experiences we experience to produce the ability to understand God so God can express through us God's Ideas.

Ancient sages realized they created matter from their ideas. This matter was alive and conscious. They realized they could alter their environment by their actions. Thoughts, ideas, and beliefs from many great thinkers agree on many things.

All suffering, pain, fear, grieving, sickness, and death are personal choices. Everything in our lives is a personal choice.

Loss is a decision. Pain is a choice. Grief, fear, and sickness are all experienced because of desire. Death comes by consent. Whatever happens in a life is because of a wish. If it's chosen, it must appear.

As we think, so we perceive. We don't need to try to change the world, only change our minds about the world.

Life is created. There is no duplication. No two snowflakes are identical. No two relationships are identical. Nothing is identical.

Nothing matters in life allowing us to add whatever meaning we choose to the experience.

Because we are a process, we are both the Creator and the Created. The important question then is do we create consciously or unconsciously? Do we experience life from the cause end of it or from the effective end of it? It is empowering to be the cause of everything.

Desire starts the process of creation. From desire, an image of the desired thing is produced and judged valuable. The images are projected outward and pronounced real and protected as the creator's property. Insane desires produce our insane world. The world we see is the same world we hold in our mind. If we change the world in our mind, we will change the world we see. The wisdom, love, and truth of God are found in each soul, expressing through us and producing our world. What we hold in our minds, is created in our world through thought, word, and deed. Therefore, to create anything, we must first have a clear picture in our minds of what we want to create. We create everything in our world through a process starting with an idea of the soul and later transferred to the mind, and finally produced in physical form. If we have ideas of perfection, we will produce perfection. If we have ideas of imperfection, we will produce imperfection. Thus, we create Heaven or Hell as we wish. Everything started out as a thought. Thoughts and words radiate out from the source in all directions to the extent of the Universe. Then they return to the source. We would do well to send positive thoughts and words out to the Universe because we create everything with our thoughts. We can create joy and peace, or we can create terror and war. We are the masters and makers of our fate.

We are constantly recreating life as we wish with God's permission or it wouldn't happen. We may recreate life in the most hideous and grotesque forms, and we have, or we may choose the most glorious and heavenly. God gives us the free will to do either. We are totally responsible for everything happening in the world. This is our part in change. We are making all the choices and we as a group can change our choices. We decide what we see, feel, experience, and achieve. Everything in our lives appears for us because we decided we wished to experience it.

Most people see themselves as separate individuals, unconnected to everything, and believe their actions have no effect on the world, but this is not true. We are One with Everything and our actions affect the whole world and can cause the collapse of everything.

We have created the world to be our joyful playground. Our creation has a duality about it where we can experience the good and the bad, and we have chosen to experience them both. Good and bad are our judgments about our experiences, and subject to change.

Our future depends on what we think about ourselves, about God, and about Life. Our reality is created from our thoughts. Our beliefs produce our behaviors, producing our experiences. Beliefs are all important.

We can choose to live in hatred or we can choose to live in compassion. If we dream angel dreams, God will help us create them and make them real. We create by thinking and anyone who thinks, creates, and experiences life.

Sacred scriptures put it this way:

"As a man thinketh in his heart, so is he" (Proverbs 23:7).

"The Lord of hosts hath sworn, saying, Surely as I have thought, so shall it come to pass; and as I have purposed, so shall it stand" (Isaiah 14:24).

"All that we are is the result of what we have thought: it is founded on our thoughts, it is made up of our thoughts. If a man speaks or acts with an evil thought, pain follows him, as the wheel follows the foot of the ox that draws the carriage.

All that we are is the result of what we have thought: it is founded on our thoughts; it is made up of our thoughts. If a man speaks or acts with a pure thought, happiness follows him, like a shadow that never leaves him" (Dhammapada 1-2).

Life can be likened to an amusement park, only we may not be amused at times. There is the Tornado Ride, the Tsunami Ride, the Earthquake House, the Flood Plunge, the Fahrenheit Fire Experience, the Fender Bender, and the Draconian Divorce, among others. There are also positive adventures like the Look of Love House, and the Compassion Experience. Each adventure allows us to experience the ride anyway we wish. Do we choose fear, compassion, or conquest? We get to be the next greatest version of ourselves or the worst. We get to choose.

Principle 14 – Everything in the Universe is for our benefit.

The Universe was set up to provide for our wellbeing, our abundance, our understanding, and all the positive things we desire. The Universe is on our side, and we can create anything we can imagine. But we may choose to bring negative things into our experience of life, and what we fear will be attracted to our world. Only our resistance to receiving these blessings can prevent our desires from appearing in our experience.

We are all co-creators. We should appreciate the diversity of our co-creators, and work with the system. We don't have to fix the system, just work with it. We don't need to try to control others. Each point of view is important. There will be a never-ending parade of issues to deal with, and enough resources to deal with them. Competition is unnecessary. There is enough.

We believe there is not enough of love, money, food, clothing, shelter, time, good ideas, us, or anything, and because we believe this, we do what we think we need to do to get what we think we need. One moment in the spirit world and we will know there is enough of everything. God never says no. We are free to decide how to live our lives. Our will for ourselves is God's will for us, and God is on our side.

It is natural to trust the Universe, but we have been taught to distrust the Universe. Trust the process. Life is the process. As part of life, we are part of the process. The process is for our good. See the perfection in everything showing up in life. It all comes down to trust. Do we trust ourselves and others? Lack of trust will lead to laws inhibiting humans doing what they want to do. Trust will lead to believing God has created natural laws allowing us to do as we please producing man-made laws affirming our freedom.

Life contains only angels and miracles. At times it certainly doesn't appear this is correct. Damning anything is not constructive. It only dooms the damner to repeat what was damned. So, bless everything to provide an opportunity to change it.

There is not a single life experience that can damage us. All life experiences where others have done something to us, we have done the same to others. These experiences have provided us with the opportunity to remember Who We Really Are. At the end of the life of our earthly bodies, we will see the Whole Picture, and we will be thankful for each moment with all the joys and sorrows. The perfection will then be apparent.

One life fallacy is we don't have enough happiness producing stuff to go around. This idea came from another life fallacy, we are separate. If we believe we are One, we would experience enough, because we would create the experience. Then we would share everything with everyone.

Many religions have charities to help those less fortunate. Unfortunately, many of these organizations provide services only to those who are members of their religion. Many countries, states, and cultural, ethnic, racial, and social groups also provide services to their own. This limited support for humanity fosters separation.

Such a narrow perspective distorts our awareness and limits our understanding of everything. Broadening our perspective allows us to realize our Oneness. We will then see we are separating ourselves from our Self. What a surprise! We will clearly see everyone and everything as ourselves. People, rocks, trees, planets, suns, and moons are all made of the same stuff we are. We all appear to be different but are composed of the same substance. We will discover when we don't treat everything as ourselves, we only hurt ourselves.

The first experience of insufficiency was within when we thought of ourselves as imperfect. We were less than the world and the gods who ruled the world. When we looked at our surroundings, the Earth, and the stars, as something separate from us, and thought how puny we were in comparison, we could only conclude we would never measure up. The truth is we are literally One with the stars. We are One with Everything.

The highest interest for humans is self-interest. This is true because the correct definition of self-includes everyone. Solving our problems is easy just by enlarging the definition of the self to include everyone. Believing we are One with everyone will stop our destructive behaviors. Believing we are One with God will allow us to create a wonderful new world.

God wants only the best for us and never wants us to suffer. God's wish for us is to be happy. When we live in Christ Consciousness, as opposed to separation, there is no limitation. God is able to supply all our needs depending on what we believe. The problem is we believe we are separate from God, less perfect, and therefore unable to create as God, but we are all One with God and able to create all things.

Expressing the love in our hearts causes us to give, and by giving we receive. If we give without expecting anything in return, we will receive abundantly. When we experience unity with Life, Love, and Wisdom, we are in conscious contact with God, and receiving abundance. We have all things within ourselves. We were created as everything. What we have is what we are. We lack nothing. God is all there is. There is nothing outside or beside God. We are therefore a part of God. All of Us are God. Everything is always with us, and therefore there is nothing to need. Knowing this we can live fearlessly.

It is impossible for us to experience death, experience genuine loss, experience separation, fail, harm anyone or be harmed by anyone, or be guilty of sin. These are all illusions of this world.

All events, past, present, and future, are planned by God to bless us. All events in our lives are for our good and provide opportunities for all of us to grow, whether we experienced the events or someone else did. In life, there is no evil, only good. It is easy to accept everything showing up in our lives when we realize everything happening, past, present, and future are all planned for our benefit.

The following wisdom from sacred scriptures emphasizes life is on our side and we can live a life of abundance:

"But as for you, ye thought evil against me; *but* God meant it unto good, to bring to pass, as *it is* this day, to save much people alive." (Genesis 50:20)

"For I know the thoughts that I think toward you, saith the LORD, thoughts of peace, and not of evil, to give you an expected end" (Jeremiah 29:11).

"Ask, and it shall be given you; seek, and ye shall find; knock, and it shall be opened unto you: For every one that asketh receiveth; and he that seeketh findeth; and to whom that knocketh it shall be opened" (Matthew 7:7-8).

Are not two sparrows sold for a farthing? and one of them shall not fall on the ground without your Father. But the very hairs of your head are all numbered. Fear ye not therefore, ye are of more value than many sparrows (Matthew 10:29-31).

"Give and it shall be given unto you; good measure, pressed down, shaken together, and running over shall men give unto your bosom. For with the same measure that you mete, withal, it shall be measured to you again" (Luke 6:38).

"Fear not, little flock; for it is your Father's good pleasure to give you the kingdom" (Luke 12:32).

"And we know that all things work together for good to them that love God, to them who are the called according to his purpose" (Romans 8:28).

"If any of you lack wisdom, let him ask of God, that giveth to all men liberally, and upbraideth not; and it shall be given him" (James 1:5).

"According as his divine power hath given unto us all things that pertain unto life and godliness, through the knowledge of him that hath called us to glory and virtue" (2 Peter 1:3).

"And this is the confidence that we have in him, that, if we ask any thing according to his will, he heareth us: And if we know that he hear us, whatsoever we ask, we know that we have the petitions that we desired of him" (1 John 5:14-15).

"Nor happeneth to you any mishap, but it is for your own handy-work" (Sura 42:29).

"Therefore the sufficiency of contentment is an enduring and unchanging sufficiency" (Tao Te Ching 46).

Principle 15 – Truth is what works to get us to where we want to go.

Truth is what works. It all comes down to what works and what does not work, depending on our goal.

What works is the gold standard of how to proceed. Through the use of science, and seeking greater competence, we will be able to move forward. Monopolistic power structures creating artificial environments and situations to force compliance of people will not serve us.

Our feelings, highest thoughts and experiences will guide us to the truth. Honor these above of all else.

Any communication from God, even if it is a sacred text such as the Book of Mormon, the Pali Canon, the Koran, the Bhagavad Gita, the Bible, or the Talmud, should be checked first with our inner understanding of truth before accepting it as truth. Our source of authority is within us. Having accepted anything as true, we should only comment on this truth as being true for us. We each have our own truth because of our own unique view of the world around us.

Safety can be found in truth and love. If we know we are love, we will know we are safe.

Here are nine new ideas to be considered as truth to facilitate our advancement:

1. We should all assume accepted truths may not be true.

2. All of us are of equal specialness. No one from history, who lives today, or who will live in the future is superior to anyone. We are all equal. Every one of us is a messenger. Our lives as we live them demonstrate to the world who we are every second of every day. Everyone who is aware of us is impacted by our lives. Jesus, Muhammad, and Siddhartha Gautama are our equals.

3. Any path will lead to God, and all are equal. All religions are equal. All prophets are equal.

4. God has everything and lacks nothing. Therefore, God needs nothing to be happy. God can be defined as happiness, so God needs nothing from anyone to be happy.

5. God is not a separate Superior Being subject to the same emotional needs and turmoil as we experience. God is immune to pain, hurt, and damage. There is no reason for God to impose revenge or punishment on anyone.

6. There is just One Thing composed of Everything.

7. Right and wrong do not exist. When judging any idea, we should check to see if it does or does not work to reach our goal. Right and wrong are judgments we make, labels of our own creation. Our values of right and wrong are decisions we as individuals and as a society make, and then change as we want changes. What is right and wrong is fickle because our definitions change over time.

8. We are not our physical bodies. We are infinite. Our bodies are perfectly healthy fully functioning learning aids our souls use to navigate this world. When our bodies are defective in any way, we have created the condition for our own reasons. We breathe life into our bodies. Our bodies can be damaged, but we cannot. Our bodies can die, but we cannot. We as souls encase our bodies. We are the energy configuration of the Universal Spirit, God. We are a force field, a radiating, pulsating energy package. We are an energy field without end. We mingle with all other energy fields. Our energy has no limit in time and space. There is only One Soul, One Energy, God expressed locally as individuals. This energy has intelligence and is the repository and source of all knowledge, awareness, data,

information, understanding, and experience. This energy is the All in All, God.

9. We cannot die, nor will we be condemned to Hell.

The Toltecs teach there is no absolute truth in this world. We each have our own truth, and this truth is the truth for each of us. It's all part of our dream world. By definition, an illusion is not true, and everything in this world is an illusion.

"To him then he said, 'There are two knowledges to be known - as indeed the knowers of Brahma are wont to say: a higher and also a lower. Of these, the lower is the Rig-Veda, the Yajur-Veda, the Sama-Veda, the Atharva-Veda, Pronunciation, Ritual, Grammar, Difinition, Metrics, and Astrology. Now the higher is that whereby the Imperishable is apprehended.'" (Mundaka Upanishad 1.4-5). One type of knowledge is the lower related to this world. The second is related to the eternal or Real World. There is the truth of this world, and there is the truth of the Real World. Knowing just one, knows half of the truth.

"And ye shall know the truth, and the truth shall make you free" (John 8:32).

"If we all worked on the assumption that what is accepted as true were really true, there would be little hope of advance," said Orville Wright (1871-1948) co-inventor of the airplane.

God does not guarantee we will know or understand the truth now. We have many times, maybe most times, misunderstood what God has been trying to tell us. What we believe now, we consider being true even though it may not be. Eventually, we will know the truth.

When it comes to solving our problems, we must find what works, the truth of the moment.

Principle 16 – Life is all about change.

Our world and everything in it including us are constantly changing. It is impossible to stop the change. We may try to perpetuate the present, but as sure as love is, everything but love will change. We get to choose how the world will change, and when we are ready for peace, we will have peace. We are evolving, and must work at the level we find ourselves. If we are in 1st grade, we must work at the 1st-grade level. We can't jump to 12th grade.

Change happens all the time. It can't be stopped. There are governments, corporations, religions, educational systems, legal systems, institutions, and organizations that will be changed out of existence because they are based on dying ideas. For any group or organization to survive, it must change in a sustainable manner or die. The most powerful country, the United States of America, will cease to exist, as the Roman Empire failed if it is unable to adapt to the changing world. Nations have risen and fallen. They have changed over time. The United States is not the same today as it was when it was founded. Someday another nation will be more powerful. And the day is coming when it will no longer exist. There are those who want to keep things as they are now. To do this requires a tremendous amount of energy and is doomed to failure in the long run. It is better to guide change to improve the world.

Change in this world is ever with us. If change would stop, so would life. Each moment, each second, we are changing. The changes might be small but changes none the less. This process of change is the process of self-creation. We may be merely watching it or actively taking part in it. We have the power to produce a change in our lives, and we can use this power to produce the highest idea of what we can be. Most of us keep trying to stop change, an impossible goal. We try to stop the aging process, and we try to recreate our hairstyle from the day before.

Religions try to keep beliefs as they were, and they have not succeeded. Change has been slow, but change has occurred. In some cases, religions have been replaced by others. Christian beliefs today are not the same as they were right after Jesus left this world. Christians like to think their version of Christianity is what Jesus taught. But with tens of thousands of different Christian sects, which one is right? Other religions have competing sects to deal with too.

Political systems, economic systems, educational systems, and social systems have come and gone and changed over time.

We tend to think the systems in place now are the best possible. Otherwise, we would surely change them to something better, wouldn't we? But we really don't want to change. Change is traumatic, and we try to hold on to what is familiar. We don't want to be wrong about what we have chosen.

Logically, change should be for the better. The problem is sometimes no one knows where the change is going to lead. So, as we make our changes, some will not take us where we want to go. Then we'll have to choose again and hope the new choice will get us there. We will make many "errors," but each step, forward or backward, will eventually get us to our goal.

The best way to deal with change is to accept the fact we don't know all the answers. There could be something out there we don't know, but if we did, it would change everything. Therefore, we should allow new ideas to be considered. Then we should try the best to see how they work, and if they don't work, consider more new ideas; try them out, and so on as we change the future.

As we make changes, there will be massive displacements. Billions of jobs, primarily in the military and allied industries will evaporate and need to be replaced with fulfilling productive jobs. Many of these people will be needed in the space program as we visit other planets, solar systems, and galaxies, and as we meet our neighbors in the Universe. This will be a massive shift for the world.

To make lasting changes in the world, each of us must change our beliefs producing changes in our attitudes. World change is not completed by thinking, working, or frantically doing some activity. To change the world, we must **be** the change. It is something within our being. It is a change of heart.

Unity leads to improving world conditions while division leads to deteriorating world conditions. Unity is constantly evolving into greater potential with God as the source. Division retards growth, uses judgment and conflict to retard unity from improving conditions. Those fostering division resist change. Stagnation is the result of division.

All problems will be solved by looking at them from a higher level with a greater perspective. Curing violence with violence cannot be done.

There is no magic bullet. Progress is accomplished one step at a time. Some steps are small. But little by little progress will be made. Rely on inner intelligence. Look for a broader perspective. Permanence is an illusion. All Earthly things change so be flexible and allow for change.

In this world, love is the only unchanging thing. Evolution is logically superior to decay or trying to remain the same.

Changing ideas about right and wrong is not a problem for we have changed these ideas in the past. The problem is the ideas we hold to be true now are considered to be perfect and correct, and everyone should believe in them. Some of us are self-justified and self-righteous about these ideas. The correct approach is to stick up for our beliefs but allow room for changes, and don't require others to believe our ideas.

Life and societies are constantly evolving. Each society must solve their problems at the level of evolution they find themselves. We presently, as a group, don't remember who we are. We don't remember we are One with Everything making us Divine. Our reaction now if faced with dealing with a despot is to stop the despotism. The abuse of anyone should be stopped. At our present state of evolution, there may be times when a country should go to war to ensure the peace. Eventually, we will evolve to the place where we will do nothing or drop our bodies and start somewhere else.

But the day is coming when we will remember who we are and then we will know we can't be hurt. If attacked, we will leave our bodies and possessions knowing we can't be hurt and we can create new bodies and possessions.

We are deciding what is good and bad, what is OK and not OK as we go along. It has to be this way, or we wouldn't be able to make any progress in this human experience. This allows for change. It allows us to replace old values with new ones.

Life is change. Everything in Earthly life is always changing. If the change would stop, Life would end. But Life can't end.

Unfortunately for us, we are constantly trying to stop the change and keep things as they are, and this creates a living hell for us.

We are constantly evolving or changing. We **must** be constantly evolving, and we get to choose how we evolve. We are both the changed and the changer. We are changing both ourselves and our world. We are constantly recreating or evolving Life as we know it.

We are constantly recreating Life as we wish with God's permission or it wouldn't happen. We may recreate Life in the most hideous and grotesque forms, and we have, or we may choose the most glorious and heavenly. God gives us the free will to do either.

We are responsible for all changes taking place in the world because we are totally responsible for everything happening in the world. We are making all the choices and we as a group can change our choices.

To change the world, we must change ourselves. First, we must select ourselves to be an agent of change. Then we must demonstrate our decision with the way we live our lives every moment. We define ourselves with every act we commit, everything we think, everything we say, and everything we do. Our lives lived, demonstrate to the world what we believe about life. And our lives have a big impact on the world. If we change ourselves, we will change our world. If we change our inner world, our outer world will change and little by little the whole world will change. If we don't do it, who will? If we don't do it now, when will we do it?

Our values of right and wrong are decisions we as individuals and as a society make, and then change as what we want changes. Our values change and change all the time. When we change what we want to be, to do, or to have, our values will change. As our perceptions, desires, and wants change, our values change.

Change is found only in the Physical World and is an illusion. Change does not exist in the Absolute World where God exists. God does not change.

Everything is changing all the time. Permanence is an illusion.

"Even the law in the Bible changed. For the priesthood being changed, there is made of necessity a change also of the law" (Hebrews 7:12).

We are all evolving all the time. We are evolving as individuals and as societies. Evolution is not a straight line up. But even digression is a step forward. Evolution can be fast or slow, but speed is not important. It's all part of the trip.

Principle 17 – Forgiveness will transform the world.

No one is guilty of anything. Everyone we meet is an angel. Until we see all as guiltless, forgiveness is the tool of choice.

Judgment causes people to feel lost, hurt, and alone. The solution is forgiveness. To be effective, forgiveness must be sincere, otherwise, it's more judgment. Judgment will stifle the development of anyone's goals. It prevents growth toward enlightenment and increases the perceived separation from God.

It may seem forgiveness prevents justice, but this is not true. Forgiveness produces transparency in anyone's life along with freedom of spirit. It reminds us of who we are and restores life. If we are transparent, we are free, wise, and an asset for all. Forgiveness brings solutions to life's problems. It starts in the heart but usually requires action. Change the perspective of the situation and eliminate judgment and any hidden reasons to continue the conflict, and release the reasons for the situation. Other methods include laughter, prayer, love, and release. Unforgiveness will limit our lives, including every relationship and goal. Why give this power to the situation?

It takes real effort to use forgiveness to solve problems. Don't use forgiveness to appease an aggressor, or to lessen the fear of additional harm. This will solve nothing. There are times when action must be taken to prevent the situation from repeating or worsening. At times conditions must be repaired, or the offender must be informed of the damage they have inflected. A release of emotion can be useful to inform the offender of the consequences of their actions. Revenge, retribution, and inflection of hurt will not bring peace.

God judges not. We think He does because we do, but He doesn't. Forgiveness is the way to end judging. God never condemns and therefore, forgiveness is unnecessary. God will not forgive anyone for anything because there is nothing to forgive.

Our world is a world of illusions. If we forgive, we release ourselves from illusions. If we condemn, we condemn ourselves. If we forgive, we forgive only ourselves.

Forgiveness knows the illusion of any offense by someone never happened. Judgment condemns the world. Forgiveness paves the way to Heaven. Forgiveness can heal all wounds, psychological, emotional, spiritual, and physical we believe have been inflicted on us. Forgiveness has enormous value for us, being a primitive society. Enlightened societies have no need for forgiveness because they know no one can be hurt. Who or what could hurt God?

Anyone who is condemned will be tempted to condemn in return. Anyone treated as inferior will be tempted to treat the accuser as inferior. Forgiveness is the solution. We should rely on justice, armor ourselves with wisdom, cover ourselves with forgiveness, mercy, and anything providing a joyful heart. We can forgive each other from our unity through our hearts.

Our unity and there being nothing outside us makes it impossible for some outside entity to judge any part or the whole of anything. Lacking a judge, nothing or no one in the Universe can be judged right or wrong, making the Whole and all Its parts perfect.

Sacred scriptures put it this way:

"And forgive us our debts, as we forgive our debtors (Matthew 6:12).

"Judge not, that ye be not judged" (Matthew 7:1).

"Then came Peter to him, and said, Lord, how oft shall my brother sin against me, and I forgive him? till seven times? Jesus saith unto him, I say not unto thee, Until seven times: but, Until seventy times seven" (Matthew 18: 21-22).

"And when ye stand praying, forgive, if ye have ought against any: that your Father also which is in heaven may forgive you your trespasses. But if ye do not forgive, neither will your Father which is in heaven forgive your trespasses" (Mark 11:25-26). What we do to another, we do to ourselves. If we don't forgive another, we don't forgive ourselves.

"Judge not, and ye shall not be judged: condemn not, and ye shall not be condemned: forgive, and ye shall be forgiven" (Luke 6:37).

"And forgive us our sins; for we also forgive every one that is indebted to us (Luke 11:4).

"Let us not therefore judge one another any more" (Romans 14:13).

"And be ye kind one to another, tenderhearted, forgiving one another, even as God for Christ's sake hath forgiven you" (Ephesians 4:32). In truth, the correct way to forgive is to see any situation as lacking the need to forgive. Whatever happen was for our benefit, and the other person was innocent. God sees all of us as innocent.

"Forbearing one another, and forgiving one another, if any man have a quarrel against any: even as Christ forgave you, so also do ye" (Colossians 3:13).

"But he who forgiveth and is reconciled, shall be rewarded by God" (Sura 42:38).

God is not conflicted. God's creation is unified and not split in two. God's Son, All of Us, could never be in Hell when God placed the Son in Heaven. There is no Hell to oppose Heaven.

If we are a part of God, The All That Is, then God would certainly not judge, condemn, and punish us because then God would be judging, condemning, and punishing Itself. If we are a part of God, then we are immortal as God is immortal. If we are a part of God, then God would love us unconditionally as God loves Itself. The correct application of forgiveness is to assign no guilt to anyone because all are innocent.

The three basic truths are: We are all One Thing, there is plenty for everyone, and doing is not important. We only have to be. If we practiced these truths, we would treat others as ourselves, share the entire world with everyone, and solve all our problems by being, that is, creating world peace by being peaceful.

Osama bin Laden is innocent. He played his part in our grand play called life. And as hard as it is to believe, his life led us all closer to world peace. When we get tired of all the killing and decide we want peace, then we will have peace. If we judge him, we judge ourselves. Forgiveness is the last thing we have to master. Forgiveness is salvation. This is not salvation from sin. Sin does not exist. This is salvation from believing the fallacy anyone can be guilty of anything.

Principle 18 – Transparency and honesty go hand in hand to demonstrate our unity.

Transparency is all about being open, honest, candid, and lacking guile or concealment. Nothing is done behind closed doors. Everything is done out in the open for all to see. In our world of illusions, we have the appearance of being able to hide things, but nothing is ever hidden. If we are all One, how could anything be hidden? Why would we want to hide something from ourselves? Transparency is what we see is what we get in action. What we hear is the truth. What we do is a demonstration of who we are, a unified whole. There are no hidden agendas. We don't hide behind a mask. We don't project the persona we think others will like. We're authentic. We're real. One important part of transparency and honesty is being honest with ourselves.

We live in a non-transparent world. We color our bodies, arrange our hair, change our odors, hang ornaments on ourselves, change the shape of our bodies, and cover our bodies to project an image of who we are not. We project a persona we think will make us accepted by those around us. The "truth" we share with others is colored to make it what we think will be acceptable to others. Our governments, religions, corporations, organizations, committees, and groups hide information and conceal how decisions are made from us. They think if we don't need to know something, we should be kept in the dark.

Much of our society is based on secrecy. We think secrecy makes our society work. Secrecy is the basis of our social, ethical, and secret codes. Our governments, businesses, and our relationships run on lies. And we lie about lying. These secrets are lies because a failure to tell the whole truth is a lie. These secrets prevent people from making intelligent decisions based on all the facts.

We live in a secret society where more truth is hidden than is spoken. We have done this intentionally. We fear by being totally honest we won't be able to reach our goals. So, to get what we want, we withhold the truth.

What we truly intend produces our actions. We may say one thing and do another, but our actions reveal our true intentions. We say we want to live in a peaceful world, but our actions say otherwise. We ignore what is so. And we lie to ourselves and to each other about what is really going on. Truly enlightened people never lie; not to themselves and not to another.

Honesty is the basis of intelligence just as dishonesty is the basis of stupidity. Honesty is important for building budgets, bridges, buildings, businesses, and producing goods and services. We should be honest with ourselves, and honest about what we perceive.

Transparency, of a nation, of a business, of an organization, or of a person, reduces conflict and increases the power to reach goals.

Anger that is wonderful, loving, and fully expressed, is healing. It is the truth, and a transparent display of our emotions. It is healing. It is the shortest path to harmony. Anger expressed as verbal or physical abuse hurts. An injury cannot heal an injury. Anger suppressed will hurt our bodies. It should be expressed to rid ourselves of the emotional energy. We should covey our feelings without physically or verbally abusing anyone. We should express how we feel without accusations.

Enlightened cultures don't hide their feelings from each other. This is the principle method of communication. The soul's language is feelings. All communication is based on truth. They know each other in truth and could never comprehend lying. Their societies are based on what is so and what works. They learned long ago being false does not work. Each person is the truth. Because they are advanced they can read each other's minds and nothing can be hidden anyway. For them, words are not necessary to communicate because their communications are based on love. Where love and caring for each other are present, words are not necessary. Where love and caring are absent, words are necessary. Real communication involves truth and is based on love. Where there is love, we will find the truth. In the presence of our beloved, the truth will be revealed. We should express our true feelings with love. It is inappropriate to fail to express our truth. Our truth should be expressed when failing to so would cause someone to believe something false, or it would compromise our integrity. The full depth of our negative feelings need not be shared.

Being totally transparent is enjoyable. We don't feel good when we're less than transparent. We have the feeling others are not totally honest all the time, so we follow suit.

Enlightened cultures observe fully what works and communicate truthfully what is so. They have no moral codes and do only what produce a benefit. They don't follow a set of arbitrary rules for living but follow only what works for society and what benefits everyone. They live a life based on what is functional and what benefits them. They believe each individual is the only authority of who decides what is and is not proper behavior for them.

Forgiveness produces transparency in anyone's life along with freedom of spirit. It reminds us of who we are and restores life. If we are transparent, we are free, wise, and an asset for all. Forgiveness brings solutions to life's problems.

Be totally honest everywhere all the time. Be honest about all actions and outcomes and take full responsibility for them. When we take responsibility for our lives, we demonstrate great maturity and spiritual growth.

To be totally loving means to be totally open, honest, transparent, fully naked, lacking hidden agendas, hidden motives, or anything hidden. Perfect communication is not possible when we try to hide thoughts from others.

It is natural for us to tell the truth, but our society has taught us to avoid telling the truth. When we become totally honest, our lives are totally transparent. We are totally visible. People can see through us because we have no hidden agendas. When we are totally honest and transparent our relationships, businesses, politics, schools, and everything in our lives will change.

Transparency is inversely proportionate to the delusion of mortality we experience.

People are not open about money. A person's wealth and financial dealings are considered private matters. Even governments and businesses are not totally open about money. Openness and transparency in all money transactions of everyone would transform the world and produce fairness, honesty, and the goal of producing the best for the collective. This knowledge would stop most of what is happening in the world now such as unequal pay. By knowing how we now spend our money, we would make it impossible to hide anything. No one could take advantage of anyone or have an edge in any dealings because the world would know what was happening.

Transparency produces appropriate behavior. Sunshine Laws are an example of this in action.

Visibility produces fairness. Period. Visibility is the truth. Knowing the truth will set us free. The powerful and wealthy know this and will not let all the truth to be known. People, governments, and corporations with the most power and money have the most to hide. They will oppose any system, political, social, or economic, based on truth and visibility.

Enlightened societies are based on visibility because these societies' goals include survival of everyone and an equally beneficial enjoyable life for everyone. No one hides anything. Everything is known by everyone. This includes wages and benefits earned, taxes paid, and costs of doing business for corporations. Enlighten societies work this way because no one is willing to get anything at another's expense.

Visibility is the best way to conduct interpersonal relationships. This includes romantic relationships. There are no secrets. Nothing is withheld, shaded, colored, hidden, or unspoken. Simply speak the whole truth without shading, manipulating, or twisting. Leave nothing unspoken that should be spoken. Visibility is about fairness and openness. Visibility is the best way to proceed to produce the greatest benefits for

All. This does not mean we disclose every thought, private fear, memory, judgment, opinion, or reaction. We can lovingly state our truth about anything without adding antagonistic verbiage. This is about being emotionally naked.

Live a life of absolute visibility. If not, why not? Lying has produced the world we live in. Is this what we want? Is the world a better place because we manipulate the marketplace, situations, and people? Does privacy make governments, corporations, and individual lives work better?

For when we die, we will meet God, who knows everything. Although nothing is hidden, there will be no judgment or punishment. We live our lives surrounded by a cloud of witnesses. We deceive ourselves by trying to hide the truth, an impossible task. Privacy does not exist. We can invade no one's privacy. Those who have something to hide, and believe they are separate from Everything, are the ones who think privacy is important. But nothing is hidden. There is only One Mind we all share. We share all knowledge and wisdom. Because we share all knowledge, nothing can be hidden. Embrace transparency, an acceptance of what is so.

Honesty is consistency. When we're honest, our thoughts, words, and actions all agree. Dishonesty produces war. When we're totally honest, conflict is impossible with anyone or anything. When we're honest, we are at peace with ourselves.

We each owe it to ourselves to be ourselves in every moment of time. Trying to be something other than ourselves doesn't make us better and deprives us of the pleasure of being ourselves and denies others and the universe of the ability to experience who we are and what we came here to convey. We betray ourselves, we violate ourselves, and we forsake ourselves when we seek to please others over ourselves. By choosing to be something other than ourselves, or by choosing to display anything less than the beauty of our own souls, we make the world poorer.

The New Testament puts it this way:

"Fear them not therefore: for there is nothing covered, that shall not be revealed; and hid, that shall not be known" (Mat 10:26).

"For there is nothing hid, which shall not be manifested; neither was any thing kept secret, but that it should come abroad" (Mark 4:22).

"For nothing is secret, that shall not be made manifest; neither any thing hid, that shall not be known and come abroad" (Luke 8:17).

"For there is nothing covered, that shall not be revealed; neither hid, that shall not be known. Therefore whatsoever ye have spoken in darkness shall be heard in the light; and that which ye have spoken in the ear in closets shall be proclaimed upon the housetops" (Luke 12:2-3).

"Wherefore putting away lying, speak every man truth with his neighbour" (Ephesians 4:25).

"Wherefore seeing we also are compassed about with so great a cloud of witnesses" (Hebrews 12:1).

Nothing can be hidden, so why try? Let's get it over with and be honest with ourselves and everyone else. The benefits are monumental.

What would a completely open and transparent society look like? On a personal level, we would be totally truthful all the time with others and ourselves. We would neither lie by commission nor omission. Our truth would not be shaded, colored, or unspoken. For example, if we are in a romantic relationship, and we find ourselves loving someone else, we would tell our significant other of our love for a different person. If we didn't like the meal prepared by a loved one, we would simply say so. If we didn't tell our truth, we could expect to receive the same meal repeatedly. We all have our own likes and dislikes, and they are not all the same as others. We needn't say it was the worst meal ever, just say, "This is something I don't like." Some people don't like coffee, but this doesn't make all coffee drinkers wrong. If we didn't like her dress, we would say it's not the type of dress we like. On the other hand, if we loved the meal or the dress we would tell them so. Appreciation is always appropriate.

Likewise, our governments would be totally open and honest. Nothing would be done without the public being aware of it. There would be no military, political, or economic secrets.

There would be no need for the government to spy on its citizens because its citizens would be totally open and honest. All money received by any government official would be disclosed. Any presents received by a government official would be openly acknowledged. All discussions on any topic would be open for public scrutiny. There would be no closed-door sessions. We as citizens should know exactly how all our tax money is being spent. And we would also know how much money was paid to the government and by whom.

Businesses and corporations would be cooperative and transparent. They would have no trade secrets, and they would be totally open and honest about costs and pricing and compensation of employees, owners, and shareholders. Technology would be shared among all business. Customers would know how much a product costs to produce as well as the purchase price. Workers would know, in addition to their compensation, how much all other employees were paid, and how much the owner(s) made from the business. Stockholders of corporations would know how decisions were made as well as the compensation of everyone.

All organizations would be open and honest about all aspects of running themselves. Nothing would be done in secret. All aspects of organizations would be open for review. Finances would be public knowledge.

Religions would be transparent. Finances and management decisions would be open for all to know, such as who contributed what, and who received what. Religions would tell the truth as they understand it about doctrines, and why they believe them to be true, and why they take any action.

We are a long way from this reality, and it will take a long time to reach this elevated state of living. It's all about being honest. Since we are all One, we should be honest with ourselves. Honesty and transparency start with each one of us.

Principle 19 – Tolerance is the way to peace by accepting and respecting everyone regardless of their beliefs or who or what they are.

The population distribution of the world is something like this: 52% female, 48% male, 60% Asian, 16% white, 14% black, 32% Christian, 23% Muslim, 15% Hindu, 7% Buddhist, 16% nonreligious, 89% heterosexual, and 11% homosexual. The numbers are not important, but the fact we have a lot of differences is. And we have many, many more differences, but we are all humans. We are One in Spirit, but we have manifested ourselves in various ways. Our differences make us a heterogeneous mixture providing us with one of our greatest strengths, and also one of our greatest sources of conflict. Life could be so much more peaceful if we tolerated the differences of others.

When we judge and reject any part of the Whole, we perpetuate separation. This rejection prevents communion with the All. It is a decision to limit awareness. None are excluded from the love of God.

We are dishonest when we judge because we lack the position to judge. We must deceive ourselves to judge, and also lack trust. If we don't judge anything, then all things are equally acceptable. Then we are all sisters and brothers.

Ending judgment ends the way most of us live. This is a great accomplishment of miracle proportions. This is accomplished by becoming grateful. Gratitude replaces any judgment and allows peace to permeate the body, gentleness to hug the soul, and wisdom to satiate the mind.

Even though we are One, we each have our own path and journey through life. We would do well to allow each to follow their personal path for each path leads Home. We each should be careful about our own selection of a path because we will have to live with our choice. And so, it is with us all. When we accept our unity, we will accept all of our fellow humans.

World peace can only be produced by the general acceptance of our Oneness, leading to the abandonment of every prejudice, anything used to produce a feeling of superiority over others. The Oneness of humanity is a spiritual principle.

Respect is important. Respect God, respect ourselves, respect others, and respect all life forms. Each is unique and irreplaceable. Everyone is part of a grand mosaic. Respect this Divine Order.

To end all conflicts and heal the world, everyone in positions of authority should say, "Our way is not better than yours. It's just a different way."

There is a battle for control. Dominance is the goal through the use of polarities. Once dominance is gained, the polarities must be maintained. Negro versus Caucasian, and female versus male are two examples.

Racism is a major barrier to peace. It prevents the ability of individuals to be their best and retards human progress. If we are all One, then there can be no racism. Till the Oneness of us all are realized by all, laws must be enforced to end this belief.

Women must be treated as equals to men for there to be world peace. Suppressing women is an injustice against half of the world's population and promotes harmful attitudes in men creating inequity at all levels of the world's society. There is no rational basis for this except to give power to men.

Baha'u'llah said in essence women and men are equal before God. Superiority does not exist. All humans are equal.

Religion is an exclusive experience. It hasn't been able to include everyone. This is because we can't agree on how we should experience religion. We have killed each other over how religious ecstasy should be experienced.

Religious exclusion wouldn't be a problem if religions were tolerant of those excluded. A person would think religions would be the ones to teach tolerance, but they haven't learned how to practice it.

When people feel their beliefs aren't being heard or honored they become fanatics. We don't have to agree with these beliefs, but they must be honored. Dishonoring someone's beliefs causes the owner of the beliefs to feel like they and their beliefs are being destroyed. For them, it's a matter of survival.

We have created the fanatics. In general, most of us find it hard to honor everyone's views, opinions, points of view, and beliefs, especially if they are diametrically opposed to ours.

"Deep down we must have real affection for each other, a clear realization or recognition of our shared human status. At the same time, we must openly accept all ideologies and systems as a means of solving humanity's problems. One country, one nation, one ideology, one system is not sufficient," said Dalai Lama, spiritual leader of Tibetan Buddhism.

"I love you when you bow in your mosque, kneel in your temple, pray in your church. For you and I are [children] of one religion, and it is the spirit," said Kahlil Gibran (1883-1931) Lebanese-American artist, poet, writer.

Sacred scriptures say this:

"But they shall sit every man under his vine and under his fig tree; and none shall make them afraid: for the mouth of the LORD of hosts hath spoken it. For all people will walk every one in the name of his god, and we will walk in the name of the LORD our God for ever and ever" (Micah 4:4-5).

"That they should seek the Lord, if haply they might feel after him, and find him, though he be not far from every one of us: For in him we live, and move, and have our being; as certain also of your own poets have said, For we are also his offspring" (Acts 17:27-28).

"Be kindly affectioned one to another with brotherly love; in honour preferring one another" (Romans 12:10).

"Give none offence, neither to the Jews, nor to the Gentiles, nor to the church of God" (1 Corinthians 10:32).

"If a superior man is reverential (or serious) without fail, and is respectful in dealing with others and follows the rules of propriety, then all within the four seas (the world) are brothers. What does the superior man have to worry about having no brothers" (The Analects 12:5)?

Seeing Everyone as One and loving Our unity will end prejudice and intolerance. How can we love ourselves and be prejudiced and intolerant of ourselves at the same time?

World Peace

We have said peace is what we want. But our actions have said otherwise. Why all the death and destruction? Why all the pain and suffering? It would be a lot simpler, less costly and less damaging if the leader of each country going to war were to fight a duel to determine the outcome of the war. Or a better solution would be for the leaders of each country to meet and negotiate their differences.

Prejudice, war, and exploitation of resources and people are characteristics of an immature civilization. We must pass through this stage to reach maturity, and along the way experience upheavals unlike any in history. Before peace can be obtained, the world must pass through a period of darkness, unrest, and war. But joy and peace come in the morning. We can make this giant step to building a peaceful world.

We will have world peace when we want it. World peace is inevitable.

Solutions

The world governments seem powerless to prevent war, prevent the collapse of the world's economy, prevent anarchy and terrorism, and prevent suffering. The idea humans are depraved has prevented efforts to create a new system based on individual freedom, creativity, and cooperation. The basic nature of humans is not aggression and conflict. World leaders must abandon unworkable assumptions, and search for workable solutions. Any attempts to justify rightness at the expense of humanity must be abandoned to produce a better world.

Love and compassion are the solutions to violence; violence brings more violence and suffering. Banning weapons is not the solution. It only deals with the symptoms. Settling individual wars is also not the solution. It only produces temporary peace. Look at all the wars we have had. The solution is a change of attitude from solutions based on exterior means to spiritual solutions. Spiritual solutions will promote the welfare of all humans. There are spiritual solutions for every social problem. The main reason for our problems is lack of spirituality, and the solution of our problems is spiritual. When we love each other, then humans will act as one nation, one race, and One in unity. Peace must be brought into existence through the will of humanity to change our thinking and beliefs. An important belief is a belief we are all One and united. Disunity can lead to terrible consequences.

The potential of each human is spiritual excellence. Each has the same attributes of God. Given the opportunity, we each can do great things. Humans are basically Love. The foundation of human well-being and development is to know and love God. Following this is to love and be kind to our fellow humans. We must think of each as a great person, and our friend. We must love each other as our self. We must love each other as if they were our self, for they are.

Our happiness is found in unity and harmony with each other. Spiritual and material progress is dependent on our love and friendship with one another. The full understanding of Oneness by humans is inevitable and will be produced by God. Although we may not know it, we are all One. We should abandon all forms of prejudice because they do not serve us well, producing war and strife. The basis of unity is spiritual. Each soul is part of One Soul. Let the whole world have one faith. Let us all be as brothers and sisters. Let us all be as One. Let all prejudices cease. Let us unite in love as One.

To obtain world peace, fundamental changes to human behavior must be made. The innate capacity of humans to practice harmony and cooperation has been subverted by religious fanaticism and diverging ideologies. Racism, the inordinate inequality of rich and poor, unbridled nationalism, religious strife, the inequality of the sexes, lack of universal education, and lack of communication are all part of the complex problem preventing peace. For these problems to be corrected there must be a change of the beliefs and the spiritual attitude of each person. It all comes down to acting on the intrinsic Oneness of humans. The solution will require several steps.

1. Stiffen the will of the people of Earth to produce world peace knowing humans are basically good.
2. Provide universal education producing knowledge of our Oneness.
3. Develop a universal language for the world.
4. Relax national sovereignty to allow the formation of a world super-government. Establish a one world government where laws will be enacted to end racism, to end religious strife, to produce equality of the sexes, and to end the extremes between rich and poor, and finally develop a love of our fellow humans where bigotry and discrimination end and we all have compassion for each other.

World peace will come in two broad stages. The first will be a binding treaty among all nations for political union. They must agree to be amiable to each other. If one nation breaks this peace, all nations must rise to oppose this nation. All nations must agree to disarm except for the forces necessary to maintain the security and order of each country. It will fix the boundaries of each country, establish the size of the armed forces in each country (strictly limited), establish the principles of relationships among the countries, and establish all international agreements. This is a materialistic step.

The wisest and ablest from the world should be the leaders of this government. This government should have a tribunal to settle legal disputes among the nations. The decision of the tribunal will be final. Lesser courts will hear lesser cases. International cases will be heard by this world court. Strife will be settled in this court avoiding war. This assembly should be formed by individuals chosen by the legislatures and nobles of all the counties of the World. In addition to a judicial branch of government, there will also be an executive and a legislative branch.

The second stage is spiritual and is the practical consequence of the spiritualization of the world resulting in the fusion of all races, creeds, classes, and nations. This peace will be built on and maintained by the spiritual principles ordained by God. Peace will now flow naturally from each individual because each will experience peace in their heart.

It is now possible to view the whole planet in all its diversity. We can now experience the Oneness of humans, and everything else on the planet. What happens on one part of the Earth, affects us all. World peace will necessitate the unification of the world's people. Disunity is a tremendous danger. Peace and security are impossible without unity.

The League of Nations and the United Nations, while helping to foster peace, have been unable to prevent war. World peace requires a change of beliefs and attitudes of all of us as well as changes in religion, economics, government, education, and tolerance. To achieve peace, an inner spiritual attitude must be achieved in each person to produce enduring solutions. The idea political agreements alone can bring peace is just wild imagining.

A replacement for the United Nations is needed a world government. The replacement would have an executive branch, a legislative branch, and a judicial branch. Each country would send representatives to the legislature. The judicial branch would settle disputes among countries. All countries would disarm except for police forces. The new super government would have the only military and the ability to wage war. All economic barriers would dissolve. The relationship between labor and capital will be recognized. Religious bigotry will end, and racial equality will be recognized. There will be a single international code of law. Each person will be recognized as a citizen of the world, with equal rights ending militant nationalism. This will be implemented by consultation with each member country. World peace will be the stated goal. A binding agreement forming a strong central government must be agreed to by all. All national boundaries, obligations, and relationships must be clearly defined. If necessary, the will of the world will be used to bring any renegade country into submission.

The short-term solution to war is to establish a one-world government. Part of the government would be a court system to settle disputes. The court would have binding decisions on all parties. A world peacekeeping force would prevent any one nation from being an aggressor toward another nation. Initially, this peacekeeping force would be busy. Sometimes to have peace, we must go to war.

Power in the world must be evenly distributed among all of the nations and not just held by one superpower. If one nation is invaded, threatened, or violated in any way, all other nations would come to its defense.

No nation would be intimidated, threatened, blackmailed, or forced to do something detrimental to their best interests or to receive assistance in any form.

A one-world government would not diminish the greatness of any country but increase it. The most powerful nations now fear this because it would diminish their influence on other nations. Under this super government, they could no longer hoard most of the world's resources, and they would be forced to share. This they don't want to do.

The big first project will be to ensure each person and nation is granted equal opportunity. This will not be possible till the most powerful and wealthy release their control of the world's resources. All leaders who have stood for the end of oppression by the powerful have been reviled.

Revolutions, civil wars, and wars between nations will happen if the rich and powerful exploit the poor through the pretext of opportunity. The perpetuation of the inequality of wealth in the world is not fair. A one-world government would ensure the resources of the world be fairly shared.

Had the educators of past generations taught our children to love everyone, war would have passed into history, but this didn't happen. World citizenship and the Oneness of humanity should be a part of everyone's education. Teaching these principles will prepare the world's inhabitants for the changes required for peace.

The worst effect on the world population is the apathy and loss of hope instigated by the misunderstanding of God's message. The paralysis of the will must be dealt with. It assumes the inevitable quarrelsomeness of humans. This has led to a reluctance of nations to subordinate national self-interest to achieve a new world order by creating a united world government. Most of the people of the world can't in their wildest imaginings visualize a world where they can live in peace and prosperity.

Peace will require the demilitarization of the whole world, and the unification of the political structure, economic machinery, language, and spiritual aspirations of the whole world while allowing for diversity. The whole system must be fluid to adjust to changing world conditions.

Existing institutions must be supported and broadened to facilitate the changes. The national autonomy of existing governments must be guaranteed allowing sane and intelligent patriotism to prevent excessive centralization. Ethnical origins and diversity must be allowed to flourish. A larger loyalty to the human race must be established. Unity in diversity is the goal.

Political unity, the unity of thought, unity in freedom, religious unity, the unity of nations, the unity of races, and unity of language are the steps leading to the unity of humanity and producing lasting peace and prosperity. This is our destiny.

The equality of females and males, the education of females, and full participation of females in life are important to obtaining world peace because females will be an obstacle to war. The denial of the equality of women and men is a roadblock to peace. God considers women and men equal. Inequality subjugates half the human race. Equality must extend from the family to the workplace, to the political arena, and to international relations. Women must be allowed full participation in all areas of human endeavor.

Ignorance and lack of education is another impediment to peace. Everyone should contribute money toward the education of our children. All countries must provide it to its citizens. The concept of world citizenship and the Oneness of humans must be part of the curriculum. If resources are limited, women and girls should be educated first because they can pass on the knowledge more rapidly. The education of women will be the greatest step toward world peace. Women will abolish war because women will refuse to allow the sacrifice of their children on the field of battle. Education can lay the foundation for peace.

Racism is a barrier to peace. We are all children of God, all part of one family. We are all part of the same original race. Racial distinction is superstitious, imaginary, and false. These distinctions are from humans, not God. In general, we all have two eyes, two ears, two arms, two legs, and one head. The process of attaining peace must allow for the diversity of ethnical origins, the diversity of languages, the diversity of traditions, the diversity of thoughts, and the diversity of habits. Racism is an attack on human dignity. It limits the human potential and progress. Enacting laws enforcing the unity of humans will be necessary to eliminate racism. Racism and all prejudice must be eliminated. Discrimination based on race, sex, or religious belief must be eliminated.

Extremes of wealth and poverty are barriers to peace. The inordinate gap between rich and poor produces suffering, instability, and conditions conducive to war. The solution is spiritual stemming from the realization we are all One. Choose profit for mankind and not profit for the individual. Choose for everyone in the world what we would choose for ourselves. Excessive wealth should be limited, and the basic needs of the poor should be supplied. Total equality of wealth for everyone is undesirable because it is an extreme unsustainable condition. Philanthropy is part of the solution to the disparity of the wealth problem.

Unbridled nationalism is preventing world peace. Legitimate patriotism is acceptable. The love of our fellow human must exceed our love of country. World citizenship must unify us all because all citizens of the world are interdependent on each other. International activities nurturing mutual affection, cooperation, and unity must be increased. We are all citizens of the world, and we should all unite as one under this banner. A person could be born anywhere on Earth and should be free to move to any place on Earth and live in any political subdivision. National boundaries are capricious and imaginary. We refer to our native land as our motherland. We could just as well refer to the Earth as our motherland and avoid all the bloodshed arising from the strife because of unbridled nationalism. Love of country, patriotism, national loyalty, diversity of ethical origins, and national autonomy are all important as long as it is maintained within the context of world unity. We are all members of the human race.

Religious strife is an impediment to peace. All of us should welcome and interact with members of all religions with love, friendship, and fellowship. All humans are the benefactors of the grace of God. All religions can trace their source of inspiration to God. The differences in beliefs can be traced to the original message being different because of different requirements of the age and pressing issues.

Religions have perpetuated confusion and misunderstandings, and a distrust of science. The principle of the "Golden Rule" found in all the major religions of the world, would argue for peace, but the prejudices introduced by these religions today, would argue for war. Communication among the various religions has been suppressed.

Religion can be a great force to create peace. Unfortunately, because of erroneous interpretations of the teachings of founders of the world's religions, confusion and barriers have been erected preventing peace. The cumulative effect of all these ideologies has deified the state, created divisions based on race, nations, and classes, created artificial superiority of individuals and groups, suppressed ideas, ignored the starving, and allowed some to live in obscene opulence.

Religion can be the best way to produce peace in the world. But when religion is corrupted, it leads to unrest and war. The original words of the founders of the great religions lead to peace. The disciples of these religions have been corrupted leading to war. The followers have misinterpreted the meaning of the original instructions. They have fostered separation instead of unity and ignored the world's poor exacerbating the situation.

Religious and philosophical ideas have been the basis for most wars. The United States' founders crafted the nation to prevent internal conflict by providing freedom of speech, by providing for the right for each to live life as each sees fit, and by allowing each to pursue their own happiness. These rights are granted to everyone.

Lack of communication is an impediment to peace. Adopting an auxiliary language would go far to resolve this problem. Being able to understand each other in language and the written word is essential for unity. Each person will be trained in their native language and the auxiliary language. Clear communication prevents misunderstandings and promotes friendship, love, agreement, and unity. A world auxiliary language would help facilitate communications among the various peoples.

War comes at great expense. First, we must stockpile weapons in sufficient numbers to defeat our enemy. Then as time passes, we must replace the old weapons with newer more efficient killing machines, with all this at great expense to each country and its people. Reducing the world's armaments is a good first step toward world peace. Weapons of war can be converted to constructive goods. Once a peace treaty is signed by all nations, the tremendous resources diverted to produce weapons can be used for useful purposes. Each nation will need police forces to keep order, and there will need to be an international police force to maintain the free flow of trade worldwide. Then poverty will disappear, and knowledge will abound. Then nations can concentrate on the wellbeing of its people. Nations will work closely with neighboring countries.

Governments should rule justly. Government job positions should be given based on merit. The goal of each government should be to produce the highest good for its citizens including security, prosperity, and tranquility.

The Baha'i Faith believes in the unity of all humans, and the search for truth, condemns all manner of prejudice and superstition, believes the purpose of religion is to promote the love of all, maintains the principles of equal rights, equal opportunities, and education for all, promotes the elimination of extremes of poverty and wealth, prohibits slavery, promotes obedience to one's government, exalts any service to the level of worship, and urges the creation of a world auxiliary language.

Baha'u'llah said in essence peace is impossible without unity. We are One and must recognize our unity.

'Abdu'l-Baha, son of Baha'u'llah, said a thought of war must be eliminated by a stronger thought of peace. A thought of hatred must be destroyed by a stronger thought of love.

The solution for conflict and war is forgiveness.

The heart is the seat of wisdom. Before we rush to war for what we think is right, we should make sure we know what is right, and then declare our position. If there is to be war, don't start it. If attacked, fight only to end the war. Love gives courage and makes a nation strong. Without love, nothing is worth the fight.

War is a cancer of society, and the individual, even if it is nation against nation, company against company, person against person, or a person within himself. It is the antithesis of commonality, and unity with others, God, and Love. A person at war with himself has no problem going to war with others. By denying the power of love, we close doors to ourselves, diminishing opportunities. When this happens, we may go to war in a desperate attempt to create opportunities.

Humans should live together in harmony, supporting each other. Individuality should not be compromised in forced conformity. Most conflict comes from non-acceptance of differences. When we see ourselves as part of One Spirit, as One, conflict will cease. This is achieved through acceptance of each other just as we are. It is helpful to see things not as opposites, but as part of a continuum. Hot and cold are not opposites but are parts of a range of temperatures. Look for wholeness in everything.

Life sustains itself. It continues even in the face of opposition. Anyone who adopts a destructive philosophy toward life becomes a lethal force against all life, including his or hers. It is wasteful and senseless with no chance of success.

Humans perceive the Sun as the source of all energy on Earth. The Sun, while supplying tremendous amounts of energy, has a finite amount of energy. There is competition for this energy leading to a belief in scarcity. If this belief persists, social democracy will be impossible to maintain. A paradigm shift is imperative to allow the utilization of the ultimate of energy. This will allow the final realization of our unity and the development of peace and prosperity for all. With this change, we will find the physical and spiritual answers we have long searched for. God is the creative source of everything. Ignoring God leads to disharmony while embracing God leads to harmony.

We have built walls and prisons with the conditions we have decreed are necessary for our civilization. We must relax these conditions. We should be more tolerant, be open to new ideas, be more forgiving, and increase our curiosity about life. There will be a need for conditions, but we must strike a balance between these conditions and fair play. This balance can be the difference between war and peace.

While world peace is a longing of human souls everywhere, it is something opposed by those who think they benefit from bigotry, war, killing, power through armies, navies, and air forces, and enforcing loyalty through fear. World peace would end their world.

The world works on the principle of right and wrong. If a person, religion, government, business does not agree with us, we make it wrong and attack it and try to destroy it. The solution and the way to peace is to accept everything and choose the best. Don't make it wrong.

The lesson to be learned from war is when we kill someone, we are killing ourselves.

There are five steps we can take to lead us to peace.
1. Acknowledge some beliefs about God and Life are unworkable.
2. Acknowledge there could be some wisdom capable of changing everything we believed about God and Life.
3. Decide we are willing to search for new ideas about God and Life.
4. Examine the new ideas and enlarge our beliefs to include them if they fit with our inner truth and understanding.
5. Demonstrate our highest beliefs by living them.

Inner Peace

There are two major steps to world peace. The first step is political, the reorganizing of the world to produce a one-world government, and the second step is spiritual and will truly eliminate war. All problems are spiritual with spiritual solutions eliminating unrest and producing inner peace leading to exterior peace. Combining both a spiritual and a political solution is the ultimate solution.

To experience peace, cause someone else to experience peace. The quickest path to peace is to accept ourselves as the great persons we are; the wonderful, compassionate, joyful, loving, and peaceful beings we are. This is who we are.

The foundation of the Physical World is chaos. To produce peace, all organizations such as governments, religions, and corporations must be integrated by aligning harmoniously. This is a spiritual process. Peace is connected to each soul. Order can't deal with chaos. Produce order in one place and chaos pops through the cracks elsewhere. Order requires more effort than chaos. Fear and anger won't help. Peace is the only solution. This is a spiritual solution. It starts with rediscovering who we are, and then returning to Spirit, the dark matter and dark energy scientists are seeking to understand. Peace cannot be understood from the perspective of physical experience. Peace cannot be found outside ourselves. We each must find our own peace. Chaos performs an important spiritual function by forcing each of us to find our own peace.

We are Love, and through Love, we may connect the law of cause and effect and miracles and then produce peace. Peace is a state of being, and it radiates from the heart. It is only when we experience this state of being and we radiate peace into the world that the world will be changed by the transcendence of peace.

Honesty is the basis of peace. Honesty is a cure for chaos. Honesty and violence are not found in the same person. World peace is produced person by person as each person produces peace within themselves. World peace is not possible by debating reality or changing individual world governments. Forming a united world government will mechanically impose peace on the world till our hearts catch up.

When we express Christ love and peace to all, then will there be peace on Earth. Peace and love are found within. When we find the presence of God within, we find strength, confidence, power, love, and peace. By expressing this, others will find this as well. Love and peace will spread from person to person till the whole world is expressing love and peace. Then all of nature will be at peace.

Each person who doesn't pursue his or her purpose in life creates chaos and disharmony. The solution is for each to go within to discover his or her purpose and live it.

Love and true compassion will produce enlightened individuals who understand good and eliminate the idea of evil. Believing in evil perpetuates this experience as does hating anything. For example, hating war only perpetuates war. The correct solution would be to love peace to produce peace.

If people's greatest happiness comes from the outside world, the Physical World, they will not wish to part with any of their accumulated wealth. Also, if the "have nots" think their unhappiness is because of lack of material things, they will seek material things. The "have nots" will want what the "haves" possess, and the "haves" will resist giving their stuff to the "have nots." Wars occur because the "have nots" want what the "haves" have. This is a misplaced desire, and misplaced desires cause conflicts.

The only sustaining peace is internal. Internal peace will allow people to know external things are unnecessary. Freedom does not need things, and this freedom will vanquish fear. Fear of not having something we think we need, fear of losing what we have, and fear of lacking something needed for happiness are all gone when this freedom is realized.

Not needing anything also frees people from anger. Anger is based on fear, and if we lack fear, we are free of anger. When our wants are not met, there is no anger because of this freedom. There is no fear of not getting it. There is no anger when others do what is not wanted because we don't need a certain action from others. There is no fear of failure to get certain actions from others. This is all true because we need nothing.

It doesn't matter if others are unkind, cruel, hurtful, or damaging. We can't be damaged because we are not our bodies, so we need nothing from others. There is no fear or anger if someone wants to take our life. What others do does not matter.

When living in inner peace, people, places, or things, present or absence, or any connected conditions, or circumstances will not affect our state of mind. In this state of inner peace, we are able to experience fully the delights of the body. The experience of the body will be voluntary where sensations are chosen.

Seeking and finding inner peace by everyone will end wars, conflicts, injustice, and produce everlasting world peace. World peace is produced by the change of individual consciousness.

All points of view are worthy of being heard. All humans are equal in dignity.

The long-term solution is a spiritual solution. The problem will be solved when humans desire spiritual truth, spiritual reality, and spiritual experience, and not things. Then governments will not impose mandatory taxes but receive donations of ten percent of incomes. People will no longer starve to death. The world's resources will abundantly provide for everyone. This will happen when we choose to be God made manifest.

Peace seems impossible in this world, but God has promised peace. Peace is produced by changing perspective and seeing peace. Peace is unavoidable to those offering peace. Those looking for war won't find peace. Anger denies peace. Where anger is, peace cannot be found. Forgiveness leads to peace.

We have chosen the material things of this world instead of peace. We have chosen littleness instead of glory.

Peace is a part of us. To experience peace all we have to do is accept every situation we face. We are everywhere as is peace.

To get to world peace, we must start with inner peace. This would lead to peace in individual lives, then peace in homes, then peace in communities, and finally peace in the world. What we are being is who we are. During war, we can be peaceful. And what we are will affect the world.

Enlightened beings live in peace. They know they are One with Everything and therefore realize they have all things in common with everyone. There can be no ownership or loss. They would gladly give what they have to anyone knowing they can create it again if they desired.

Violence

Violence prevents a life of joy, love, and peace. In our world, strength decides the outcome of events. We haven't learned to observe what works and what doesn't. We haven't observed that if we use force against a person or nation, this person or nation will retaliate with force. We haven't noticed we hurt ourselves when we use force.

War is a largely male activity. Women tend to seek justice, freedom, and love.

Disagreements are natural manifestations of individuality. Violent solutions to the disagreements are proof of exceptional immaturity. Rationally, nations should avoid violent conflicts because of massive death tolls. Apparently, we aren't rational.

When nations use force to gain their goals, they are sowing the seeds of their own destruction. Rome captured much of the known world through force and eventually was destroyed by force. Revenge is pointless because violence solves nothing.

An attacker sees their attack as a defense. We have only defenders, no attackers. We can then say we were forced to kill them because we were only defending ourselves. This is the way attackers see their situation. This applies to all situations of conflict whether in war, in bedrooms, and in boardrooms.

Violence is part of our culture. We perpetuate it and encourage it in many ways. Violence is illustrated and demonstrated in our movies, television shows, comic books, video games, and descriptions in many other forms. By constantly placing violent images for us to view we have taught ourselves and our children violence is an acceptable way to deal with conflicts.

The idea we can solve conflicts with violence is widely spread throughout our world. This idea is shared with everyone including our young in many ways. We, and especially our young, form beliefs about this idea. The idea is eventually put into action, with violence popping up everywhere.

The problem of violence has been present in our world for a very long time. But our present-day technologies allowing us to instantly and graphically display violent content exacerbates the problem to human extinction proportions. Mass violence has become a part of our culture.

Historically our sacred scriptures have been interpreted to include God's blessing on violence. These same scriptures foster the illusion of disunity, evil humans, and unworthiness of humans resulting in dysfunctional and violent behaviors. We are violent because we believe we are isolated and must act violently to preserve, protect, and defend ourselves in an evil world. We must protect our bodies. This is a key motivator for violence. When threatened, we attack in self-defense, because we don't want to die. The common belief is death is our end. Death does cause the body to stop functioning. But we are not a body. Misunderstanding this is the cause our fear.

One of the many fallacies we have about Life is we can kill one another to solve our differences.

To end violence, ask the attacker, "What pains you to the extent you feel you must injure me to stop the pain?"

The problem with mistakes is they can be equated with being immoral instead of just an operational failure. A mistake can then become a sin. In some societies, a mistake can be equated with an offense against God, with severe consequences. If we disagree with these standards, we may be labeled an apostate and killed. This situation creates all the ingredients necessary for war. We would now be defending the faith if another group disagreed with our laws. This holy war would be authorized by and required by God. This has been happening for hundreds and thousands of years. A different way of looking at this removes God from this mess by separating morals and mistakes.

We insist on considering other countries, other cultures, and other people as being separate from each other and from ourselves. This allows us to treat them as we do. We may consider ourselves as being united with God, being God's people, and following God's plan for salvation, but we can still believe the others don't fall into any of these categories. This kind of thinking leads to killing and war.

Presently, some of us believe we can serve God by destroying life. Some of us believe God demands we kill in his name. We will eventually mature to the point where we could not imagine doing this.

When we are attacked, we can defend ourselves, attack, or ask why we were attacked. If we find out why we were attacked, we can then seek for reconciliation, forgiveness, and collaboration to reconstruct our relationship with the attacker.

Any attack is a request for help. A proper response is to determine what help is needed. Ask directly. Many times, the attacker believes the one attacked did or is doing something requiring a defensive response. Determining the cause of the attack is an important step in reconciliation.

Do we want to live together in peace, joy, good health, happiness, and harmony? Because we see each other as separate beings, we have been inflicting pain and suffering on ourselves. When we see ourselves as One, then we will see this as self-inflicted injury and we will stop the injury. The solution is to be stewards of the truth by speaking and living the truth we are all One. Then we must be stewards of each other. And then we must be stewards of the Earth. A steward is someone who takes care of something. Therefore, we must care for the truth, each other, and the earth.

Three Steps

One giant step for mankind we could take now is to reconcile differences between races, genders, nationalities, and religions. This would include an acknowledgment of all past offenses to each other and a sincere apology. Compensation for past losses should be made where possible. Offended people should be allowed to be who they are.

Poverty and lack of education, more than anything else, produces lack of opportunity and awareness. This stagnates our evolution. Reconciliation is the first step in correcting this and closing the gap between rich and poor would be part of this.

The second step is recreation. We must reinvent and redefine ourselves. Old ways, old habits, old ways of thinking, and old justifications should be replaced with a new vision of who we are. What does it mean to be human, successful, abundant, and happy? Our definitions for these are out of date. Education will help accomplish this, but we as individuals, governments, and other organizations around the world will need to get involved.

The last and most important step is reunification. If this is accomplished, everything will change forever. Reunification means experiencing Everything as part of the One Thing we call God. This can be achieved through education for all ages.

Many religions teach we are separate from God. The truth is we are united with God. This truth has not been believed preventing us from creating a peaceful world and preventing us from experiencing unity with God and each other.

When we see our Oneness, we will cease to fight, and wars will end.

We consider ourselves highly civilized, but, other societies are more civilized than us. We haven't learned to live in peace and they have. We have turned our technology against our best interests. We have not provided the rest of the Universe with an exemplary model of living to be emulated. We are all citizens of the world and it is in our best interests to live in peace.

Natural disasters like earthquakes, famine, and hurricanes, will cause us to divert our resources from war to fighting the disasters. Our caring will cause us to remember love and to work for the benefit of humanity. These disasters are blessings in disguise uniting us.

We should join groups to influence our governments for peace by practicing our duties as citizens of countries and of the world. All loving people of the world should unite their voices and demand peace in any legal way.

Final Thoughts

Harvard psychologist Steven Pinker in his book, "The Better Angels of Our Nature: Why Violence Has Declined," shows by statistics violence has declined over time. Based on deaths per 100,000, the number of people killed in battle is down over a thousand-fold, genocide is down, murder is down, rape is down, discrimination against blacks and homosexuals is down and capital punishment is down. The number of authoritarian countries has decreased while the number of democracies has increased. Some of his suggested causes for this trend include, the rise in empathy, increased respect, better communication, overcoming superstition and religious intolerance, decreasing beliefs of superiority, increasing the belief peace is appropriate, and the feminization of the world.

Joel Andreas, Johns Hopkins University sociology professor, in his book "Addiction to War," says addiction to war has a high cost: higher taxes, and environmental degradation. Social services, education, and health care suffer because the money goes to the military.

Edgar Cayce, the American psychic, said, "Peace in the world must begin first within the heart, purpose, and mind of the individual…[for] as individuals change themselves and their interactions with one another, eventually the world cannot help but follow."

Sacred scriptures say this:

"Ye have heard that it hath been said, An eye for an eye, and a tooth for a tooth: But I say unto you, That ye resist not evil: but whosoever shall smite thee on thy right cheek, turn to him the other also. And if any man will sue thee at the law, and take away thy coat, let him have thy cloke also. And whosoever shall compel thee to go a mile, go with him twain. Give to him that asketh thee, and from him that would borrow of thee turn not thou away. Ye have heard that it hath been said, Thou shalt love thy neighbour, and hate thine enemy. But I say unto you, Love your enemies, bless them that curse you, do good to them that hate you, and pray for them which despitefully use you, and persecute you" (Mat 5:38-44).

"Then said Jesus unto him, Put up again thy sword into his place: for all they that take the sword shall perish with the sword" (Matthew 26:52). This infers violence produces violence.

"Promote peace among men" (Sura 2:225).

"Now arms, however beautiful, are instruments of evil omen, hateful, it may be said, to all creatures. Therefore they who have the Tao do not like to employ them" (Tao Te Ching 31).

In summary, we live in a violent world. We make matters worse by displaying violence on TV, in our movies, and as part of our video games. Our religions have given God's blessing on violence. From little on up, our children learn violence is an acceptable way to solve differences. This must stop.

We must educate our children and ourselves to live differently. Violence in any form is unacceptable. It should not be depicted in our actions, in our TV programs, in our movies, and in our computer games. Our religions must reevaluate our understandings of God's commandments. What does God really want? Does a God of love truly foster violence? Could it be we have misunderstood our sacred writings? If we are One and eternal, and we are, why is there a need for violence? There is no need. There is no need to defend ourselves because we can't be hurt. The solution is to care for the truth, care for each other, and care for the earth. All of us should universally apply the golden rule, to everyone.

World peace is not only possible, it is inevitable. Violence in the world is slowly decreasing. World peace is a personal thing eventually producing a global experience. Each of us personally can experience peace during a war. And when enough of us experience this peace on the inside, our world on the outside will experience peace. The probability of this happening anytime soon is remote. This may take a thousand years or more, but it will happen.

To find the ultimate solution, we must change our perspective from solutions based on exterior means to spiritual solutions. The solution for all our problems is spiritual. Spiritual solutions will promote the welfare of all humans.

World peace will necessitate the unification of the world's people. Disunity is a tremendous danger and the cause of all wars. Peace and security are impossible without unity. In the end, we are all members of humanity. We are all members of the human race. We are all One spiritually, each soul part of One Soul. Unity with our tremendous diversity is the correct perception. Our happiness is found in unity and harmony with each other. The basis of unity is spiritual. Our Oneness must be reflected in our government, our political structure, spiritual organizations, our trade and finance, and our language and written text.

Certain governmental structures can produce a framework for world peace, but only a change of heart in each person can yield a lasting peace.

Sex, Marriage, and Nudity

More than anything in this book, this chapter will upset the most readers. We are still in denial about our sexual nature. We still haven't recovered from the Victorian Era. At the very center of our being, we are exchanging energy all the time with everyone. On the spiritual level, this is sex, and it is normal and natural. On the physical level, we repress our sexuality. We say sex is for the dark, sex is to be hidden, and sex is not to be discussed or exhibited in any manner.

Plants and animals openly express and exhibit their sexuality. Flowers, the sexual parts of a plant, are usually the showiest parts of a plant. Bees and other insects are openly invited to assist in procreation. Animals openly copulate in the presence of other animals of the same and different species without shame or self-consciousness.

There is nothing more natural than the physical expression of love. Sex is the ultimate physical demonstration of love. We have suppressed the physical expression of love by law and social custom creating all manner of social dysfunction and fostering the commission of sex crimes. What does this say about how we feel about love?

Maybe not for a thousand years or more, but the time is coming when it will be just as natural to see humans openly copulating as plants and animals. But not now. We are so stigmatized by this thought most people will feel revolution just imagining this possibility.

We were created naked but cover ourselves to be modest we say. Of course, in cold climates, this is a necessity. Years ago, missionaries were horrified to find naked natives in remote parts of the World. The natives felt comfortable with their nakedness. The missionaries didn't. For most people, seeing a naked body walking around is disconcerting. Just the thought of walking around naked in front of other naked individuals makes most people shutter. But first we must master our climate, and yes, it will happen.

In the meantime, we must change our attitude about our bodies and sex.

Marriage is basically a license to practice sex with a commitment of fidelity. Historically, it provided protection for children and the mothers who bore them, and it provided for the survival of the species. Males provided this protection in exchange for sex. This is not to say love was not involved because it was.

But marriage as we have known it is dead. What has constituted marriage has varied widely over the years, and is changing now, and will change into the future. We have already decided marriage is not working. The divorce rate is an indicator of this dysfunction. Marriage will survive in some form, just not as we now have defined it.

Here's some wisdom about sex, marriage, and nudism in sacred scriptures:

"Therefore shall a man leave his father and his mother, and shall cleave unto his wife: and they shall be one flesh. And they were both naked, the man and his wife, and were not ashamed" (Genesis 2:24-25).

"For in the resurrection they neither marry, nor are given in marriage, but are as the angels of God in heaven" (Matthew 22:30).

"Men should love their wives as Christ loved the Church" (Ephesians 5:25).

We have allowed society to dictate to us what is acceptable. Unfortunately, what is acceptable changes from time to time, and place to place. When we allow the expansion of love to take place, we are experiencing our true self. It doesn't matter if this love is expressed between a man and a woman, or between two men, or between two women, or a parent and child, or a child and a pet. Expressing love is always appropriate and should be blessed as a manifestation of our true nature. Express love continually and love freely.

Love freely, and freely love; no strings attached. Allow each to be who they are and allow them to walk their own path. Allow each to experience what they need to experience, loving them all the while.

Sex

Sex can be the most wonderful experience two people can share. Sex can also involve more than two people at the same time. This is the experience and common knowledge of the average person who has had the experience. The judgments and opinions of religions, governments, parents, and others call it shameful, and dirty. Rather than dispute these judgments, we have agreed with these judgments producing conditions fostering rape, and untold mental, emotional, and spiritual turmoil leading to suicide. Our prejudices and judgments prevent us from openly celebrating our sexuality. We would rather openly make war than openly make love.

God provided sex for us to use to enjoy the most physical fun with the body possible. Like any tool, it can be misused negating a great experience. Using sex for anything other than pure joy and ecstasy shared in love misuses sex and reduces the quality of a great experience. Sex is joy, but as it is commonly practiced now, joy has been removed. Sex is also sacred, and sacredness and joyfulness is the same thing.

We have made sex an experience of fear, anxiety, scarcity, envy, rage, and tragedy. Sex has been repressed, and we have made sex shameful. Moral codes, religious restrictions, social taboos, and emotional norms we use to regulate sex prevent us from celebrating who we are.

All we have ever wanted to do is love one another. But we devised all kinds of barriers to prevent it. We display violence without shame, but not sex. We can't say or show how much we love sex without being called a pervert.

Sex is a heavenly manifestation of love, whether it is the love of another, of self, or of life. God created nothing shameful; not our bodies or any of its functions, including sex. We have been given intense feelings of attraction and desire to embrace others. This is natural and as it should be.

Love what you like. Love sex. Love yourself. Love self-gratification. What is loved is drawn to us. Enjoy sex as an observance of love. By abundantly pleasuring ourselves, we'll be able to abundantly pleasure another.

Tantric sex is a very high expression of sex, allowing prolonged unions of bodies and souls. A two-hour experience might start with self-pleasuring of the partners and may or may not end in intercourse. Giving ourselves joy, pleasure, ecstasy, or anything making us feel good is the road to Heaven. Believing we are all One makes it very difficult to hurt another. Experimenting with sex within this belief will allow the experience of an unimaginable life. Self-denial is self-limiting and self-destructive.

Enjoy sex lovingly, frequently, and creatively producing a totally euphoric experience. Sex is for a reunion of souls, with procreation a side benefit. Love is all there is, and sex allows the physical experience of the spiritual union. The climax of this union is the experience of Oneness.

Most people don't want others watching when they have intercourse. However, there are some who openly have intercourse such as the Aboriginal and Polynesian cultures. These cultures we call "pagan" have great respect for life and know nothing of rape, and few killings. Our society puts sex, a normal and natural function, in the dark and hides it from view, but kills people in the open for all to see. To us, sex is embarrassing, dirty, shameful, and forbidden. Public sex doesn't make it better. It's our attitudes about it that are important. Seeing sex as other than normal and natural human behavior perverts our experience of it. Failure to participate in some sexual activities because of propriety is more than limiting. It can deprive us of joy. As in all of life, any sexual behavior is acceptable as long as there is mutual consent among all participants and those affected. What would love do is the deciding factor in determining what is acceptable.

An enlightened view of sex, money, power, security, possessions, and other bodily experiences is an appreciation of these, and not addiction and compulsive behaviors. Kinky sex, interracial sex, loveless sex, and gay sex are all OK as long as no one is hurt, and all participants agree with the activity and all give their permission. But doing anything without love misses the grandest part of any activity. As Shakespeare said, nothing is evil lest thinking make it so.

In general, our society instills shame about our sexual body parts to our children resulting in our children behaving awkwardly or inappropriately to sexual urges as they mature. We tell our children not to touch their genitals or masturbate.

A better way would be to allow our children to experience to the full their very being, including their sexuality. The sexuality of parents should not be hidden from their children. There is nothing shameful about naked bodies and hiding them from sight is not necessary. Sexual functions are natural, and children should be informed of their wonderful nature. Sexual intercourse expressed by parents in full sight of their children will convey to the children the joy and beauty of the sexual expression of love. Ultimately, parents model behavior for their children. Children will learn from subtle hints of their parents about how they feel about everything including sex.

In societies where sex is not shameful, and openly and freely practiced, rape, prostitution, crimes of passion, sexual inhibitions and dysfunction are rare.

Today, open sexual intercourse would traumatize our population. There are laws to prevent it. But we must end the shame, guilt, and repression associated with sex.

Parents should teach children nothing is shameful or wrong about any bodily functions. Teach them nothing sexual need be hidden. Parents should allow them to observe their romantic side by demonstrating hugging, touching, and gently fondling for them, to illustrate their love for each other in physical form.

This demonstration should convey the idea physical love is natural, wonderful, and desirable.

Children should be allowed to connect the sexual feelings, curiosities, and urges experienced with an inner sense of joy and celebration. Shame and guilt have no place here.

It's OK to allow our children to see us naked. They should be allowed to experience our sexual identity. Presently most children see their parents as asexual because parents present themselves as asexual. This instills rage, guilt, and shame in children who think they should be asexual, as their parents, and they can't figure out why they feel sexual.

It's healthier to talk and laugh about sex and demonstrate how to celebrate their sexuality. This all starts at birth. Touching, kissing, and hugging the child and each other is a healthy demonstration of our love for each other.

By being clear and understanding the meaning of our own sexuality, we will be in a great position to tell our children about sex when they are ready. Incrementally as they ask, tell them what they want to know. We need not go into greater detail than the children request.

When our children are not allowed to experience themselves as the wondrous sexual beings they are, they cannot celebrate themselves and the use of their bodies.

In sexually open societies where sex is discussed and experienced freely and joyously, few sexual crimes are committed, few unexpected births occur, and no illegitimate or unwanted births happen. In these societies, each birth is a blessing, and all mothers and babies are cared for by the loving society.

Most people hide what they are ashamed of or what they want to keep private. People hide their sexuality because of this.

A good test for determining if something is desirable for the human race is to examine the consequences of having everyone do it. If the outcome is a disaster, then it is not desirable for anyone. In the case of celibacy, it's easy to see it's undesirable.

Somehow, we humans have elevated celibacy as something to be admired while sexual expression in any form is baser and shameful, but this is not true. Notice who made sex and the desire to experience sexual fulfillment, God. A sexual experience is a natural experience, and sexual desire is controlled by genes and is a biological essential. It is an urgent drive to experience sexual passion, and this drive is not to produce life, but to experience abundant life; to experience Oneness.

Enjoying sex is noble, and holy. It can be and is better if it is experienced on the three levels of soul, mind, and body. Experiencing sex with just the body is only a small part of the peak experience possible when the ultimate can be experienced while engaging the mind, body, and spirit in love. This is a *wholly* experience. This is a *holy* experience.

Sexual expression and every form of love starts as something being experienced with someone else, but ends as an experience of Oneness, being with our true Self.

Love a person for who they are, and not what they give, and remove shame from love and sex. This kind of love is unimaginable for us, so we can't imagine a God who loves this way. The lesser love we believe in has created a great sadness in the world, and a whole lot of killing.

Sex is a celebration of Life and of God. The shame experienced in connection with our bodies and sex is taught by our societies. Human sexuality was meant to be a joyous and glorious celebration and expression of life and Godliness, lacking embarrassment, shame, guilt, restrictions, or any limitations unless we desire limitations.

Sexual expression does not hamper spiritual awakening. However, a focus on too much sex or too much of anything creates an imbalance preventing enlightenment. Enlightenment is possible only traveling the middle path. But an active sex life has no negative impact on spiritual awareness.

We would be wise to abstain from sexual activities with others who do not wish to engage in sex with us, and those who would be negatively impacted because they were too young, or those who were mentally or emotionally unstable.

Rape is an assault and not sexual expression. We as humans are in agreement this is an activity we do not want to happen.

Sex crimes and dysfunctional sex result from repressed sex. Laws limiting sexual expression are not beneficial. They produce anger, shame, and guilt, causing us to hide our sexual activities from others.

In the past, and even the present, there are and have been laws regulating human sexual activity where there has been no civil damage. We should explore whether such laws are needed or should be enforced.

Society, in the past, has defined homosexuality as being wrong, but this is like saying it's wrong to be left-handed. If a person is left-handed, that's what they are. It's not right or wrong. This is a judgment having no basis in fact because right and wrong are human constructs that change over time. At one time being left handed was judged to be wrong and children were forced to use their right hand to write.

Marriage

In truth, we are all married to all of us. And it is impossible to divorce ourselves from any of us. We are all One, immortal, with no death to separate us. At the very least our marriage vows must be reconstructed to reflect this truth and consider our unlimited freedom. If we perceive someone is providing us with love, we tend to experience loss when this someone is shared. Loss is impossible. In truth, no one can be a source of love for us. Relationships do not provide love. Relationships are holy, providing members with the opportunity to realize only love is real. Love is not possessive. God is loving through us. We should be allowed to physically express our love for anyone, anytime, anywhere, among consenting adults. This too will happen, but not in the immediate future.

In enlightened societies, freedom is taken for granted. Each person is free to love others in any manner that is true, authentic, and appropriate at the time. Laws, social taboos, religious restrictions, psychological barriers, tribal customs, or other unspoken rules and regulations relating to who, when, where, or how people may love one another do not exist. This works because each person decides what love would do now, and each person is an adult, mature, and capable of making such decisions for themselves. In a three-way relationship, each person speaks their truth, and they each can decide how they will proceed from there knowing loving another does not mean loving themselves less. There is no sacrifice and no abuse. Loving another does mean allowing them full freedom. Love would never declare who someone else is or must be. Jealousy will end our love for another, and very likely their love for us.

We have relationships with everyone and can never end them. We can change these relations, but the question facing us is what kind of relationships we choose to have.

Over time in our past, marriage has been an exclusive intimate relationship between one woman, and one man, between one woman and one woman, between one man and one man, among one woman and many men, among one man and many women, and among many women and many men. It is regulated by some religions and not by others. It is regulated by some governments, and not by others. Marriage has economic implications. Recently there is a trend where couples live together without being married religiously or legally. There are temporary marriages, forced marriages, and marriages of convenience. Some marriages are arranged and in others, each spouse chooses their partner. We humans being the creative beings we are have created a variety of possible marriages. Most possibilities are outlawed by some religions and some governments. Being the unlimited beings we are, we will eventually explore all possibilities. This exploration will produce consequences we must be willing to take responsibility for. Over time, the consequences will increasingly include forgiveness.

Nobody marries in Heaven.

None of us needs anyone. We are complete unto ourselves. If we love someone, then we would allow this someone to love someone else. Love allows freedom of choice. If we love someone, we love them for who they are, not what we want from them. Love lacks conditions, limitations, and need. If someone loves us, but we love another, we would tell them clearly and immediately. We would transparently tell our truth all the time. Love in its highest form is honesty. There should be no shame in the truth. Infidelity would not occur. The marriage could be dissolved or altered to allow the beloveds to be with each other.

Marriage should not be based on obligations. It should provide opportunities for growth. Each should be allowed full expression and should be allowed to develop their highest potential. The goal should be for a full reunion with God through the full interaction with each other. Loving unconditionally, honestly, unlimitedly and without need, allows us to grant total freedom to the subject of our love. This leads to relationships different from current societal conventions.

We are married to everyone and are united as One, now and forever. We are loved and free to enjoy everything, and there are no limits placed upon us. Interracial marriage is OK.

It is appropriate to love everyone to the maximum, and it is the most joyful way to live. Special, restrictive relationships are inappropriate, and marriage, as we have constructed it today, falls into this category. We are free to express love without restrictions, for the soul is the essence of God's limitless freedom. God is limitless, and therefore God is freedom. We, being a part of God, are unlimited freedom. We deny ourselves when we accept restrictions and our soul rebels at any limitation.

Children are good examples of this freedom expressed. They think they can do anything, and think they can love everyone, and believe they can live forever. To them, there is nothing ungodly. They can run around naked hugging everyone.

Most people have a difficult time dealing with the promises, and constraints of marriage. The worldwide divorce rate illustrates this. But we are free to choose marriage or not. Initially, marriage was to provide the female with support and ensure the survival of the children, while providing the male with sex and companionship. It was an attempt to create security, but, it is an artificial social institution created to govern our behavior. All laws relating to marriage are unable to prevent people from breaking marriage promises because these laws go counter to natural law. We are love, and love is unlimited, eternal, and free. The marriage laws as we have constructed them impinge on our unlimited and free nature. Marriage excludes.

Because we are unlimited, we will try to experience unlimited, eternal, and free love. Marriage was an attempt at the eternal but failed in being unlimited and free. By its very nature, it is limited, but if a marriage is a choice, it is free. Marriage should never be an obligation. We should be open and honest about our truth in word and deed. This is the only sacred promise we can make in any marriage, and any other promise limits freedom.

We are change, and we are constantly changing. So, we can't promise to stay the same, and the time may come when we choose to leave a marriage.

It is difficult to keep promises. First, most people don't know what they are doing in any situation, and it is difficult to act consistently in all situations. Life is constantly changing. Second, most people can't predict the future, so a promise cannot be made truthfully. Third, a person's truth evolves, changes over time eventually producing a conflict between what was promised and what the person's current truth is.

Therefore, when confronted with whether to keep a promise or not, remember the highest betrayal is a betrayal of ourselves even if it is an effort to prevent betraying another.

People are constantly changing. No one should expect anyone to keep a promise. No one should be forced to keep their word because they didn't want to or felt they couldn't. Forcing anyone to do something they don't want to do is an aberration of free will.

We imagine marriage is based on love, but it is actually based on fear. It is an institution constructed to guarantee the fulfillment of our needs. It was designed to insure the present state would always be. Without the need for a guarantee, marriage would not be needed. It would be based on love if it allowed our love to be unlimited, eternal, and free.

As we have constructed marriage, we employ an external institution to provide the security we intrinsically have within. We use marriage to punish if we don't get this security, we use marriage to limit the love of another, or prevent the sexual expression of love with another, and we declare our marriage as a special relationship above all others.

The enlightened, and God, hold no one more special than another. Special relationships with a special person are unnatural. Everyone is equally special with God, and we would do well to organize ourselves in a similar fashion. Marriage vows as we have constructed them are therefore a sacrilege. God's love is unlimited and unconditional. Anything less for us is limiting and stifling for our evolution.

Marriage could be based on love. It could be formulated in such a way to make it unlimited, eternal, and free. Such a marriage would be inclusive, including everyone.

Marriage, as we have constructed it, does not supply us with love, joy, peace, and security in the long run, and the longer we stay with it, the further from these we are taken. About half of all marriages end in divorce, a method of extracting punishments and rewards, with many of the remaining marriages containing couples who are very unhappy. Some end in murder suicides.

Love requires nothing. A love with requirements is a fake love. Marriage vows as we have defined them shackles those married in a way love would never do. Conversely, a marriage without limiting expectations or any requirements is based on love.

Everything in life is done for ourselves, because there is no one else. We are all One, and so love is not about giving to someone else. There is no one else. It is impossible to give to another, because there is no one else.

Doing or not doing something for another is the same thing as doing or not doing for us. What's good for one of us is good for all of us. What's good for all of us is good for one of us.

No one should get married for security, and no one should get married expecting someone else to provide anything for them. All security, all needs, all love, all wisdom, all power, all knowledge, all understanding, all nurturing, and all strength lies within each of us. No one should get married to limit, control, or restrict another. Marriage should provide opportunities, not obligations. Life in marriage should be a metaphor for life as One with Everything, the union of two as the union of the All with the All. Marriage should be a partnership where everything is shared equally, and should be an institution where there is unity, and a joining. It is not a possession, entrapment, or restricting of another, and it is not a promise to love, honor, and obey. The length of a marriage, or any relationship, is not an indication of quality. We should always be true to ourselves even if it means ending or changing a marriage or relationship.

Love and freedom is the same thing. The implications for marriage are tremendous considering current thoughts about the institution. True love would grant total freedom to all members of a marriage. To experience being hurt by another's free will choices is a sign of forgetfulness about who we are. To choose to experience hurt is to choose to be a victim. We may decide to define marriage any way we wish, and we have chosen many variations in the past. Marriage like other parts of society will be continually evolving. No rules and regulations should be placed on it. It would be wise for all connected to a marriage to be open and honest about their truth, decisions, choices, and preferences, and to accept the resulting outcomes and consequences. Everyone gets to choose what they say, do, and be. If there is a conflict, everyone gets to decide how they will react to the conflict, and as time passes, everyone continues to choose who they are in every situation as the relationship evolves. All take responsibility for their actions, eliminating the possibility of there being a villain or victim.

Marriage should only be entered after careful consideration and was not intended to provide ownership of one person over another. There can be times in a marriage, even a good one, when to allow for greater growth, each must go in different directions. The marriage should not be continued just to provide stability or to provide the appearance of solidarity. A marriage should not be dissolved without careful thought, and not because of temporary pressures.

Marriage is the perfect symbol for relationships. The greatest marriage is the union between God and souls. Other marriages are between humans and work, friends, and family.

The union of two or more with love, for any purpose, creates a bond within God. If money, convenience, social advantage, or any number of other inappropriate reasons to marry is the basis of a marriage, the marriage has already been adulterated.

For a marriage to succeed it must be based on love with sincerity, and a genuine commitment by all involved.

Nudity

Enlightened cultures create, control, and care for their environments. Because they can control the weather, environmental conditions are comfortable for living without any clothes. So they wear nothing at all, except ornaments indicating rank or honor. They have no concept of shame or modesty, and they wear nothing to make themselves prettier because they believe the naked body is the pinnacle of beauty.

In our society, our natural self is considered bad, evil, and something needing to be controlled. If we act in a natural way, we are considered to be sinful, evil, and indulgent. It is considered sinful, perverted, dirty, and unlawful to appear in public naked. In some societies, this applies to women who expose their face, wrists, or ankles. We have been taught to act in very unnatural ways, against our basic nature. Our basic nature is to be totally loveing, to love everyone and everything. But we are taught not to.

We have associated shame with our normal bodily needs, our normal bodily processes, our normal bodily noises, and our normal bodily odors because of the way society has raised us from little on up. Infants and toddlers are not ashamed of their bodies or bodily functions. Our society changes this as they grow up.

By adorning our bodies, we prove we feel guilty with them. Any concern for our bodies indicates we believe we are mortal. Any attempt to beautify our bodies indicates we think they are imperfect, flawed, inadequate, shoddily constructed, and defective. It is an attempt to hide behind a mask. It lacks transparency.

Summary

Sex is great! It's the most fun we can have with the human body. However, society, in general, thinks it is embarrassing, forbidden, dirty, shameful, and something to be hidden. We have incorporated fear, anxiety, scarcity, envy, rage, and tragedy into sex. This inhibits the full experience and celebration of something joyful, and leads to rape, mental, emotional, and spiritual turmoil, and sometimes suicide. This perverts our experience of sex. Most people would feel very uncomfortable having others watching them engage in intercourse. In cultures practicing intercourse openly, life is greatly respected with no rape and few killings.

Copulation and marriage are both metaphors in the Physical World for our Unity. In the Spiritual World, our Unity is experienced as a matter of fact, a place where there is no copulation or marriage.

We are in the process of redefining marriage. Marriage, as we have defined it in the past, is not working as illustrated by half of all marriages ending in divorce, and the fact many couples are living together without being married. In the past, marriage was important for the raising of children, and with the dissolution of marriage, children have suffered, mainly because of the war between the spouses, or the added pressure on one person trying to raise children. The remedy for this is found in the chapter on Education and Raising Our Children.

As we have constructed marriage, presently it is a religious and legal ceremony with economic implications. It is an artificial social institution created to govern our behavior. All laws relating to marriage are unable to prevent people from breaking marriage promises. The marriage laws as we have constructed them impinge on our unlimited and free nature. Marriage excludes and is based on fear. It's an attempt at security. All of these, religious, legal, and economic attachments to marriage, should be removed, and it should be a simple act of love. The marriage vows should be simple statements of love with no future requirements. "Till death do us part" must go because we are eternal beings. It is not based on the truth of who we are. Marriage should be inclusive by including everyone, should have no requirements or limiting expectations, should provide opportunities for growth, should act as a partnership where all is shared equally, and should facilitate a union of souls. True love would grant total freedom to all members of a marriage. Love is unconditional.

How two or more people marry, and the sex and race of the individuals involved should be irrelevant. Freedom of expression should be the hallmark of our society because it logically follows from freedom of choice. And freedom of choice should apply to all marriages with no obligations imposed on the members. Each should be allowed full expression and full growth to develop full potential. The goal of marriage should be to help each member of the marriage to fully reunite with God through their relationship. Leaving a marriage should be as painless as entering a marriage, and both entering and leaving a marriage should be simple to do. The decision for marriage or divorce should be done carefully and deliberately and should only be done after careful consideration. The economics of the world should be changed so no one feels trapped in a marriage. No one should be forced to decide to either stay in an abusive marriage or leave and starve.

We have been taught to act in very unnatural ways, against our basic nature. We are love, and our basic nature is to love everyone and everything. But we are taught to be careful of who or what we love. We should feel free to love everyone. Marriage can be a beautiful thing when constructed to be eternal, unlimited, and free. It should be based on pure love unadulterated by any other desires, and with all involved being open, honest, and transparent. Such a marriage provides an opportunity for unlimited growth. When it has served its function, the members should be allowed to go in peace and love to other life-expanding opportunities.

As we were created and as we are born, we have been naked and unashamed of our nakedness. God created nothing shameful including our bodies or any of our bodily functions, and yet it is considered sinful, perverted, dirty, and unlawful to appear in public naked. In some societies, this applies to women who expose only their faces, wrists, or ankles.

When we learn how to control the weather, we can adjust the climate to allow us to be naked all the time. By then, we may have evolved enough to comfortably walk around naked. Nothing need be worn except signs of rank or honor. The naked body is the peak of beauty with nothing needed to adorn or improve it, contrary to popular belief. Any attempt to beautify our bodies indicates we think they are imperfect, shoddily constructed, and defective. It is an attempt to hide behind a mask. It lacks transparency. And it confuses who we are, spirit, with our bodies, something we are not. This is a high ideal, and it will take a thousand years or longer for society to embrace this way of life. This is not a requirement, and we are free to live as we like.

Religion and Spirituality

A religion is an institution dedicated to organizing, interpreting, and regulating beliefs in spiritual matters. Spirituality is life as it is experienced. The one is an organization and the other is a personal thing.

There have been people from all religions with God as its focus, who have had a personal relationship with God. This is a personal thing done by the individual with the religion having nothing to do with the experience. The religions provided doctrines and their explanations of how humans relate to God and to life. But it is the individual who establishes the relationship.

Over time people have changed their ideas about God and life. But this change has been slow because of religion.

Once established, a religion acts as a person with the preservation of itself as a goal, and in most cases, it says it is the one true religion, an act of self-preservation. Any new ideas about God and life are considered a threat to its survival causing the religion to impede change. When major new ideas arrive on the scene, a new religion has had to be formed. When Christianity appeared, it was rejected by the Jewish Religion, forcing the formation of the Christian Religion, and the same thing happened when Islam appeared.

A religion finds itself in an awkward situation when confronted with change. Does it abandon the teachings of the founder for the new ideas, or does it stand by the original teachings? How does it decide the path to take? How does it react to new religions competing for members? Is it possible for a religion to reinvent itself by accepting new ideas? Does it really matter what a person believes?

Religions face the two-edged sword of maintaining their truth. If they say this is it, and nothing can be added or deleted, then when a new truth comes along, they are forced to reject the new truth. And if they welcome new ideas as truths, they run the risk of changing their truth to something less than true.

New truths can be overlooked, ignored, rejected, or accepted. If people don't search for new truth, it's easy to overlook a new truth. A truth not found is continued ignorance. If a new idea shows up and is noticed, but nothing is done about it, the idea is ignored and again, continued ignorance if the idea contains truth. If a new truth shows up and is rejected, the result is the same with continued ignorance. Finally, if a new truth shows up and is accepted, positive evolution takes place.

When Jesus showed up, the Jews had a dilemma. Was Jesus the Messiah foretold by the prophets, or just a pretender? The Jews decided Jesus was a pretender, but Christians thought otherwise, and a new religion was born. If the Jews had accepted Jesus as the Messiah, there would be no Christianity, just a larger group of Jews. This same dilemma has played out in millions of forms in millions of places. The fear of making a wrong choice has caused people to err on the conservative side by rejecting new ideas. This has infinitely slowed the spiritual evolution of the world. Unfortunately, in the past, for new ideas to be accepted, a new religion had to be formed, most times with its own scripture.

Another problem religions face is an interpretation of what the original writers meant centuries ago when the scriptures were written. All scriptures become out of date as time passes and new challenges arise unheard of at the time of the original writing. Is the interpretation of the scripture correct? Most scriptures are so vague a person could prove almost anything with it. Different interpretations have led to the formation of different sects within the same religion.

The Problem with Religion

The main reason for our problems is lack of spirituality. The solution to our problems is spiritual. In the contest between religion and spirituality, spirituality will win. Religion teaches a person should learn from the experiences and thoughts of other people, while spirituality teaches a person should learn from their own experiences and thoughts. When a person learns from their own experiences and thoughts, they can come to conclusions different from what religion teaches, and religions don't like it.

Our most basic beliefs have come from exclusivist organized religions. Initially, these beliefs came from our earliest mystic teachers who passed their teachings onto their interpreters and followers. These teachings were then passed onto others who passed the teachings onto still others. This passage of the information caused misinterpretations and distortions. This information then formed the basis of today's influential religions. These religious beliefs formed the beliefs of society and the basis of the laws of our various countries.

Our ideas about ourselves come from our ideas about God and Life. Our ideas about God and Life come from our religions. The ideas we get from our religions carry moral authority. This moral authority behind these ideas makes it difficult to object to any of them. Unfortunately, religions haven't had a stellar history disseminating ideas worthy of emulating as exemplified by the Christian Crusades.

Killing, domination, suppression, and terror have been inflicted by religions in the name of God, with the Christian Crusades a good example of killing in the name of Christ.

Religion has been beneficial in the lives of individuals, but social evolution has been slow because of religion's refusal to accept new ideas, and religion has not produced a significant change in worldwide consciousness. Though they have put forth a great effort, they have failed because of lack of understanding and stubbornness. There haven't been any significant new ideas introduced into most major religions in hundreds or thousands of years. Any new idea is thought sacrilege. Religious leaders refuse to consider new ideas, and they cannot accept there might be something they don't know that could change everything, because they think they have all the answers.

When it comes to war, for example, we can resist our government by becoming a conscientious objector. But what do we do if our religion tells us to go to war?

Religions hope we will believe their ideas come from God. So, if we oppose their ideas, religions hope we will believe we are opposing God's ideas. And who would oppose God?! The bottom line is religions want we humans to follow their beliefs no matter where they lead.

Religions have used fear to control people, and these same religions teach God is ruthless, self-serving, unforgiving, and vengeful, just like people.

Religions have used the mystery surrounding the spiritual to control people. God sees us just as God created us, sinless, unchangeable and eternal. The second coming of Christ is the realization by all of us the Christ is found within each of us and then living and expressing the Christ within each of us by all of us. The idea of Jesus returning to remove the saved from Earth is a figment of our imaginations.

Fighting between religions has caused wars and restricted progress in all fields. Now religions must decide how to resolve their differences. Can they respect each other's beliefs, submerge their differences, and work for understanding and peace?

The purpose of God's Prophets is to enlighten mankind and provide for their peace. They provide for our well-being. Their teachings lead to unity and peace. True religion has advanced civilization and has the potential to lead the world to love, and unity. However, humans in the name of religion have impeded advancement and contributed to divisions, wars, and unhappiness.

Some religious leaders have caused all kinds of difficulties for the world because they wanted power and wealth or were misinformed. Some religious leaders persecuted prophets who were teaching the truth.

The main reason for strife in the world is the misinformation spread by uninformed religious leaders because they say their form of religion is the one true religion, and all other religions are false and the other religion's adherents are condemned by God. This produces discord, contempt, disputes, and hatred, but if these religious prejudices were removed, peace and harmony would follow.

Churches are not wholly to blame for strife. Each of us must live our own lives, and each of us is responsible for our life lived. No one can live for us. The power of God has been given to each of us to create our own life. The Source is within each of us, and all our needs and desires can be supplied from it. Nothing outside us satisfies. God's purpose for us is to express the Divine in our lives. This is something we each must do for ourselves. God may have a purpose for us, but we are still free to express it as we choose.

All true religions have proclaimed the unity of God and humans. They teach love and aid for each other. Humans should live in unity, love, and harmony with each other. Oneness is the essential truth of all true religions.

Any religion opposed to science is superstition. When we oppose knowledge, we welcome ignorance. The truth of any religion is supported by science. For humans to evolve, science and religion both are needed. Science by itself will lead to materialism. Religion by itself will lead to superstition.

True religion is basically one message from God presented to the world at different times by different prophets in terms appropriate for the time and location where it was delivered. When spiritual information is given by God to humans, it is best suited to the time and place where it is given. This information has a spiritual part and a practical part. The spiritual part remains the same and deals with the inner world. The practical part deals with the exterior world and changes depending on conditions of the time and place where it is delivered. Just as advances are made in science and technology, so advances in religion must be made.

From the beginning of time, people have received inspiration from God. Each has received their message and has added their own ideas about the inspiration, thinking they alone have received the message, and only they can deliver it, and their message was the only true message from God. The messages from God have thus been diluted and subverted from the original truth. This has resulted in disharmony, and conflict in the world.

Many religions have subverted the word of God from the original truth to something they feel comfortable with even though it creates hardships leading many away from love. Religious leaders have used and continue to use the history of religions to manipulate members to continue this history. Religions and people are not their histories. If we continue to live now as we have lived in the past, there will be nothing new. One of the great calamities humans have fostered upon themselves is trying to perpetuate the past. Life should be allowed to select the future. To find the future, we should allow the past to die.

Religion first tells people they don't have the answers, and then, it, religion, has the answers. Third, religion conditions people to accept their answers as truth and not to question them. It conditions people to doubt their thinking ability. Religion must keep people from coming up with answers different from theirs.

For some people, this has resulted in believing God doesn't exist. Religions taught their followers to fear God because of the wrath of God, to worship God, and to be ashamed of their bodies and the body's natural functions. Religions taught their followers they need an intermediary to go between them and God and to adore God. They have also taught their followers disunity, and taught this disunity has a hierarchy of God above man, and man above woman making women spiritual second-class citizens.

Many religions tell adherents to follow their collection of dogmas and practice, and certain rites and ceremonies, all external in nature. These dogmas, rites, and ceremonies vary from religion to religion. They are often confused with inward truth. The differences sow seeds of discord, hatred, and disunion. Frequently, religion and science are thought to be at odds with each other. Most religions teach reflection and logic have nothing to do with religion. Much hatred would cease if the harmony of science and religion were accepted. Humans should apply their intellect and reasoning to religion.

Prejudice in the form of religious bigotry and fanaticism has created hatred in the world. The sources of scriptures have agreed with each other. The followers of these sources disagree with each other resulting in antagonism and hostility. The greater the cooperation, reciprocity, communication, and unity among humans, the greater the accomplishments humans will create. Love and fellowship among humans is the purpose of true religion. Denying higher revelations from successive prophets will prevent this unity.

Each person must seek reality for himself or herself. Obsolete doctrines mask the truth and must be abandoned. There is only One Reality and having different versions of it leads to division.

Fundamentalist religious beliefs are causing dysfunctional behavior. As we change these beliefs we experience a fuller sustainable life.

Create a unified theology. Our separation theology has created artificial ideas of separation in all parts of our lives leading to all form of suffering.

Intrinsically we know God is kind, gentle, and loving, but our religious leaders have told us God should be feared because God is vengeful. But God is joyful, loving, accepting, blessing, and grateful.

We have been taught to feel guilty, a learned response. Our parents have told us we are bad. Our religious leaders have told us we were born less than perfect in original sin. But could God create anything less than perfect? Religious theologies have been built around original sin to justify the idea of an angry God. If there was no original sin, and there is no sin, religious teachings of an angry vindictive God wouldn't be needed. If there's an angry, vindictive God needing appeasement, then there's the need for a religion to save people from Hell. This gives power to the few.

One set of beliefs is we were born in sin, we sin throughout life, and we can die in sin. We are reconciled to God only by accepting Jesus as our intermediary. But the question remains: why were we created that way? Did God make a mistake? This implies God made imperfect beings and then required them to be perfect or be damned. The short version is the Son saved us from what the Father did.

In truth, we are under no obligation to God. God has given us unequaled opportunity to be the highest ideal we can imagine for ourselves.

Our religions have created illusions separating us from God. These illusions are insanity. Religions, in general, cannot teach our unity because this truth means we are all equal, no soul pleases God more than another, all souls go to Heaven, and all paths lead to God.

Our biggest, most powerful religions rob us of self-esteem. They teach we are separate, not worthy of God, shameful, guilty, born in sin, and undeserving of God's presence. They say we are not magnificent, and so we must beg for mercy for our many sins.

If we have our self-esteem taken from us, we will take it from others. If we don't love ourselves, we can't love others. If we see ourselves as unworthy, we will also see others as unworthy. Most organized religions teach fear, guilt, and self-denial, not joy, innocence, and self-celebration.

Religion is an exclusive experience unable to include everyone. Religious groups can't agree on how its members should experience religion and have killed each other over how religious ecstasy should be experienced.

Religious exclusion wouldn't be a problem if religions were tolerant of those excluded. Religions should be the ones to teach tolerance, but they haven't learned how to practice it. Our current beliefs are only stepping stones to greater understandings of the future. None of our current beliefs about God are complete, so none of us can judge or criticize anyone.

One of the biggest problems in the world is organized religions; not all, but most of the largest. Far from being a solution, these religions are leading millions of people blindly. This is because their beliefs about God are false. The problems of the world are spiritual, and most religions haven't helped.

Where God is thought of as a small, petty, jealous, capricious, impulsive, demanding deity, God becomes the worst of humanity. We claim to want to be God-like, and using this definition, we have succeeded magnificently, and we have organized religion to thank for this distorted version of God. Religions who say, "we are the only true religion," create major problems for the world. They teach a separation philosophy and an exclusive theology. Their spiritual teachings while untrue, have a huge effect on the world.

We decide if we want to suffer or not. If we refuse to express ourselves as God and take control of our lives, eventually the evidence and our suffering will be so great we can't ignore it.

Humans natively have known they have the answers. The source is within. Humans natively have known they could joyfully reach out to God and have known they could expect God to help them. Humans natively have known the joys of their bodily functions and have known they are intimately connected to God. Humans have natively adored God, and in our knowledge of our Unity with God and Everything, we have known no one is higher than another.

Because men, like nations, want more power and refuse to share it, they have constructed God in their image. They have created a God who wants power, refuses to share it, and desires to exercise it. God shares all power with us.

All religions can be improved. All philosophies and ideologies can be made better. Be receptive to new truth. Invite the possibility of new truth to improve the current understanding. At the edge of our comfort zone life starts. Refusing to change our current truth impedes the flow of life.

Civil and Moral Codes

Currently, we believe our own code of conduct comes from God and is THE one to follow. This belief, resulting in the formation of the many codes of conduct of the many religions, has prevented the consideration of new ideas about God and Life that could lead to a new workable universal code of conduct. In the past when we lived in widely scattered communities, we may not have functioned well, but at least we could survive. Now we are an interconnected, interdependent worldwide community. We really are One even if we don't believe it. Any disruption in any part of the worldwide community affects the whole. If we want to continue to survive we will have to function as One.

We act as if God is confused. Each culture has different codes of conduct, all said to be based on the Law of God. If this is true, then God is very mixed up.

Repressive religious societies have been around a long time. While their leaders say their laws are based on the laws of God, they are based on the fears of the leaders who fear their people will stray from the path chosen by the leaders, and the leaders' fears are probably correct. These are societies based on fear, and fearful people will find new ideas more attractive than the present beliefs.

Such societies arise because of their incorrect ideas about God. Most of us believe God's society is ruled like this: God requires us to love God, requires us to believe God's teaching, and requires us to act in certain ways or else. This is the way a god of fear would act.

A God of love would act totally different. Love has its own allegiance.

Wrong can be used in two different ways. It can mean mistaken or immoral. The problem with mistakes is they can be equated with being immoral instead of just an operational failure. A mistake can then become a sin. In some societies, a mistake can be equated with an offense against God, with severe consequences. If we disagree with these standards, we may be labeled an apostate and killed. This situation creates all the ingredients necessary for war. We would now be defending the faith if another group disagreed with our laws. This holy war would be authorized by and required by God as believed by those who think this is true. This has been happening for hundreds and thousands of years.

An example of a basic belief that doesn't work is morality. It is only an idea created in our minds. It has no substance. It is a concept built on false beliefs. Morals are ideas based on what we believe about God and Life that we use to determine how things are and how they should be. These are our ideas and not God's. The problem with morals is they haven't changed in a very long time, creating the problems of today.

Our various cultures have constructed morals and values we consider absolute. They are not absolute, but only thoughts and beliefs we think to be true. These values include gender expectations as well as all cast, race, or other group stations in our societies. If we changed our morals and values, and they can be changed, our world would change.

Different cultures contradict each other with their beliefs. For example, eating animals is a sin for Hindus while Chinese believe it's unhealthy to be a vegetarian. Deciding what to believe can be fearful, but fear is unnecessary. We each have our own path, and we would do well to be true to ourselves. Our own path is the most spiritual for us.

There is a problem with any religion fostering divisiveness, strife, and killing because of religious doctrines because it dishonors our unity. Any religion limiting us to "one true way" is limiting our ability to be who we are and create our own pathway through life. The best possible way to live life is to nurture ourselves, creating an unlimited life to allow us to see our true magnificence.

God gives us all we need to have a wonderful and happy experience. Among these is free will. We have corrupted this idea by saying God has taken away free will by saying exactly what we are to do, think, say, and at times, how we are to dress and eat. Some countries have based their civil law on religious law. This is a problem because Life evolves and changes, and these countries try to prevent change. They are fighting Life, and Life always wins. As the difference between the evolving society and the law of the land widens, new and more practical standards of behavior will pop up. The old ways will be defended by those afraid to change. This creates huge problems. Ironically, freedom is what God is, and free will is God's greatest gift, but both are severely restricted by religious governments.

Expressions of freedom include the human rights of personal liberty, equality under the law, and fair trials, equality of men and women, and freedom of beliefs.

For us to change our world, we must be willing to give up some of our sacred beliefs. Unfortunately, many of us would rather die than be wrong. When enough of us die, our experiences will finally prove our beliefs were mistaken. We will finally realize what doesn't work, was a mistake.

To have lasting change, we must change people's model of Life. We must change their beliefs. This affects the source of people's actions.

For peace and harmony, now is the time to expand and change our beliefs. The problem is once we have a belief, it stays a belief until proven wrong. Even then, some will not change. The first step is to be willing to look at our beliefs to see if some are not working. The presence of conflicts in our lives is proof the fallacies about God don't work. The conflict would have ceased long ago if our beliefs about God were correct. The telltale sign is a lack of perfect peace in our relationships with anyone or anything because of our beliefs about God. Our incorrect beliefs about God cause conflict.

Ridiculous ideas have not stopped us from believing them. One such idea is God is unhappy and needs to be placated. We have killed millions of people, including the sacrificing of babies, to please God. Our belief we have caused God's unhappiness is the insane belief of insane religions that causes people to act insanely. It is arrogant to think we could cause the Creator of the Universe to remove Peace and Love and replace them with unhappiness. Doing this is impossible. Peace and Love are what God **is**. This fallacy is part of the basis of the way **we** act.

Very early in our existence on Earth, we decided God separated from us because God was unhappy with us. We do the same to each other, so we assumed God would act the same way. Because we believed we were separate from God, we also believed we were separate from each other even though we are One with Everything. The moment we believed we were separate from God, we experienced separation from everything in life. And we believed we were separate from God because organized religion told us so.

Religions took these early stories, codified the separation experience, and converted the myth to dogma. The illusion of separation from God and all of life was complete.

Modern religion has failed modern humans in leading us to the truth, but now we can find the truth if we're courageous. We can take our religious beliefs and enlarge them and drop or change what does not work.

The moment we believe we are One with God; we will experience our unity with everything in life.

We believe what we believe because of where we were born and the early training we received. Our beliefs are the result of our cultural environment, not necessarily the eternal truth because we usually don't question what we are told, especially if it comes from our parents or religious leaders.

We may choose to question our beliefs, but changing our beliefs presents a problem because of who we might make wrong. If we believe in right and wrong, we have a problem. We will be more likely to fight for what we believe to be right. We will not want to change if we make us or someone we love wrong.

On the other hand, if we embrace the "what works" paradigm and critically analyze our beliefs based on what works, changing is easier.

Once we experience the bliss of total unity with others and the Divine and start talking about it, we will be told to be wary of the experience.

Because of the fallacy of separation, we do to others, things we wouldn't do to ourselves, even though we are doing it to ourselves. Unfortunately, we don't see it as doing it to ourselves.

Religions have practiced discrimination because of the Life fallacy stating some humans are better than others. Most religions refer to God as "he", a blatant form of discrimination saying men are better than women. As our spirituality changes, we will end this discrimination, even though it will be opposed by those in power, men.

The idea of "better" is the most harmful idea conceived by us. Using it we have justified and rationalized our worst behaviors. Some Christians think they are better than Jews. Some Jews think the opposite. Some whites think they are better than blacks, and some blacks think they are better than whites. And the list goes on. In some circles, "in the eyes of God" has been added to these contrasts, elevating the betterness. In some religions, only males can be members of the clergy. Some religions think they are superior to others because only through their religion can we find salvation.

Unfortunately, the better we think we are, the worse we act. We need to expand our awareness and notice this.

Organized religions clearly state in their scriptures killing is acceptable and proper to deal with our differences. This is opposite our instincts, but organized religions have changed our thoughts. Some religions have told their followers that killing others with suicide bombs is what God wants.

"We are One with Everything, and our way is just another way, and not better than any other way" are two powerful statements for changing the world. Our political and religious leaders could not say this phrase because they would undo everything they taught us and undo the basis of their actions.

It has been and will be very difficult for us to change our basic beliefs. Even when presented with incontrovertible proof in the past about the inaccuracy of our beliefs, we have refused to change our beliefs.

For us in the past, great truths have started as blasphemies. Today we still look at great truths as blasphemies. For example, God continues to speak to us today, nothing is demanded of us by God, and we are One with God. The greatest blasphemy for many of us is many of our beliefs are false.

Atheism is learned. Deism is a deep-seated knowing, a cellular level awareness. However, the deep-seated knowing is not always what is believed about God.

What is God's Law? Each religion has its own. This produces divisiveness. The solution is to agree on one set of laws unrelated to any religion. Create a spiritual community based on spiritual principles and eliminate religious communities with their doctrines. The new spiritual community would be based on all the new ideas about God and Life including the idea, Everything is One Organism. There is just this One Organism, and Everything is part of this One Thing.

We have insisted we must do God's will, and then we have defined God's will as we pleased. God's will has been used to rationalize and justify our most horrendous behaviors. They have been unfair, contrived, and ungodly, and used to attack unsuspecting and innocent people. We have used God's will to get our way, not God's.

God's will and our will are the same. Seeing them as different causes problems. If our will was different from God's will, God's will would win out, and we wouldn't have free will.

We have had little practice acting as One, and many feel threatened by it. So, we continue to allow our dissimilarities to produce divisions.

"A house divided cannot stand. Every kingdom divided against itself is brought to desolation; and every city or house divided against itself shall not stand" (Matthew 12:25).

It is possible to practice Oneness and still be different. It doesn't mean sameness. Unity and individuality do not exclude each other. Differences do not mean we must have divisions and conflicts.

Our various body parts don't look like each other, for example, eyes and ears, but they are all part of the body. Each has an important function. By working together, the whole-body benefits.

Deciding on the Truth

How does someone decide what to do? We have studied the sacred scriptures to determine God's will in matters from killing another to making promises. No matter what we determine God's will to be, we haven't implemented it. We have tried the system of rewards and punishments for millennium without success. The truth is our will is united with God's will, and God has no preference except ours. This is free will.

So how do we decide what to do? What is good and what is bad? What is the best of all the possibilities?

Given this freedom, we never have to worry about rewards or punishments from God. In all matters, we are free to decide what we want.

The old belief of separation where we have right and wrong, good and bad, crime and punishment, and everlasting rewards and everlasting damnation has not solved our problems. Believing We are All One will change the way we treat ourselves and others ending suffering, torture, and killing.

The purpose of religion is to connect us with God through our souls. We are worthy companions of God having no limitations. Religious services may include various ways to help the members of the congregation to evolve and get in touch with God, but the most important part is to have a period of twenty minutes of quiet meditation. Meditation, or any contact with Spirit, is limited without compassion. Love, joy, and imagination should be part of all religious teachings. Religions should be providing opportunities for full spiritual development through direct revelation and inner knowing. Members should always be pointed to the Kingdom of God within where they commune with the Holy Spirit and the soul. There we will be guided in living our lives. It is variously called prayer, contemplation, and "Be still and know." We should be encouraged to expand our awareness beyond Earth to the life existing throughout the Universe, and to explore and visit our neighbors with love.

Theology and arguing the meaning of scriptures is non-productive. The simple approach to religion is to love God with all our hearts, love our neighbors as ourselves, and equally important, love ourselves. Live love. Be love.

Trying to understand any holy book by interpreting its exact wording when it was written for past ages will be misleading. The basic concepts found in any holy book are the truth. Our interpretations of these books must be expanded to know the truth. No holy book is the final word. Life evolves and changes and new understands will be constantly needed in any present age. Over time, God has sent may teachers resulting in the formation of many religions. We have used these religions to form separate groups dividing us from one another. Separation was never God's intention. It's something we did. The goal of all these teachers was to unify us, not divide us. If we examine all of the world's teachings and look for the universal message in all of them, we will realize our unity and end our divisions. All codes will need to be updated as time passes, except for the basic message of peace, love, and forgiveness.

Meditation is an important preparation for the transition from a material body to an energy spirit. We existed before "birth" and will continue to exist after "death." All religions should teach the all-encompassing nature of God, the importance of loving God, our identity as a soul being a part of God, and our divine immortality. We can celebrate the diversity of our religions without feeling our religion is superior to any other religion.

Habit-forming substances, such as alcohol and drugs can degrade the spiritual matrix of the mind and emotions as well as impair the body. We will need disciplined minds, clear emotions, and non-violent attitudes. Nothing should be put in our bodies causing us to lose control of our peaceful behavior, and no substance should be used to replace a peaceful mind and loving heart.

One goal religions can and should apply themselves to achieve is world peace by loving one another, living peacefully, and cooperatively with everyone. We must not only say we want peace, we must be peaceful, and demonstrate it with the way we live our lives by actively being peaceful and loving in our governments, businesses, and industries. Loving behavior brings peace. Expensive buildings and organizations are unnecessary for this. Greed has led many astray.

Nothing can substitute for the voice within, not even rituals. Listen and believe. Only those priests, rabbis, preachers, ministers, swamis, lamas, gurus, and teachers who demonstrate love and peace, and address us as God's evolving creation are worthy of our trust. They are the ones who have found their own inner soul connection and are helping us to connect as well. The purpose of any religion should be to help us have our own personal connection to God. This leads to world peace. Without this, we have war in all of its various forms creating all kinds of suffering.

We are magnificent beings and are part of Everything and are constantly enveloped in unconditional Love and acceptance. God has only compassion and unconditional love for us and never judges us. Living the same way is our natural reaction to life.

We are complete and perfect just as we are. All our parts, ego, intellect, body, and spirit, are perfect. We have nothing to do, including forgiving, letting go, or attaining anything to be perfect. We are not "less than." In practical terms, we are more than we have imagined. Any religion, guru, teacher, or master who teaches we are less than their deities, and in some cases even the same as their deities, is not teaching the truth. We don't need to be saved, to be enlightened, to be educated, or to do anything to be improved. However, if we change our beliefs from those based on false ideas to those based on the truth, life on Earth will be closer to Heaven.

When we live as One, religions will support and use as the basis for their beliefs awareness, honesty, and responsibility. These concepts will make possible unconditional love, unlimited sharing, and emotional and physical healing.

We have said our sacred scriptures, and there are many, have given us the authority to treat each other as we have been treated. We have read our scriptures, but have we listened? We have decided what the scriptures say even though our understanding is different from the original message. All sacred scriptures basically say the same thing. The problem has been we are willing to kill each other over our differences of **interpretation**.

The truth is there are many sacred scriptures, but we act as if there is only one, and we have decided our chosen scripture is the one true scripture, and all else is less reliable or worse. And then there is only one way to interpret it, ours. This spiritual arrogance is the cause of our greatest pain. And it's all because we insist on being right. We have decided our chosen scripture, our chosen God, and our chosen prophets are the basis of our one and only one true religion.

The solution is to transcend our current beliefs and open our minds. This means to go beyond our current beliefs, picking the best from them and add new beliefs to them. We have more than just two choices, to reject or to accept our current beliefs. We can hold to the best of the old, rejecting what doesn't work, expand some of the old to make them work better, and add new beliefs to make the whole package work better.

Actually, no one has any wrong beliefs. We just didn't have enough information to formulate our beliefs properly. Transcending current beliefs adjusts the belief system to make it workable without rejecting the old system entirely.

Every human being is Divinely inspired. Religions say otherwise. That is why they say no books written today are the word of God. Religions could not tolerate new teachings from a new Messiah.

Religions may not be able to agree on which books are the true word of God, but they all agree the books are old, and they all agree God's revelations stopped long ago. The truth is, God's revelations never stopped and never will.

Most people agree God can inspire humans with Divine wisdom, just not today. If it's an old idea, it could be God inspired. If it came from an old person today, it's not inspired by God.

Some of the major fallacies about God, leading us away from peace, are God needs something, God may not get what God wants, God withdrew from us because we didn't provide what God needed, God now requires we provide this need from our separated position, and God will damn us if we don't provide this need.

Our actions reflect our beliefs about God. Some of us think we can act with each other the same way we believe God acts with us, and believe by creating crisis, violence, killing, and war, we are meeting God's requirements, and this helps to provide God's needs, and a context for believing God's will is for wanton killing.

The wrath of God is a fallacy about God. But we believe in the wrath of God, and the appropriateness of venting our own wrath on each other. Religious leaders have used this argument to call "all true believers" to "kill the apostate."

As long as we base our lives on the major fallacies about life leading us away from peace such as we are separate from each other, things needed for human happiness are limited, we must compete with each other for this limited supply, some of us are better than others, and killing is appropriate to resolve differences, we will continue to create a world of anger, violence, loss, sorrow, and terror. Our beliefs, not other people, are the source of all of this, and the solution is to change our beliefs. Other means such as political, or economic will not.

There are other problems in the world such as hunger, poverty, crime, corruption, political unrest, governmental abuse, corporate greed, plus others. But all our problems are spiritually based. If we knew who we are, who God is, how life worked, that love is the basis of life, and fully knew unconditional love, our problems would not exist.

Unfortunately, problem religions will not permit a full spiritual understanding, because they prevent contemplations beyond their own doctrines. So, the world is forced to try to solve our problems by treating the symptoms and not the root cause. We've tried politics, economics, education, social programs, and bombs, and failed because it's impossible to succeed using these methods. Our basic beliefs are causing the problem, and they must be changed to solve the problem.

Fundamentalists believe going back to the exact words of the scriptures and applying them literally is the way to go. They can be found in every religion. The problem is the words must be interpreted. Once they are interpreted they are our words about the Word of God. So, are our words about the Word of God correct or not? There's no way to know.

Some religions have conferred infallibility on scriptures or some supreme authority to get around this. The problem with this is all humans are fallible. And being always right makes someone else wrong. Disagreement and conflict are the result. A pride in being always right replaces the humility expected of religions.

Society is constantly evolving, and all holy texts should be examined within this context. These texts were written at different times, places, and circumstances than today. In all writings, the underlying principles should be sought. Interpreting the words literally will lead to misunderstandings or possibility the loss of the original wisdom they were based on. A wiser course of action would be to be open-minded to the possibility of new applications of old wisdom. We should follow our hearts, but shouldn't impose our interpretations on anyone, and never by force.

For those who say God requires they enforce certain beliefs, why would God give us free will only to have it taken away by someone? Who are we to deny free will to anyone?

There are false beliefs we have used to create our present religious institutions, economic systems, political structures, and educational programs. These false beliefs are wrecking our society and should be replaced with beliefs reflecting reality. We can change our society for the better by deeply examining our religious wisdom and allow new expressions of our spirituality to be experienced. We can open ourselves to new ideas, thoughts, and revelations to explore innovative spiritual expressions. The whole of society needs a major renovation based on new beliefs reflecting reality.

Looking at religions' track record in solving world problems, we must admit little has been accomplished. We face the same problems today faced thousands of years ago. We still have greed, envy, anger, righteousness, inequity, violence, and war. These problems have been aggravated by problem religions, and have caused estrangement and separation from God, and not communion for society. These religions have in general prevented community and integration by saying God's plan was to separate varying races, cultures, and nationalities, preventing commingling, marrying, and co-creating. These religions instead of bringing joy and freedom have brought limits, restrictions, and prohibitions specifying what can be worn, eaten, thought, done, and enjoyed. Guilt has been heaped on us about what we enjoy doing. Money, sex, power, music, dancing, and just being seen have all been called evil by religions. Cover, hide, protect, and be ashamed of ourselves. Religions have taught all this.

But the message from God has been worthiness, tolerance, integration, unity, liberation, freedom, joy, acceptance, and unconditional love.

Are we willing to boldly go where we haven't before? Will we explore new ideas and create a new spirituality by expanding the old beliefs?

Religious beliefs are based on convictions these beliefs are correct, making it difficult for these beliefs to change. A starting point might be to ask some questions. Are followers of the major organized religions angry, intolerant, rigid, abusive, and engaged in wars? Who was fighting in the war in Ireland, Middle East, Balkans, Indian-Pakistani border, Afghanistan, and many others? Who is responsible for intolerance of gays, for women's inequality, and minority discrimination in the United States? Religion is not alone. Nationalism is also involved in many struggles. The spiritual beliefs of politicians and business leaders impact and support our political and economic systems. The whole community should reevaluate their spiritual beliefs.

It is important to see we have problems needing correction. If we can't see there are problems needing correction, there is no hope of improvement. Organized religions are based on fallacies about God. Nationalism is the result of fallacies about life. Organized religion and nationalism have produced constant turmoil on Earth for centuries. Improvements can be made by just looking at these fallacies and replacing them with new ideas that work.

Is reincarnation true? In the Real World, the Spiritual World, Ultimate Reality, or Absolute World, four names for the same place, the answer is no. In the Physical World or Illusional World, the answer is yes. Reincarnation is an illusion just like our bodies and time are. In the Physical World, each of us lives an average of 600-800 illusional lives here on Earth, not to mention other lifetimes on other planets. In the Spiritual World, there are no lifetimes in different time periods because time is an illusion, and we don't use different bodies because our bodies are illusions, and we are not our bodies. What is finite is an illusion, and our bodies are finite. We are all One Thing so having separate lives is an illusion. We are all One powerful spiritual Being capable of doing anything, so we can imagine an infinite number of lifetimes all at the same "time." But reincarnation is a useful idea in that it portrays the concept of multiple illusional lives. Reincarnation is just another illusion in a world full of illusion.

By pondering the diversity of spiritual traditions in the world, we will notice each provides for the specific needs of some segment of our diverse population. These spiritual traditions all help us control our mental states, conquer our negative inclinations, and achieve our inner potential.

All of us are of equal specialness. No one from history, who lives today, or who will live in the future is superior to anyone. Jesus, Muhammad, and Siddhartha Gautama are equal with us. We are all equal. Every one of us is a messenger. Our lives as we live them demonstrate to the world who we are every second of every day. Everyone who is aware of us is impacted by our lives.

The Dalai Lama said on May 6, 2009, "Everyone is my spiritual peer. You are my spiritual peer."

"Verily, verily, I say unto you, He that believeth on me, the works that I do shall he do also; and greater works than these shall he do; because I go unto my Father" (John 14:12).

All paths to God are equal. All religions are equal. All prophets are equal.

God's Requirements

It has been said we have been made in the image and likeness of God. ["And God said, Let us make man in our image, after our likeness" (Genesis 1:26).] Could religions have made God in the image and likeness of us? Check it out. If we don't get our way, we become angry. If we still don't get what we want, and we really, really, really want it, then we condemn and destroy the ones responsible. This sounds a lot like the image of God painted by religions.

Religions teach what they say is God's preferences, but God has no preferences. We made them all up. Having a God with preferences makes life easier because we don't have to figure out what to do. We do as God says. But we don't know what God says because we believe God hasn't said anything in thousands of years. So, we have to rely on those who tell us what God said when God spoke to us. The problem is there are huge numbers of teachers and teachings. The bottom line is we must decide for ourselves what is true. The solution to this dilemma is to become a good observer. Notice what works for what we want to accomplish.

The thousands of religions in the world have produced many different beliefs. There are a few beliefs shared by most of these religions and are the foundations of these religions. The most important of these is God needs something to be happy. Even though God is omnipotent, under certain circumstances, God becomes unhappy, then angry, and finally applies retribution.

A fearful god uses fear to get its needs and wants. So, shouldn't we? Shouldn't we do it in the name of God? This is a vicious circle creating viciousness on Earth.

These religions believe God needs us to be in certain ways, act in certain ways, and have certain things, and God needs us to not be in certain ways, not act in certain ways, and not have certain things. God has these requirements and expectations, and we are in big trouble if we don't meet them. An example of these requirements is the Ten Commandments.

Unfortunately, all these religions are incorrect about this. God is Everything now, in the past, and in the future. There is nothing outside God, so there is nothing God needs. There is nothing to get. It is all located right there in God. So, God wants nothing because there is nothing to want. God does not demand, command, require, compel, order, request, insist, nor expect anything. God is total happiness requiring nothing to be happy. So, God needs nothing of us or anything in the cosmos.

God requires only what is within the Everything God is and therefore needs nothing. We were made in the likeness of God and need only what is within us. We need nothing to be perfectly happy. What we have cannot be destroyed or lost. Our bliss is within, and nothing outside of us can compare.

We have trodden on each other because of our beliefs, and this is permissible by religions, if we don't tread on sacred beliefs. Religions believe it is ill-advised to tread on sacred beliefs and ancient traditions. But when we know deep down in our hearts these sacred beliefs and ancient traditions are incorrect, do we have the courage to contradict these ideas?

In Tom Moore's June 7, 2014 newsletter, *The Gentle Way News,* he states less than 25% of what is in the Bible is correct. He also states the reason for this is the initial information was passed from person to person for generations, and centuries before the information was written down, allowing for the introduction of incorrect information. This also applies to all the other ancient religions.

Tom Moore's May 1, 2014 newsletter says Muhammad, who was illiterate, eventually passed the information from his visions onto a trusted friend who wrote them down. The trusted friend, who thought Muhammad was too soft, edited the love messages to produce the passages about conflict.

The true test of sacred scriptures is to see if it works. If it doesn't work, it should be discarded. Every sacred text should be tested this way.

Every sacred text was written by a human who was fallible. And everyone who passed on these sacred texts was fallible, possibly passing on inaccurate information. There were some writers who wanted to get humans to act in certain ways, so in an attempt to keep order among the population, these writers said the commandments came from God.

God is the creator and the created. God does not order because who would God order. There is only God. Who would be punished if there were an infraction? There is only God. Would God slap, the right hand of God with the left? There is only God.

Our spiritual leaders have told us to fear God because God is vengeful, fear the wrath of God, tremble in the presence of God, fear the terrible judgment of God because God is just, and all this justifies our obedience of the laws of God.

All this sounds like a tyrannical egomaniacal insecure despot. They are ungodly demands. Any thinking person who closely examined these descriptions of God would realize God is not this tyrannical egomaniacal insecure despot who makes ungodly demands.

We have created in our minds a God who seeks revenge and imposes punishment. But the real God is not a separated super individual residing somewhere inside or outside the Universe. This true God lacks the same emotional needs and emotional agitation as humans. God is immune to hurt or damage, and therefore has no need for revenge or punishment.

We are always in the wonderful grace of God, but we have imagined God often feeling hurt or offended. This is impossible. God can't be upset or made angry. We have also imagined a god who is like us but only bigger and more powerful. This god is something of a parent figure having ego needs and emotional turmoil like us. The real God is not like the little god we have imagined God to be.

Religion is an institution. Religions have created ideas about how things are. Once these ideas have been accepted as truth, they become unchallengeable dogmas and doctrines. We are required to believe these teachings.

Spirituality is an experience. We are required to believe nothing. Spirituality invites us to observe our experience, the source of our authority. We need not rely on what others have told us. Religion requires we approach God in a particular way. Spirituality does not.

Of the many different religions there are, each has its own directions on how to reach Heaven. The thing is, we don't have to follow any of them. God has no requirements we must follow to get there. In fact, we are already there. The Kingdom of God is Heaven and we are there because the Kingdom of God is within. There is nothing outside us in truth. The Physical World makes it appear we are small, with the vast majority of the Universe outside of us. Just remember the Physical World is an illusion. We can experience Heaven any time and any place. The hellish experiences of the world are only illusions.

We have deep emotional attachments to our beliefs, especially our religious beliefs. We find it difficult to change our beliefs, especially our religious beliefs. Changes in all aspects of life have been faster than changes in religious beliefs because of this.

Even though religions mean well, and are based on some sound spiritual precepts, their understandings are incomplete. It has been impossible to improve religious beliefs because the adherents to the beliefs feel it would be blasphemous and heretical to change them. Most of us believe the new ideas about God and Life are impossible and believe nothing new is possible because everything is known and understood.

Unless we are willing to say there might be something we don't understand about God and Life that would change everything, then we might end up destroying ourselves and everything else.

God

I am you, and you are me. We are also everyone else, and everything else. We are One with Everything. In a word, we are God. Where the Bible says, "Inasmuch as ye have done it unto one of the least of these my brethren, ye have done it unto me," (Matthew 25:40), it meant literally whatever is done to anyone is done to All.

God holds no one more special than another. Religions tell us otherwise perpetuating a fiction. Religions as we have constructed them exclude. God includes. Everyone is in fact joined to God. There can be no exclusion. When religion is unlimited, eternal, and free, then it can support us as we grow and evolve. Anything less is faulty. There is no right or wrong about religions acting exclusively. However, such actions do not work to get us to peace and harmony.

Religions have God appearing to be mysterious and causing its followers to fear God. Religions have failed to change how we act. We're still killing each other. We are still judging each other as wrong, all with the help of religions. Religion is not supplying us with what we want from religion. The longer we practice a religion, the further it takes us from love, joy, peace, and security.

In God's name, people create and destroy, accept and reject, and reward and punish. But God neither destroys, rejects, nor punishes anyone. Many can't accept this because it removes the moral authority claimed by them. People have used God as the reason things are done, using the power of God to justify what is done. Our beliefs and the beliefs we have about God are killing us.

We have been taught about a god who is characterized as being angry, supporting war, death, destruction, guilt, and retribution. This is all an illusion. The true God is a God of inner peace and unconditional love. We move and have our being inside this God. Knowing and experiencing this can change the world.

We cannot in our religious worship discover and cultivate a relationship with a loving God by teaching a doctrine of judgment and punishment.

To fully understand God, we must realize we don't know everything there is to know about God. As Werner Erhard, author and lecturer, said, there may be something I don't know, but if I did, it could change everything.

God is a process, not a person, place, or thing. God is a being, energy in motion. God is always changing, and this is the unchanging truth. God is unchanging in that God is always changing. Many religions relegate God to the past and the future, while God dwells in the present.

God loves all of us just as we are. All of us are lovable. Based on our individual view of the world, none of us does anything inappropriate. We can't do anything to cause God to stop loving us.

God is never sad because there is nothing God has to do. God will not punish us because God cannot be harmed in any way. And because we are a part of God, we cannot be harmed in any way.

There is a difference between the reality of God and churches' teachings of the reality of God. To know God, religious teachings may have to be rejected. God loves us unconditionally, welcomes all of us into paradise without restrictions, refuses to punish us, and talks to us all the time, contrary to religious teachings. We can know God and know God as a friend, the kind of friend we would choose as a friend.

Religions have constructed their "one true way" to salvation, reinforcing the illusion of separation. They have gotten the everlasting torment and damnation idea wrong. Nothing like that exists. We can do anything we wish without fear of being punished by God. God will never forgive us because there is nothing to forgive.

Religions use fear to attract believers instead of love. Religions are not willing to say theirs is not a better way, only another way.

We each have our own path to God in that no two paths are the same. There is nowhere to go except to God because God is Everything. Therefore, all paths lead to God because all paths are within God. Each path may have many twists and turns and usually takes many lifetimes to complete. The path to Love may lead through hate and fear. There is no one correct path to God. There is no one true religion with one true path to God. In fact, there is no path. We are there already. We never left God, nor can we leave God, since we are One with God.

Is it logical to believe in a God who trades Heaven for our love, and live our lives imitating this God we have constructed and making love conditional?

Religions agree we have free will, or the ability to freely choose how to live, but how free is it when they say we will be damned to eternal Hellfire if we make the wrong choice?

They have created the myth of the jealous God because they have jealously guarded God's love for us. Most religions consider themselves the one true religion and believe God loves only their members. Religions call it blasphemy if someone says God loves all people, faiths, and nations equally when in fact God does. This jealousy extends to our loved ones, jobs, hobbies, children, other things, and it is killing us.

Our true Self and God are One. There is more than one way to God, and to our true Self. The religions of the world should note this. Our imaginary self, our ego, our present personality, and body, are just one in a series of personalities and bodies used by our true Self. Our true Self uses these imaginary selves to experience life on Earth.

Changing Our Beliefs

What is necessary is for everyone to see things in a new way. See what is true, admit it is true, eliminate self-righteousness, and notice we are evolving, adapting, and changing the rules as we progress. All this is necessary.

To make lasting changes in the world, each of us must make changes on the inside. Our beliefs must change to lead to changes in our attitudes.

Humility in our religions is a good thing. The theologies of our religions tend to assume they include all knowledge. This assumption leads to not knowing anything. When a theology is assumed to be incomplete and there is a searching for more knowledge, the searching leads to knowing. Seeking for new information could lead to finding some bit of knowledge that could change everything. Not seeking leads to not finding.

The greatest gift we can give someone is self-realization. Self-realization is God's will for each person. It's called free will. It is inappropriate to try to coerce anyone to believe anything. Be love and we will act appropriately. No one knows what is best for another. No one knows how another can best express himself or herself. So, don't try to force someone to think and believe according to any religion or doctrine.

Religion should not limit or control the approach of humans to God. Permissions and protocols should not be used. Religions have repeatedly over time established rules and regulations to gather power to themselves. These rules and regulations have shut the door to heaven for people. Simplicity is best, and the best is to allow each human to have a personal relationship with God.

Knowing God increases our understanding of reality. Religions can only tell about God. Knowing God is a personal thing done by the individual. Move toward knowing God and God's ideas, and life flows. Move away, and life must be forced and manipulated.

The major obstacle to creating our Heaven is overcoming the fear of going against the prevailing beliefs, even though these beliefs are killing us. Most of us want to change but were afraid to say anything. Saying something would acknowledge our present beliefs aren't working.

We have a major choice to make. Do we change our spiritual beliefs, or do we allow our way of life to die? We have already lost our safety and security. We now must get them back. We can do this physically with war, or we can do it spiritually by changing our beliefs.

Spiritual ignorance is the cause of many of our problems. Our only limitations are spiritual. New spiritual perceptions will eclipse physical perceptions.

Spiritually, we can believe we are safe and secure, and our previously perceived loss of safety and security was only an illusion. Based on human terms, we have lost them, but spiritually, it's impossible to lose them.

The ego is destroyed by mercy. The ego, our fictitious self, refuses to allow us to believe we are love. It uses unworthiness to establish this fallacy. Any religion employing unworthiness as a doctrine facilitates ego development. Love is who we are with individual abilities, dreams, desires, gifts, and viewpoints. Jesus taught a turning from an egocentric life to a spiritual life based on God, the source of everything. This "repentance" is different for each person, requiring no conformity, leading to the knowledge they are love and a part of God. "Salvation" is not restricted to only members of any specific church.

Religions have been founded on great principles. But when these principles are used to manipulate large populations, it is time for a change. The change may be painful or graceful, and the Reformation is an example of a painful change.

Beliefs will be reexamined. Religions will face a crisis and emerge revitalized with a new dogma emphasizing the relationship between the individual and God and how the individual can have an intimate relationship with God.

When humans develop an intimate relationship with God, humans will change as they accept and develop their inner abilities. This will lead to humans treating members of other races, sexes, occupations, or stations in society as equals because all are members of One Thing.

To end our nightmare, we must acknowledge all our actions and beliefs up to now have not been working. Then seek for new ideas to replace the old beliefs. New revelations are possible. Humanity needs to be empowered to reveal our Divinity to humanity. We have the great qualities of God; love, compassion, caring, patience, acceptance, understanding, creative abilities, and the capacity to inspire. We don't always act like this because we believe in the many fallacies about God and Life and use these as the basis for our mental constructions thus creating social conventions that don't work. Examples of these social conventions are violence can solve our problems, and declaring God commands, allows, and rewards us for killing others.

Love or fear is the basis for all actions and reactions. For us, most of our behavior is based on fear. Our mental constructions and social conventions are designed to protect us from something.

To protect us from God's punishment, we constructed morals. To protect us from being treated unjustly, we constructed justice. To protect us from having our possessions taken from us, we constructed ownership. Unfortunately, none of these constructions protect us over time.

When we replace the fallacies that cause our fears, our social conventions will change to reflect the truth found in Life principles.

We frequently change our value system. This is because our value system is based on fallacies, making our value systems nonfunctional. One fallacy is morals having any real value never change. Our religious leaders tell us moral values are changeless. In truth, they change. What works in one time and place may not work in another. Morals working in one millennium rarely work in another.

Currently, our beliefs serve the body's agenda causing massive dysfunction. The body's agenda is for survival and pleasure. It wants food, water, shelter, and anything to stimulate the senses.

A good way to proceed is to select core beliefs that work, so they're functional, will adapt as conditions, awareness, and experience change, so they're adaptable, and that serve the soul's agenda, so they're sustainable. Such core beliefs will never need to be abandoned.

The soul does not seek safety and pleasure, because the soul is safety and pleasure.

If we decide to recreate our world, we must start at the level of belief. The cause of our problems is what we believe. People today have beliefs causing the unbelievable, and have produced horror, devastation, destruction, cruelty, sadness, suffering, oppression, anger, hatred, conflict, warring, and killing.

We must carefully evaluate our beliefs. After testing them to see if they produce the results we want, make any additions, deletions, or corrections clearly needed. This is an individual decision. Then openly, honestly, and courageously explore and examine any new ideas presented to our open hearts. The new ideas presented here would be a good starting point. But don't accept them without careful evaluation. Is there any truth for us individually and collectively?

We must change ourselves to be what we choose to be first and allow our doing to flow from our state of being. Doing something just to do something without changing our being is hard, if not impossible. Doing has been tried and has failed.

Producing lasting change in ourselves will produce lasting change in our world.

It is impossible to **do** peaceful, but we can **be** peaceful. It is impossible to **do** loving, but we can **be** loving. It is impossible to **do** united, but it is possible to **be** united. Seek to first change the self, then the world will change. Change ourselves and our doing will automatically change.

When it comes to changing ourselves, we must first decide who we are, what God is, and how life works, and then live these decisions. As we change, so will the world. But remember, inner peace does not come by being agitated because of the inability to achieve outer peace.

Sharing our experiences is OK, but it is inappropriate to tell others what we think their experiences should be. In teaching others, tell them they have their own answers.

Don't expect the way we live our lives to impact others. Expecting such results is counterproductive. Experiencing a lack of results can be frustrating and self-defeating.

The purpose of changing ourselves is to evolve. Having others follow our example is irrelevant. Evolving is our personal joy. This is our reason to change our beliefs, not to get others to change their beliefs.

Trying to get others to change their beliefs creates resistance. Change is an act of free will, not compliance. Evolution is done creatively. If we want peace in the world, be peaceful first. This applies to all change and is done on the inside.

Doing anything to achieve a state of being is very difficult. A state of being is achieved by choosing it and bringing it into existence or creating it. We can decide ahead of time what state of being we wish to be in any situation. Try being peaceful, loving, understanding, sharing, forgiving, and compassionate in any situation we meet. Doing so will cause the world to lose any control over us. Persistently demand to be ourselves regardless of what the whole world is being. But we must know who we are. We are what we are being.

Most of us are afraid to try. Did God really give us the power and authority? Most of us are afraid to believe the wisdom of divinity is within us. We are afraid to talk to God, be a friend of

God, and have communion with God. Fear and guilt are our greatest enemies. We fear God and death. For us humans to survive, we must replace fear with love as our guiding principle. We cannot die, nor will we be condemned to Hell.

Religions tell a different story. They agree with us being immortal but strongly believe in God condemning some of us to Hell. Some have taught we will go straight to Heaven for killing people for the right reasons and going straight to Hell for believing in God for the wrong reasons. None of this is true. These are the words of humans, not God. Humans have taught God is angry, vindictive, revengeful, retributive, petty, nitpicking, particular, and exclusive, just like humans. These humans imagined God set up a system of rewards and punishments for eternal life, just as humans designed a system of rewards and punishments for life on Earth.

Humans have replaced God's unconditional love with rewards and punishments, a human social convention. Rewards and punishments mimic adaptability. This system was a way to get other humans to adapt their behavior to what was thought to be God's will. Because of the distortions by the fallacies about God and Life, some humans act like demons.

As we reinvent ourselves, and we must, let us honor the past as we imagine the future. Enlarge old beliefs instead of rejecting them. Alter old beliefs as appropriate. Old religious beliefs should not be rejected but fulfilled.

To correct our fallacies about Life and God, our present theologies need to be enhanced, and our religions need to be revitalized. Religion is just another word for beliefs. Our beliefs are the foundation of our civilization and create our behaviors. This is true no matter if we believe in God or not. So, our beliefs need to be updated and revitalized.

Things to Consider as Truth

Not only does God speak to everyone all the time, but since we are One with God, God is speaking through all of us all the time.

God is present in everything and everyone. When we look into the face of a perceived enemy, we are looking into the face of God. Strangers, friends, family, homeless, householder, starving, well fed, smelly, dirty, clean, poor, rich, sick, and healthy, All are God. God has Its being in, as, and through everything.

God is Love, freedom, joy, peace, and unity. And we are God. God does not exist separate from us.

The answer to all questions can be found inside from God.

Most of us see God as a bigger more powerful version of us. Because we see ourselves as being needy, we see God as being needy. We have made God in our image.

However, the Bible says we are made in the image of God. This means we are not a physical form. We are Pure Energy powerful enough to create. We are Infinite Wisdom and Unconditional Love. We can take any form we choose at any time, and we have. Our energy surrounds and creates our bodies. We are Life Itself expressing as we wish when we wish.

The Word of God, the Truth of God is found everywhere. No single writing contains the whole Truth. The Koran, the Upanishads, the Bhagavad Gita, the Bible, the Torah, the Book of Mormon, the Book of Hidden Words, and all other sacred texts taken by themselves are incomplete understandings. Every book is sacred, and every messenger is holy. Likewise, every person is holy, and their lives lived displays their most sacred truth.

No message should be considered dogma and then turned into a god.

True spirituality builds bridges as does true religion. These bridges can connect different religions, cultures, races, and nations, joining together all things thought to be separate.

All churches are God's churches. All faiths are God's faiths. All souls are part of God's soul. Everything is part of God. Nothing is outside of God.

The form of the god most of us believe in is not true. The concept of this god is something we made up.

The true God is the God who gives us free will to do as we please without any interference from the Divine.

The true God is the God who sends many messengers to us all the time, constantly, to inform us of Who we are.

The true God is the God who talks to everyone constantly.

The true God is the God who tells us there is another way to experience God and Life. Our differences need not produce divisions and conflicts. Our various beliefs need not produce violence.

The true God is the God who tells us there is another way we can create by being open to new ideas and changing our old beliefs as needed to produce an enlightened world.

The true God is the God who invites us to believe, live, and experience ourselves as the highest idea of Who we are, not a god who tells us how we should live.

The true God is the God who doesn't require us to believe in God.

The true God is the God who lacks gender, size, shape, color, or other properties of individual beings.

The true God is the God who is united with everything, present everywhere, and in everything, past, present, and future.

The true God is the God who is the extraordinary process of Life. The true God is not a Super Being, or a bigger more powerful version of humans, as many humans have created God.

The true God is the God who doesn't change in that God is constantly changing, expanding, and becoming.

The truth is Love is unconditional, Life never ends, God needs nothing, and we are all miracles of God. These truths have been denied by our minds, our bodies, and our religions. But our hearts know the truth.

Believing in the false ideas about God has produced war, dissonance, unhappiness, tears, anger, violence, bloodshed, anguish, and destruction. Believing in the true God will produce peace, harmony, happiness, and the Golden Age of Enlightenment.

Life exists. Life lacks shape, form, gender, color, fragrance, size, shape, or form. Life is Everything. Life creates Life. We are Life. Life is us expressing as us. Life is God, and God is

Life. Life is constantly expanding, and becoming so it can function, adapt, and sustain itself. We have called this evolution.

In truth, we are immortal, sinless, unchanging, eternal, and are created in the image of God. The truth stands as it is, and we should evaluate it and decide for ourselves its validity.

Everyone born into this world is perfect. Each is a member of the Sonship of God, the Christ, and the Messiah. It may take some time for each to remember this. We please God just as we are. We are pure, perfect, holy, divine, and One with God.

Jesus was a human, just like us. Jesus had the presence of God within, just like us. Jesus was the Christ, the Messiah, just like us. The only difference is Jesus knew it. Jesus is our elder brother, showing us Who we are. He has shown us what we are capable of being.

We are never separated from Love, nor are we ever alone. We can never die or experience genuine loss. Separation from Everything or God is impossible. We can only succeed. We can neither harm anyone or anything nor can we be harmed. It is impossible for us to commit a sin.

These beliefs have evolved over time and will continue to evolve in the future. These evolved beliefs will eventually affect the enactment of laws.

We demonstrate our spirituality by the way we live our lives. Our politics, economics, education, relationships, sexuality, parenting, and the way we live our lives demonstrates our spirituality.

Sacred scriptures have this to say:

"Mankind was but one people" (Sura 2:209). Originally there was just one religion.

"Let there be no compulsion in Religion" (Sura 2:258).

"And who hath a better religion than he who resigneth himself to God, who doth what is good, and followeth the faith of Abraham in all sincerity? And God took Abraham for his friend" (Sura 4:125).

"Are not the friends of God, those on whom no fear shall come, nor shall they be put to grief" (Sura 10:63)?

"And God said, Let us make man in our image, after our likeness" (Genesis 1:26).

"So God created man in his own image, in the image of God created he him; male and female created he them" (Genesis 1:27).

"And in all things that I have said unto you be circumspect" (Exodus 23:13).

"And when he was demanded of the Pharisees, when the kingdom of God should come, he answered them and said, The kingdom of God cometh not with observation: Neither shall they say, Lo here! or, lo there! for, behold, the kingdom of God is within you" (Luke 17: 20-21).

"[God] Neither is worshiped with men's hands, as though he needed any thing, seeing he giveth to all life, and breath, and all things" (Acts 17:25).

"For the perfecting of the saints, for the work of the ministry, for the edifying of the body of Christ: Till we all come in the unity of the faith, and of the knowledge of the Son of God, unto a perfect man, unto the measure of the stature of the fulness of Christ" (Ephesians 4:12-13).

"Having a form of godliness, but denying the power thereof: from such turn away" (2 Timothy 3:5).

"And the scripture was fulfilled which saith, Abraham believed God, and it was imputed unto him for righteousness: and he was called the Friend of God" (James 2:23).

"I [Krishna] am the self-seated in the hearts of all beings" (Bhagavad Gita 10:20).

As we grow and develop from early childhood, we adopt the beliefs of those around us, as our own. If we grow up in a society where we are never taught to think critically, or we are taught to never question the beliefs of those around us, then the sins of the fathers are passed onto the children unto the third and fourth generation. Of course, there is no sin, but the fallacies of one generation are passed onto future generations this way.

We act as if God is confused. Each culture has different codes of conduct, said to be based on the Law of God. If this is true, then God is very mixed up. Estimates of the number of religions in the world range from thousands to billions, depending on the definition used for religion. The larger religions are further divided into sects with differing beliefs. For the Christian religion, it is estimated there are about 45,000 different sects. This proves we can't agree on what to believe, and the intolerance of our differences has produced wars. The differences go farther. Each person has their own unique set of beliefs. Just like snowflakes, we are all different with our own sets of unique beliefs and our own unique paths to God. Although we don't agree on what we believe, it's time to allow each person to hold their own beliefs without prejudice.

God does not guarantee our understanding of truth. We have many times, maybe most times, misunderstood what God has been trying to tell us. What we believe now, we consider being true even though it may not be.

The accuracy of ancient sacred scriptures is called into question and for good reason. This accuracy is further diminished by translations, some by several translations before we get a chance to read it. There is also the confusion of applying ancient cultural understandings to present-day cultural understandings. The best we can hope for in any written material is something written in our own language and written in our present time. We are blessed with many present-day writers as God continues to speak to us today. Old does not make a text better and definitely makes it less applicable to today's problems. The old writings were written for their times and problems. This does not mean we should ignore the ancient writings. There are nuggets of truth found in them. All writings were written by humans who are fallible. Just remember the same fallibility applying to ancient writers also applies to today's writers. In the end, we are each responsible for deciding on the interpretation of the writings and deciding what is true. We each have an internal source to guide us to the truth, accessed through meditation.

Spirituality is our relationship with God, our fellow humans, and our environment. This is a personal thing, and we each are responsible for our own experience. We can all experience God as a friend, and we can see each person we meet as the God/Goddess they are, and care for our beautiful holy/wholly environment. Anyone from any religion, or from no religion, can cultivate a friendship with God. The most important thing we can do in life is developing a close ongoing relationship and communication with God. This is not about following a list of do's and don'ts.

Stalin lived in fear of losing his power. This was a self-imposed hell. He killed any and all whom he perceived to be a threat to his power. Joseph Stalin blessed us with an example of how not to live. God still loves him with unconditional love as God loves all of us. Stalin played his part in the great play called Life and was never judged or condemned by God. His life demonstrated for us how not to rule the world.

Abraham, Buddha, Jesus, Muhammad, Baha'u'llah, and many others have shown us how to live and love. We each have the potential to do greater things than they. We are each a Great Person. We are powerful magnificent spiritual beings.

Most of us are afraid to change our beliefs. We are afraid to believe the wisdom of Divinity lies within each of us. We are afraid to be a friend of God. Fear and guilt are our greatest enemies. To change we must replace fear with love.

In the future, religions will be stronger than ever. As new revelations from God are made, religions will do a house cleaning of sorts to remove outmoded and ineffective beliefs. Each religion has much good to offer the world. But a belief such as God is angry, jealous, and a punishing Deity will be removed from belief systems. Any moral justification for vengeance and retribution also will be removed. No religion will claim to be exclusive or better than any other religion. The intimate experience of the relationship of each person with God will replace the importance of codified texts and teachings.

The many religions in the world will eventually lead all their followers to the truth. They will teach their followers there is something they should possess but failed to receive. This knowledge of something missing will drive them to search for it till they find it. All the churches will someday be one church. Eventually, no organization will be needed when we live as One.

Our basic beliefs are causing all of our problems, and to solve our problems we must change our beliefs! THIS IS IMPORTANT. Our basic beliefs are causing all our problems, and to solve our problems we must change our beliefs! The problem is our beliefs are the foundation of our civilization and create our behaviors. Our beliefs in fallacies have created the world we have today.

We don't need to change to please God, but we may change to please ourselves. God loves all of us unconditionally, and we always please God.

Science, Technology, Health, and Medicine

Today's science fiction is tomorrow's reality. If we can imagine it, we can create it. We will have transporters as on *Star Trek* to transport our bodies instantaneously from one place to another, we will be able to control the weather, we will have access to free energy except for the machinery to produce it without requiring fossil fuels, we will have access to DNA therapy putting today's medicine in the primitive category, and extending life expectancy well beyond anything we now imagine possible, and we will travel to the ends of the Universe visiting unimaginable beings.

The "Big Bang," came from a place where time does not exist. There was no "singularity" to produce the start of the Universe. God did indeed create the Universe. Time does not exist where God resides, thus the "Big Bang" is happening **now** just as the Universe is collapsing in on itself to produce the nothingness when the Universe disappears. Time is an illusion.

Life is eternal. It has no end or beginning. It has always existed. Over the illusion of time on Earth, the forms of Life have changed. And the forms of Life are limitless. Life exists on Earth in forms we have not discovered or imagined. This is true on other planets, galaxies, and universes. Life exists throughout our Universe and in other universes. There are billions or trillions of stars in each galaxy, and there are hundreds of billions of galaxies estimated to be in the known

Universe. Scientists can only account for less than 5% of the material in the Universe. What the other 95% plus is, is unknown to scientists. We now call this unknown stuff dark energy and dark matter. As much as we have progressed with our science and technology, we know so little about our Universe let alone other universes. Life is much more fantastic than we have imagined.

We have made tremendous strides in science and technology in the last century. But they all will pale in comparison to what we will achieve in the future. We will explore our solar system and eventually the whole Universe where we will meet and communicate with other life forms. Now we are limited by our technology and such ideas are only dreams. But these dreams will someday be a reality.

The implication of Unity or Oneness on everything is this: all of us, all our planet, Earth, all of our solar system, all of our galaxy, the Milky Way, all of our Universe, and all universes are all part of One Thing, God. We all compose It. The Oneness agrees with itself with no internal conflict. It is united and unified. Nothing happens by accident, and there are a grand design and purpose for everything.

Science and Technology

Science has a problem. It deals with the physical. But there is more, much more than just the physical. And the physical is all an illusion anyway. Scientists have learned when conducting experiments, the observer impacts the results, skewing the results. However, the experiments of the past have helped us to better understand our physical Universe. Science and religion are both looking at Life but from different directions. Both will meet in the middle with God.

Any religion opposed to science is superstition. When we oppose knowledge, we welcome ignorance. The truth of any religion is supported by science. Science and logic support the Unity of God. For humans to evolve, science and religion both are needed. Science by itself will lead to materialism. Frequently religion and science are thought to be at odds with each other. Most religions teach reflection and logic have nothing to do with religion. Much hatred would cease if the harmony of science and religion were accepted. Humans should apply their intelligence and reasoning to religion. What works is the gold standard of how to proceed. Science, and seeking greater competence will aid us in moving forward.

Honesty is an aspect of intelligence. Dishonesty is based on stupidity. Intelligence cannot be applied to anything in life without honesty. Honesty is essential to finding solutions in science, law, and the management of society. The goal of science is not to verify a theory, but to find the truth. Honesty while being essential to finding the truth, is also the easiest way to find the truth.

What we perceive affects our lives. The world is not what it seems to be. Quantum physics shows our lives are dependent on what we look for in life. This is based on the principle of complementarity that says knowledge of the universe is based on the observer's decision of what to observe. For example, how we perceive ourselves affects how we perceive life. If we think of ourselves as friends, we will act one way, and if we think of ourselves as enemies we act in a totally different manner. This also applies to scientific inquiries for if research is aimed at one part of a problem, the other aspects of the problem are ignored. This makes it difficult to determine where research will be most fruitful.

Life works through the principles of functionality, adaptability, and sustainability. Life functions, that is, it works. Before it becomes dysfunctional, Life will adapt to sustain Itself. Life is eternal and self-sustaining. If we mess up the environment to the point of dysfunction, Life will adapt to ensure sustainability. This adaptation may make life for us humans a living hell. Consider the hurricanes, tornados, earthquakes, and rising oceans as adaptations. These are not judgments and punishments from an angry God, but natural outcomes of our actions. They are the consequences of what we have done. If we stick a finger into an electrical outlet, we can expect to get shocked, a natural consequence of our action.

Everything in the Universe is alive. Each rock, planet, sun, and we are all part of a living system. We are each a living part of a much bigger living Thing. God is the heavens and the Earth. God is One with Everything and breaths as humans, allowing us to experience ourselves as manifestations of God interacting with other manifestations of God.

The Living System of the Universe is huge with every part interdependent on all the other parts, a matrix of waves of energy all interconnected and interweaving creating matter, form, and everything else. Matthew 14, Mark 6, Luke 9, and John 9 all recount the story of how five loaves of bread and two fishes were multiplied to feed thousands, an illustration of matter being created. The System is self-regulating, rarely requiring intervention. Higher life forms like us humans have impacted the System negatively requiring the System to adjust to ensure sustainability.

The Living System of the Universe is huge compared to our bodies and are huge compared to the cells of our bodies. Any speck of our bodies is important to the body and we are all important to the Living System. Each part, no matter how small, is composed of the same stuff as the Whole.

Nothing is ever still. Things in motion stay in motion, and all things are in motion. The faster things vibrate the faster they will vibrate. This motion is evolution. This is one of the failures of the laws of thermodynamics.

Everything in Life down to submolecular particles has intelligence. Because of the intelligence of these particles, they move with intention. They produce specific and predictable outcomes. On a large scale, we have the cosmology of the universe. On a small scale, we have particle physics.

A paradigm shift will occur when humans see the possibility of energy generation based on attraction and not resistance. Our present ideas about how to produce energy are based on polar resistive, friction-generated processes. If we limit our view of life, we will limit our understanding of life and everything connected to it. When we broaden our perspective, we will be able to see primary magnetism as having attractor fields in the future. It possesses primary attractor fields produced by scalar abilities with continuous attraction. Now we see it as electromagnetism, a derivative, but it is also the primary. These attractor fields have no polarities or resistance. When we have this understanding, energy will cease to be a commodity fought over. Energy will be abundantly available.

When the paradigm of energy as force changes to energy as attraction, great advances in science will take place. 98% of the physical Universe is space, making density largely an illusion. It should be obvious there is a problem with force having very little to act on since it works only with densities. Force and density work together and only in close proximity. It is impossible to travel across the Universe with technology based on force. Space responds magnetically to love. Magnetic cohesion is the basis of our Universe. Harmonic non-toxic energy will be possible with this shift. The shift will start with a respect for the ultimate power of love. When faced with love, force loses its control of our consciousness, and change will be rapid.

Today's technology is a poor indicator of the technology of the future. For example, wind powering sails in the past has little in common with steam power produced by various fuels used to propel ships today. Our technology is based on force. The technology of the future will be based on attraction, and it's a whole new ball game.

It was thought by scientists of the past theology would bias objectivity. This is just as true now as in the past. Theology has its own biases. God is reality, and reality objectively observed will lead to a better understanding of both God and the Universe. Unfortunately, all measurement instruments interact with the observed. At the finest levels of observation, nothing can be viewed objectively. This returns us to the realm of theology. The best we can do is evaluating the collected data within the largest dependable context possible.

We must understand the relationship between truth and reality to have science. Truth is workable, useful, and improves life. Truth is fulfilled and verified by understanding the consistent repetition of experience. It brings equilibrium to life. Reality, the Spiritual World, is perfect just as it is. It is the mother of truth. God is not separate from an imperfect creation, the Illusional World. Scientific observation must avoid preconceived ideas about the Universe, and avoid careless observations, dishonesty in writing reports, and justifying results to achieve self-serving goals. Science should verify reality, not prove a theory. Distilling truth from reality will continue forever.

We are about to determine a new definition of truth. There is the truth of what our spiritual self is. And there is the truth of the physical body part of us. If we know only one, we lack the other. The two together provide the whole truth. The truth will lead us to God. God cannot be separated from reality.

The point of perfect equilibrium of the implicit and explicit of the Universe is where matter, energy, space, and time have no resistance producing infinite potential. It is the source of all patterns, rhythms, ratios, and harmonies. As this is understood, our concept of ideals will change as we finally know ideals are implicit to the Universe.

Love is the source of power for everything. The physical agent for love is magnetism causing compression. Love is reason, particles uniting, and relationships forming. Love causes union. It brings everything together. Love is more than just affection. It's where two complementary forces change places in the presence of a stabilizer. The complementary forces are compressing and expanding forces at a zero point, producing a magnetic vortex as the energy is transferred. In the physical world, this is primary magnetism and compression. Compression generates energy, and expansion releases it. Each compression produces new energy. This process takes place among all primary particles and energies. DNA operates in this way.

Prior to the "Big Bang," there was immense compression. The "Big Bang" released photons, light as the constant of motion in the thermodynamic field as the Universe was created. The release of the compression created space, energy, time, and matter. The energy released by the "Big Bang" was a reversal of its original condition. This energy maintains itself as a fixed amount through similar energy reversals. Because of this, all structure is limited and is constructed by this energy reversal, demonstrating the law of conservation of energy.

The unified field of energy conservation is the largest structure in existence. It is stable and has a fixed amount of energy. It is constructed of exact and finite structures. In addition to this field is a free and infinite field of primary particles activated by love. It is available for current and future compressions thus making available an additional infinite amount of energy. To understand these primary particles, scientists must address the properties and the completeness of infinity.

Contained in the conservational field of the Physical World is magnetism. It is electrically created with defined amounts of magnetism created by defined amounts of charged particles in motion. This prevents direct access to a source of energy through magnetic potential. Magnetism has no direct application for producing energy. However, a higher function of magnetism is pure energy. In attractor fields, the primary part, magnetism is put into motion by infinity alignments. To utilize magnetism, we must change our preference for electrical methods to a preference for those based on attraction. Within the spectrum of attractor fields, the alignments of infinity can activate magnetism.

Primary particles are particles of infinity. They are indivisible particles. They are the building blocks of all of existence. To understand these particles, scientists must first understand the characteristics and incorporated unity of infinity.

The basis of Everything is constant in that it is constantly changing producing unlimited potential for motion and life. It is indefinable. This essential sub-stratum of existence, the ground of infinity, is dynamic, unbiased, omnidirectional, unchanging, and enduring, but providing the potential for unlimited change, life, and motion. It is a mixture of primary particles, Love, and Spirit with qualities the Physical World cannot define or quantify because it produces our world. One quality it possesses is stasis providing the ability for wavering capabilities, and for contraction and propulsion of potentialities.

The substratum is very simple and acts as a web connecting everything.

The quality of infinity is expressed as an angle. Infinite quantity is a proportion progression approaching zero but never reaching it. The constant relative to infinity is not an absolute, but a factor, attribute, possibility, or static point for a particular circumstance. This constant marks the starting point, an index of equilibrium, of all variations and accelerations allowing measurements. An example is Einstein's use of the speed of light, demonstrating for the first time, equilibrium in motion as a constant relative to energy. The Milky Way is an equilibrium in motion. Find its anchoring point and we've found the constant. Think outside the box of the fulcrum of a seesaw as a point of equilibrium. A real equilibrium is lively, reciprocal, and synchronistic. Contrary to appearances, this generates the most potential although considered to be the "constant" point for associated variables.

The mathematics associated with infinity and primary energy involves angles and proportions to produce probable quantities. The angular proportions resolve to zero providing for a common source point with indeterminate potential.

Infinity is a universal agent allowing the translation of quanta to qualities and qualities to quanta. It is involved in the transmission of potential in all dimensions. Through infinity, primary particles synchronize with Love power.

Energy equals potential. Potential is defined mathematically by a quantity, a constant, and a quality. The equation will be stable even if the constant varies because the equilibrium point is the zero point of hypersynchronicity, found in all phenomena. Hypersynchronicity cannot be observed externally.

Energy does not equal mass. Energy equals potential and is inter-dimensional. $E=MC^2$ is universally true because it includes a quantity (mass), a constant (the speed of light), and a quality (the square). Energy is potential and can be compressed into matter. Potential consists of quantity, quality, and a constant. It is based on the ultimate zero point of equilibrium. This understanding will lead to a comprehension of infinity. Infinity has relevant magnitudes and is also simultaneous and qualitative while existing in space but not shaped or influenced by it. This wisdom is hidden from all who look externally for it and found by those who know they are One with it. The false thinking energy equals mass is an attempt to control or rule the Universe.

Two particles traveling in opposite directions at the speed of light relative to mass will travel at 186,000 miles per hour. If we perceive the same two particles traveling in opposite directions from a point of equilibrium, a zero point, based on their combined impulse to perform, they can be observed to travel at twice the speed of light. If these particles then hit other particles causing a multiplication of the process, it can speed up events such as the creation of the Universe. This is accomplished by a process of qualitative transmission and replication, mutually beneficial with any quantitative factors or constants. The important part is the zero point or origin from where angles of infinity extend.

Zero Point energy is the source of energy in the physical Universe. Related are the power of now for time compression, and the increased power of synchronicity and simultaneous occurrence.

Everything we perceive in this world is part of and held together with God. There is life in everything. We are all united in this Universal Energy. Attraction is the source of this energy. This energy can be released by uniting with this energy, and by abandoning ideas based on scarcity, resistance, and force, as they relate to energy forms, ideas, and practices.

Zero-point field energy is not generated by friction. Quantum physics has proven our physical world to be a large body of energy manifesting and disappearing in milliseconds in consecutive cycles. Our experience of solidity is an illusion.

Our world is created by ideas one at a time from this ocean of energy. Everything in our world started out as an idea. We create what we think about the most. We were before the Universe was created, and we all helped to create it. Being One with God makes us equally creative. If we don't like something we create, we can uncreate it and recreate it differently. Nothing happens by accident, and all agree with what happens. We are united in all we do, and we can create a Universe of illusions where we appear to be separate and not in agreement. To discover the zero-point field we must understand our inner world. This will be accomplished by discovering our unity with Universal Energy and then bringing it into our world through practical ideas. This will produce free and endless energy.

Scientists define the zero-point energy of a quantum system as the lowest-energy state possible, or ground state. It is the lowest energy a system can have. The zero-point energy of empty space is called vacuum energy. The sum of vacuum energy in space, known as the cosmological constant, is dark energy, an unknown, and something other than a vacuum. This force is thought to cause the Universe to expand.

Tom Moore in his August 31, 2013 newsletter, *The Gentle Way News,* said technology based on both cold fusion and magnetics would produce almost free energy for our use soon.

Chaos theory is correct in taking simultaneity and qualitative replication into account since infinity is this. But it will not be productive in the long run because there is no single numerical constant for each instance of chaos.

The Physical World lacks singularities, but the substratum, because it is undefinable, provides the function of a singularity by providing the unifying force without being a physical singularity, and the quality of adaptability to circumstantial requirements without being limited by them. The result is almost everything is space.

The laws of thermodynamics cannot describe everything in existence. They are useful for certain fields of densities involving thermal energy. Energy is defined as a function of matter isolated from a background of some unknown. They can't handle "dark matter." This leaves a huge void in our understanding of physics. This unknown has been separated from the rest of science because scientists don't know how to deal with it.

Black holes are three different phenomena. Ruptures in the energy grid showing the power of equilibrium and the power of magnetic attraction are one form. Stars are born in this the first type. Quasars are a second form exerting attraction across galaxies. They are huge mature vortexes acting as energy fountains without becoming completely solid. And last are the collapsed energy fields of aging stars. They no longer have the ability to balance time, energy, matter, and space in motion around them. These collapsed systems are nearing infinite density.

Antimatter and matter, created at the same time, are two streams produced as pure energy. Matter is compressed into densities. Antimatter is uncompressed and disperses. Their complementary natures are in dynamic equilibrium. The two are not in perfect symmetry based on structure since matter has both positive and negative charges, and antimatter has minor amounts of mass. Matter collects in concentrations and antimatter disperses in major compression fields. Normally the two repel each other, except under extreme compression. The attempted expulsion of antimatter attracts antimatter and leads to decompression. This can lead to a huge explosion.

The law of the conservation of energy limits our thinking to beliefs of scarcity. Humans perceive the Sun as the source of all energy on Earth. The Sun, while supplying tremendous amounts of energy, has a finite amount of energy. There is competition for this energy leading to a belief in scarcity. If this belief persists, social democracy will be impossible to maintain. A paradigm shift is imperative to allow the utilization of the ultimate of energy. This will allow the final realization of our unity and the development of peace and prosperity for all. With this change, we will find the physical and spiritual answers we have long searched for.

Science should be the pursuit of solving everyday problems by understanding how life works. This involves finding what works and applying solutions at the location of the problem. It included respect for life, infinity, and the whole of existence. But the dominance of high technology and military competition has subverted science as a servant to science as a dictator.

The answers to all our problems are right in front of us. All we have to do is ask the correct questions to receive the correct answers. We must approach our problems with a humble inquiring mind, free of judgment, and clear perception to receive the answers we need.

A panacea does not exist for all our problems. Each problem must be solved where it was created. Love is the answer, but it must be applied problem by problem at the place of breakage. First, locate the place of fracture. Is it the foundation, window, door, or roof in a house? Is it a broken relationship, broken plan, broken heart, or broken word? This is where it is fixed.

We have believed in the panacea of the drug. Take a pill to solve any medical problem. This kind of thinking has produced some strange situations. If someone has a financial problem, this person might develop a health problem, so it may be dealt with a pill.

When we believe in God as a reality and the source of all the answers to our problems, then all the answers are in front of us because God is everywhere and in everything.

God is everything there this, and everything there isn't. Once upon a time God decided to create "here" and "there" and the "space in between." There was a huge explosion and relativity was created, allowing for relationships to form. This is the spiritual explanation for the "Big Bang" and the Universe created allows God to experience Itself. This "Big Bang" sent particles flying creating time because first, a particle was "here" and later the particle was "there" and the duration between the two could be measured. These particles defined a relationship relative to one another.

Before the "Big Bang," there was only the Absolute (Spiritual) World. Now there is an Absolute World and a Relative (Physical) World. The Relative World is not real even though it feels so real we accept it as real. Now in the realm of make-believe, we may act as God would act instead of knowing we are God.

Many physicists think the Universe came from a microscopic dot, something that sounds like science fiction. Even if we think it came from nothing, what created it all? Could this first cause be God?

Time and space are identical. This means time as we experience it is an illusion and everything is happening now.

Everything in this world is an illusion. Space is an illusion. We are on Earth, and at the same time, we are at the furthest reaches of the Universe.

Time does not exist. Everything in the past and everything in the future is happening now. There is only now. Physical objects because of their separation in space creates the illusion of time. Physical objects like us, move relatively slowly and experience the illusion of time, while non-physical objects move instantly, requiring no time. Mathematically we have proven if we travel fast enough we can circle back over a long enough distance and see ourselves start the trip. Thus time is a field we move through and not a movement. Time is only our way of counting movements through space. Einstein realized time was a mental construction relating space and time, and if he wanted to alter time, all he had to do was change the distance between the start and finish or change the amount of speed of travel. Einstein and others theorized there are "folds" in the framework of space allowing for the passage across great distances in very little time, and this is correct.

Predestination does not exist. Even though everything is happening now, we still have the power to change our future because it hasn't happened to us yet.

We create our physical bodies through a process where the energy we are slows its vibration to produce matter. Spirit, also called Soul, is pure energy. There is only One Soul, but parts of this One Soul produce individual Souls that produce individual bodies. We co-create our experiences and our world.

The physical Universe comprises less the 1% of all that is. This small proportion of everything is based on chaos. Over 99% of everything existing is Pure Spirit. As mentioned earlier, the dark matter and energy making up over 95% of the universe, is part of the 99% of Pure Spirit. To deal with chaos, science can produce order through constructive effort. The chaos in the Universe is responsible for the second law of Thermodynamics stating the transfer of energy moves toward entropy. Only peace can deal with chaos. Order is not the solution. It requires more energy than chaos. Fear and anger won't help. Only peace will prevail.

Matter is not solid. Atoms are attracted by perpetual motion. We have evolved through minerals, plants, and animals to get to where we are today. We are not matter. Only the spiritual is real. Matter is an imperfect image of the spiritual. Our thoughts and ideas produce the Material World we see.

The Universe has closed systems leading to death, and open systems leading to life. The closed systems tend toward disorder and loss of energy. Open systems, the living Universe, for example, move toward order and more energy. By changing our perspective from separate objects to the relationships of the united whole, we will be able to utilize the power of Life. Life is found in both open and closed systems. It can be found thriving under extremes of temperature and other environmental conditions. Life will be discovered to exist in intangible electromagnetic fields with the ability to move throughout the Universe. It will be found in what we now consider space. This space is filled with Life we now call dark matter and dark energy. When we understand open systems better, we will discover better forms of food, medicine, and energy. As our understanding of ecological systems expands, we will find abundance increasing for everyone, ending competition. This connective Life throughout the Universe allows telepathy and connection to the Devine.

Life, health, and happiness will cease to exist if both open and closed systems are not utilized. A balance between both systems is needed. The unity of everything allows for this balance. Each part of this unity impacts on all parts. Life is immortal because there is a creator. Closed and open systems come in all sizes and shapes and are defined differently depending on what branch of science is being discussed. On a personal level, there is our body. At the large end of the spectrum is God, All That Is, with the Universe in between. If we utilized only our bodily system, our physical life, health, and happiness will suffer, and the same applies if we utilized only God. As for the Universe, it appears to be isolated from anything else and stuck with whatever energy and matter are found here. This is an illusion, for energy is being added to the system.

The Universe is composed of Love, Spirit, and a particle smaller than anything found by scientists in the past. This primary particle is what creates matter. Scientists have referred to it as the "Higgs boson" or the "God Particle." On July 4, 2012, CERN, the European Organization for Nuclear Research, announced they had discovered a particle fitting the description of this particle. Experiments are now underway to understand this particle.

These particles are the building blocks of the Universe. The whole Universe exchanges these particles in a manner like breathing in and out. An imbalance of these particles causes disease. Love restores balance. This is why prayer and touching an ill person restores health.

These particles connect everything and everyone creating what we call the web of life, although this web extends much farther than we understand. The web extends to everything. Learning of our connections and being responsible for them will expand our evolution and enhance our exchange of these particles leading to positive advances in all areas of human endeavor.

Science seems to think there are accidents, and some religions believe there are none, we are predestinated to experience what we experience. Religion for its part has retarded science by imposing its beliefs on science, as in believing the Earth is the center of the Universe. Science seems to think we begin life at birth and life ends at death. Most religions believe life continues after death while some believe life was before birth. Scientists have problems with time even though there are a lot of theories about it and a lot of practical applications of it. Einstein thought time was an illusion. The Bible says time will end: "that there should be time no longer" (Revelations 10:6).

Everything in our lives, past, present, and future is existing simultaneously as if time doesn't exist. Everything we are attempting to achieve, we have already achieved. The good, the bad, and the ugly of our lives are all parts of the whole, perfect, and perfectly balanced. Every part is a step to produce the perfect balanced whole.

One of the main sources of conflict between those who believe in God and those who don't is evolution. Atheists tend to believe in evolution, and those who believe in God tend to believe in creation. Could it be both are correct? Could it be God created the Heavens and the Earth, and everything has been evolving ever since? The answer is yes.

Advanced cultures have developed a means of transportation where they disassemble and reassemble their bodies based on physical and mind technologies, as demonstrated on *Star Trek*. They can be wherever and whenever they choose.

When two subatomic particles are linked, called quantum entanglement, with each particle spinning in opposite directions, and when the spin of one particle is changed, the other particle changes its spin instantaneously. This communication is faster than the speed of light. Einstein and two colleagues, Podolsky and Rosen wrote a paper known as the Einstein-Podolsky-Rosen Paradox where they point out mathematically it's impossible to travel faster than the speed of light, but here communication apparently between the two particles is. Quantum entanglement lays the foundation for teleportation, the ability to move atoms, and whole beings over great distances instantaneously. This technology was demonstrated in 2004, but it will be a long time till it can transport large objects.

One part of the quantum theory is the theory of the Multiverse where there are many universes. These many universes contain every possibility available in life. This theory is a good description of God since God is Everything. We, as we live our lives can reach out and bring any possibility into our lives, being the unlimited beings, we are.

We as observers affect what we see. Electrons, when shot through two slits in a metal plate, will produce a pattern consistent with waves when no one is watching, and produce patterns consistent with particles when someone is watching. If no one is watching, electrons are just a mathematical possibility.

Neils Bohr, the Danish physicist, suggests in *The Copenhagen Interpretation* a phenomenon called *non-local phenomena* or *non-locality* is demonstrating the possibility the two particles are not really separated but were part of a larger whole. This is considered a fundamental principle of quantum physics and changes our understanding of time and space. It's more like a thought than a physical reality.

Rupert Sheldrake has reported the non-local behavior of birds in England. When a certain number learned to open milk bottles in the 1930's, birds all over Europe began doing the same thing. It happened so fast, it wasn't possible for the birds in England to educate the birds in Europe. This type of behavior has been demonstrated with other animals and human actions. Humans can and do transmit information this way.

Physics today implies consciousness created the Universe and this consciousness is not restricted in location. It could be said the Universe is consciousness.

This universal consciousness can be accessed by our individual consciousness, and many people who have experienced this have left us a record of it. They have told us about a core of truth, power, beauty, and love. This universal consciousness is the Universe and can be called God.

Meditation is important for scientists to prevent harming the planet and the rest of the Universe. When it comes to peace and love, we are still children. Some of us are scientific monsters lacking a conscience and having no respect for creation.

The Universe is full of other life forms. We are not alone. Meditation, prayer, and contemplation are important activities to prepare us to greet these other beings with love. Treat the entire Universe with dignity, love, and respect. Space is not empty and should not be abused. It should not be used as a dump, and we don't own it. We are only custodians.

Enrico Fermi posed the Fermi paradox, i.e. if there are other life forms in the Universe, where are they. It's theorized an advanced civilization based in the Milky Way could spread across the entire galaxy in less than a hundred million years, a small fraction of the 13.7 billion years the Universe has existed. SETI, search for extraterrestrial intelligence, supporters suggest the aliens haven't contacted us because of a non-interference policy. This is true, but about to change.

We must invent with love. What we send out to others, returns to us in full measure. Fear, hatred, and violence sent to others will return to us. Our inventions should be intended to help others, and not harm them. We as citizens must insist our governments work for peace and cease producing weapons to destroy others. By ceasing to develop new weapons, the military will be restricted.

Health and Medicine

Science and spirituality are the same disciplines with different perspectives. They both study life. Science will soon tell us what spirituality has told us. This will cause major ethical and philosophical problems.

Spirituality has said we are immortal. Science will show us how to extend our lives for unimaginable lengths of time. Spirituality has said we create our own reality, and we possess within us the power and secrets of life. Science will soon confirm this and show us how to use this information. Spirituality has said we are united with God, Gods in human form. Science will soon show us this, and how to use this power to impact life.

When we understand this, there will be decisions to be made. Are we playing God? How far do we go with things we thought only God does? How far do we go with miracles? What does God want? Does genetics belong to God or medical science? With these questions, we inject moral issues, right or wrong, and not whether it works or not. No matter how promising these scientific discoveries appear, some of us will insist it is wrong and immoral. There is no right or wrong, and indeed this is true. But issues like this will cause some people to bring up these old beliefs. Does it work or not should be the rule used to determine whether or not to do something.

Religions have taken the lead in the past with these decisions and are hoping to continue to lead into the future. But without expanding their beliefs, they will fail in the future just as they have in the past. In the past, we have gotten little guidance with the decision to live or to die. Do we choose extinction or not?

Each decision we make now affects the ultimate answer to this question. Our ultimate survival is never in question for we are immortal, but we can cause our extinction in the Physical World.

Now we are only interested in short-term solutions. Long-term solutions can wait. We make life and death decisions all the time. We pollute our environment and then live in it. We poison the soil and then eat the poisoned food grown there. We eat and breathe things that will poison the body. We choose these short-term solutions while we ignore the long-term outcomes are the death of the body. We will have to face decisions in the future like how shall we live and how long? We will eventually replace short-term gratification with long-term goals. The decision to live or to die will finally be decided in favor of living.

Future discoveries in medicine will prove blood is Life itself.

Scientists cannot agree on a definition of life. But Life is a process. Life is God, and God is Everything, therefore Everything is alive.

To improve health there will be joy-filled healing communities, covering all aspects of the human experience, developed in the future with a minimal charge to stay in these communities. Much of the healing will be accomplished through the practicing of unconditional love, and the sharing of love among members of the community. These communities will be places of great natural beauty with trees, open grassy areas, and flowing water. They will be places of great peace - peaceful landscapes, and with peaceful souls living there. Some will live there permanently, and others will visit periodically to provide services. The public will visit for periods of time for healing. These places will be sanctuaries in the world but separate from the world.

Each healing community will be filled with music. There will be physical music and music of the soul. The tones and vibrations of these sounds will be healing, leading to remembering the frequencies of energy we are. Colors will be a means of healing. The frequencies of different colors in the color spectrum will lead to wholeness. Color has more uses than just for aesthetic purposes. Our medical profession could utilize colors for healing purposes, but unfortunately, most doctors don't use them. Blue has gentle sedative properties and produces peace and relaxation, while red has the opposite effect. Different vibrations of sound and color can be used to balance the body and heal.

A broad spectrum of healing methods will be used, including physical modalities, nutritional belief systems, and emotional integration yielding the integration of mind and spirit. Joy will be the greatest healing therapy. This will be accomplished through freedom of expression. Restrictions will be removed. The whole community will be integrated with nature.

In the future, work will be a source of joy and fulfillment. A child-like attitude will infect everyone while doing activities from physical labor to paperwork. Work will be creative, joyful, and playful. All this will make humans healthier.

The process of community development is well underway. Fellow souls will be uniting to start and sustain these communities. The development will be in concert with Mother Earth. The use of trees to build structures in these communities, done with honor and respect, expands the understanding of community.

Good health will be seen as based on the wholeness of energy. The energy patterns of the whole body will be monitored and adjusted to restore good health. Technology may assist in this process, but ultimately it will be understood the knowledge of the body is all that is necessary, and energy will be shared from one to another through the chakras. Using technology to produce sound and light vibrations and using the body itself to tone and sing through the voice to open and balance the chakras will be used to heal. Chakras are intersections, meeting points of energy channels of the energy or spiritual body located at corresponding points in the physical body at the confluence of veins, arteries, and nerves. Various nutritional supplements will be used to remind the body, and the cells of the body, they are formed from light energy. This is all an extension of present-day modalities such as Acupuncture, the Healing Touch, Royal Touch, Reiki Touch, and the laying-on-of-hands spoken of in the Bible.

To get the most from our bodies, we must love them, respect them, listen to them, and give them proper care. Do what is necessary to keep them in good operating condition. Exercise each day. Meditate. Discipline and exercise the mind. Health is a mind, body, spirit experience. Don't abuse the body.

Smoking cigarettes, eating red meat at every meal, and drinking large amounts of alcohol have a negative effect on the Earth and everything on it. Alcohol and smoking, taken into the body demonstrate a death wish on the part of the user. Alcohol impairs the mind, and the effects of smoking are well documented. We must stop denying what is so. Eating animals produced by filling them with chemicals is not healthy, yet we deny this is true. It's cheaper to produce meat this way, but not healthier for our bodies. It has been demonstrated it is unhealthy to eat meat, to smoke, and to drink large volumes of alcohol, yet we ignore this information.

The medicines we have developed replacing the body's natural defense mechanisms have created resistant organisms capable of devastating our population. The bacteria of the world have access to a single gene pool. They have access to unlimited adaptation possibilities through endless DNA recombinations. They can adapt to any antibacterial agents. The continued use of these agents is useless and disastrous. The solution is to devise stimulants to cause bacteria to develop a symbiotic relationship with us. Caring and love will produce these outcomes. Fear and hatred will lead to disaster. Scientists seeking to understand life should enlarge their perspective to include all possibilities. Look for expanding patterns and relationships and how they're integrated. Loving one another, and all life forms leads to eternal life.

Genetic engineering and cloning can be beneficial. However, if done with insufficient care, we can create the greatest disaster know. Messing with genetics is messing with the building blocks of our illusional life forms. We can never be harmed by anything we do, but we can really mess up this video game called Life. Messing with genetics is like changing the programming code in a computer game. If we don't know what we are doing, we can really mess up the game.

Tom Moore in his July 7, 2012 newsletter, *The Gentle Way News,* said we must be proactive to improve the health of our people to lower health care costs. We must determine the causes of illnesses and make corrections to improve our health. This is dealing with the cause, and not just treating symptoms. In the July 27, 2013 issue, Tom Moore said genetically modified organisms used as food, a high reliance on drugs to maintain health, and foods and drinks contaminated with poisons are not health-producing. We must eliminate these problems, exercise more, and use vitamins to produce a healthier population. The October 5, 2013 issue said using DNA manipulation and gene therapy, in the future, we would be able to cure most diseases. Gene therapy is just in its infancy but it has been used to treat blood disorders, defective vision, and HIV infections.

Genetic engineering and DNA manipulation are similar because they both juggle genetic material. Breeding is a form of genetic engineering where genetic material through sexual reproduction is combined to produce a newly improved individual. But today it is possible to inject genetic material from another source other than the same species through genetic engineering into an organism not possible with breeding. After the DNA has been changed through genetic engineering, we now have a new organism capable of replicating itself, and the results can be devastating if due care is not exercised. It is possible for the new organism to escape into the wild with devastating consequences, or new super biological weapons could be produced. This is playing with the building blocks of a living organism. This new organism can now pass its offspring and humans who eat it new molecules, some possibility capable of producing illness, if not immediately, eventually over a long period of time. Genetically modified organisms have been produced using transgenic technology by tweaking a gene here or there to produce an organism with new properties.

Synthetic biology is the engineering of new life forms. Remember the stories of creatures composed of half-man and half-beast? These are not myths, but historical creatures created in the past. Such creations are possible in our future through genetic engineering by messing with DNA. The outcome will be our responsibility and we will suffer the consequences. Any changes should be for the benefit of all. All of life is interrelated and messing with just one part can have devastating consequences for the entire ecological system. All parts of the system are connected to the whole, and each part supports life for the whole. Our science should ennoble us, improve all of life, and respect all life forms, no matter where they are found in the Universe. We co-create our Physical World. Because this is so, we should demand the scientists engaged in genetic engineering follow an ethics code established by the general population.

DNA manipulation has the same potential to muck up the building blocks of nature if due care is not exercised. But correcting defective genes has a bright future. More knowledge is needed to determine what a defective gene is and how to correct it, but all this will happen.

Our health-care system is based on caring for the sick. Little is spent on preventing disease with most of the money being spent on managing sickness. The system is profit motivated. More money should be directed toward teaching us how to live our lives to be healthy by acting and eating differently.

We have created the illusion of using money to buy food to prevent starvation. We have created the illusion saying we need pills or antibiotic injections to provide us with good health. We have created the illusion saying we are alone if no other body is present with us. Our religions have created illusions separating us from God. These illusions are insanity.

Our bodies reflect our internal state. If we are aware of our greatness and our connection to God, our bodies would self-heal. Any healing modalities will be more effective if we trust it to heal our bodies. Lacking this trust, the modalities will have less chance of success. Our mental and spiritual condition is the cause of most of our diseases. Treatments aimed at correcting our mental and spiritual abnormalities will be more successful than those aimed exclusively at the body. Treatments with an underlying cultural trust will also have increased success.

Obsessing about a disease is counterproductive. If sick, we should not spend our time trying to get rid of a disease. We should employ those modalities we trust, live fearlessly giving the disease no attention, and spend our time happily doing stimulating positive creative activities. It is helpful to accept our health, to be happy, and to spend our time living in the present. Live each minute to the fullest.

China, Japan, and India have a lower incidence of cancer than the Western part of the world. Part of the problem in the West is due to diet, as well as fear of the disease, the constant reminder of the disease, and the mindset to detect cancer rather than live healthier lives.

There will be radical changes in our understandings about science and medicine in the future, correcting past misunderstandings, and discovering unknown truths.

According to the World Health Organization, in 2013, about 6.3 million children died before the age of five worldwide, and approximately 289,000 women died from preventable causes related to pregnancy and childbirth throughout the world. Many of the deaths were preventable, but due to lack of access to therapies, death resulted. We can do more to prevent these deaths.

Here are some quotes from sacred writings:

"Wisdom is the principal thing; therefore get wisdom: and with all thy getting get understanding" (Proverbs 4:7).

"For wisdom is a defence, and money is a defence: but the excellency of knowledge is, that wisdom giveth life to them that have it" (Ecclesiastes 7:12).

"O Timothy, keep that which is committed to thy trust, avoiding profane and vain babblings, and oppositions of science falsely so called" (1 Timothy 6:20). Avoid false knowledge.

"In the sight of true wisdom, there is no difference between the creator and the created. Even physical science has come to recognize that cause and effect are but two aspects of one manifestation of energy. He who fails to see this, being engrossed in the visible only, goes from death to death; because he clings to external forms which are perishable. Only the essence which dwells within is unchangeable and imperishable.

This knowledge of the oneness of visible and invisible, however, cannot be acquired through sense-perception. It can only be attained by the purified mind" (Katha-Upanishad 4:11).

Final Thoughts

If all this sounds like science fiction, just remember television was science fiction two hundred years ago. In fact, the vast majority of people living on the Earth then probably never imagined the possibility. There was also a lack of context for understanding such a possibility.

Science has a problem facing the idea of God. Presently it is unscientific to mix God with science, but as time passes scientists will be faced with the possibility of God. Even now, more and more scientists are embracing this fact. To make truly great discoveries, God's place in the cosmos must be recognized.

There is the Spiritual World or the Real world, and there is the Physical World or Dream World. Everything in the Physical World is an illusion. For science and medicine, the greatest illusions are:
1. Space or separation; we are all One and there is no separation
2. Time; everything is happening now
3. Birth as the start of life; we were alive before "birth"
4. Death as the end of life; we continue to live after "death"
5. Scarcity or limits of anything including energy; there is plenty of what we need
6. Ignorance; we know everything, and we just forgot so we can remember
7. Pills and antibiotic injections make us well; our beliefs heal
8. Failure; for we can only succeed.

In the Physical World, we have space or separation, and time to deal with, and science has defined these well enough to do great things. This is the "truth" of the Physical World but is only half the truth if we ignore the Truth of the Spiritual World.

When we know the truth of the Spiritual World, in addition to the "truth" of the Physical World, we will know the Whole Truth. Jesus knew the Whole Truth and was able to do "miracles." Once we know the Whole Truth, what we call a "miracle" today, will be just an understanding of the way things work. If we showed a television to someone from 1800, they would think it a "miracle," and us gods.

Science has done an admirable job dealing with the illusions of this Physical World in the past, and they will do better in the future.

Politics

The job of being a politician is difficult. Politicians must know a lot of information about a broad spectrum of subjects. A functional politician should be honest, transparent, and serve the constituents she or he represents, and not special interests. As a group, they should be co-operative to facilitate the accomplishment of the people's work. And they should pass workable laws. All unworkable laws should be repealed.

Henry David Thoreau said, "I heartily accept the motto, 'That government is best which governs least.'"

Leo Tolstoy wrote of governments, "That this social order with its pauperism, famines, prisons, gallows, armies, and wars is necessary to society; that still greater disaster would ensue if this organization were destroyed; all this is said only by those who profit by this organization, while those who suffer from it - and they are ten times as numerous - think and say quite the contrary."

Governments and Beliefs

Governments are based on exclusion because we have formulated a God who excludes. God includes everyone. Governments will function better if they include everyone. Governments should be unlimited, eternal, and free. Then they can truly support their citizens as they grow and develop.

Governments, as we have designed them, are supposed to provide us with peace, freedom, and domestic tranquility, but they don't. Instead, they provide us with war after war, less freedom, and increased domestic violence. Our governments haven't been able to stop starvation, keep us healthy and alive, and provide equal opportunity for all.

The way we practice politics demonstrates our spirituality.

Organized religions and governments should be separate. Governments should not establish religious doctrines, and religions should not influence how governments govern. It would be unfair for a religion to control how a government governs because one single religion cannot speak for everyone in a country.

The sum of our cultural values and sacred beliefs should impact the political process by having people elected who will enact laws embodying these beliefs and values. The elected officials should vote their consciences. This works best when our beliefs are based on the truth.

The whole world is voting their consciences and we have high violent crime rates, poverty, intolerance of race and sexual lifestyles, lack of medical care, lack of suitable nutrition, lack of decent housing, lack of safe communities, and lack of two-parent families. A better future is only a dream. Most of the world is refusing to admit we are mixing politics and our beliefs. We have been trying to create our society based on our best understanding of what God is. Apparently, our beliefs are based on fallacies because something is not working.

What we believe is the problem. Our beliefs are taking us in the wrong direction. We will never have a world of peace, harmony, and happiness believing what we believe at present. Our spiritual beliefs are adversely affecting the way we govern and our lives as a result. The defects in our beliefs are our beliefs in separation, superiority, retribution, and violence.

Most religions believe God is omnipotent, creator of everything, omnipresent, unlimited, totally free, and omniscient. Eventually, we will include all-inclusive, peaceful, lacking vengeance, and possess equality among all Its parts. In the future, we will finally admit we wish to define ourselves this way, and will finally define our politics this way too.

When people perceive their most sacred beliefs are being challenged by another culture, they feel their very survival is being threatened. This has led to religious wars in the past, and even now among countries and smaller groups who hold divergent beliefs about how life should be lived and about God. Our divergent beliefs have produced discord in the world.

While military force may be used, it is really a struggle to control the hearts and minds of people. Military force may conquer, but victory will not be achieved until the minds of the people align with the victors. The problem is spiritual. Once this is realized, all of life will be changed to achieve a solution. We will all hold more of our fundamental beliefs in common. The way we apply our politics around the world will be more uniform.

Some governments have tried to remove God altogether from society and have failed. We instinctively feel a connection with Divinity.

While some countries have chosen to keep church and state separate because of historical problems, the relationship between spirituality and state is different, because Spirituality is universal, and is Life itself. Everything is a part of Life and Spirituality. Church and state do not go together, but spirituality and state do.

If Spiritually is Life, then Spiritually is Life-affirming, and can be combined with politics to produce Life affirming political activities and decisions. This we are trying to do. All political systems try to allow their citizens to live harmoniously, happily, and peacefully thus affirming Life.

Unbridled nationalism must yield to love of humanity. All people must realize they are part of one country - Earth. We are all fellow citizens of the same place. Literally, we are joined to everyone through the internet, economic interests, and by advances in science. All countries are now interdependent whether we want to admit it or not. One can still love one's country and still, consider himself or herself a world citizen. With all countries working together, we can make tremendous advances in every field of endeavor. Unity of endeavor in everything from education to science should be encouraged.

Governments and Peace

Anything accomplished in this world is by people. This is the way God works. We may pray to God for peace, but only we can produce it.

Political unity, the unity of thought, unity in freedom, religious unity, the unity of nations, the unity of races, and unity of language are the steps leading to the unity of humanity and producing lasting peace and prosperity. This is our destiny.

The only problem in the world is lack of love. Love leads to tolerance and tolerance leads to peace. Intolerance leads to war. To reach peace fastest is to see all of humanity as part of our family. End separation. All nations of the world must unite. A new world political organization must be formed where each nation-state would have equal say in the world's affairs and would share proportionately in the world's resources.

We need to learn to care for one another. We do love and care for family members. We just need to enlarge the definition of family to include everyone. When we see ourselves as part of the same family, humans, and believe it is in our own best interests to care for and help others when needed, we are ready to change the way we live and govern ourselves. We are ready for a one-world government.

Albert Einstein felt the only way to keep nations from fighting was to have a world government, and he spent much of his time working for this goal. Einstein was for peace. He thought each government felt the need to protect itself from attack from other governments and would build up its military strength because of these perceived needs. He proposed two choices: prepare for war or create a world government where war was unnecessary. The United Nations was a step in the right direction but inadequate. A strong federation is needed to bind the nations of the world together.

This one action alone would free billions of dollars a year to end starvation, to clothe the needy, to provide housing for the poor, to care for the elderly, and to provide health care for everyone. This would end the cause of crime. New jobs would be created as money is pushed back into the economy.

Governments could be reduced because there would be less work.

The billions of dollars would come from the money saved by not building defenses and weapons of attack. The military would not be eliminated, but drastically reduced. Local police could be strengthened. Taxes would be reduced, and eventually eliminated as enlightened citizens would donate 10% to progressive governments to provide for society's needs. This would happen globally.

Now the richest nations can't conceive of going defenseless fearing invasion by the have-nots. To neutralize this threat, the world's total wealth and resources could be shared with everyone. Then no one will need what someone else has. Also, a system to resolve disputes to eliminate war should be created. A great example of this is the United States of America. This type of government currently covers only a small portion of the world, but it could be expanded to cover every country.

The U.S. was able to successfully unite a loose confederation of individual states into a united federation. Before, each state made its own trade agreements with other countries and each other, enacted its own tariffs, fought wars with each other, built and maintained its own armies and navies, and printed their own money. Eventually, each state realized it benefitted them to join together in unity. They realized merchants would have increased profits because they wouldn't have to pay taxes enacted by the individual states. States governments saved money because they didn't need to protect themselves from neighboring states. Citizens had greater safety and prosperity through cooperation and lack of fighting with each other. Each state achieved greater greatness through unity, and this can happen for each nation of the world through unity.

Even with this political solution, disagreements will still happen. Through a system of laws of agreement, and a court system, and the ability to enact new laws to address new situations, disagreements can be reconciled, and wars can be averted. This same system should work with nations.

The main obstacle to having a one-world government is the people who control the power now would rather hold onto their power than improve the quality of life for everyone. The powerful know a World Federation would improve life for the less fortunate but believe it will be at their expense. They refuse to give up anything.

They don't necessarily need to give up anything. Over a trillion dollars spent annually for war would be available to improve living conditions for the less fortunate. No more money will be necessary, nor will wealth be needed to be shifted from the haves to the have-nots. It could be argued the reason we don't have peace is because we depend on the military-industrial complex for our abundance and survival. If so, our source of abundance is misplaced.

Just as the federation of states in the United States of America ended wars among states, so too can a federation of countries among the nations of the world. But the true solution to ending all conflicts is a spiritual solution. Since Life is spiritual, the solution to all problems is spiritual. The only sustainable peace is the internal peace of each person. This will come but in the far distant future. In the meantime, a world government will impose world peace.

The government of the world should be tiered with local, national, and world assemblies. Periodically, the national assemblies would elect representatives to the world convention to govern the world. This world government would have administrative, legislative, and judicial bodies.

These governments should rule justly. The wisest and ablest from the world should be the leaders of this government. Government positions should be filled based on merit. The goal of any government should be to produce the highest good for its citizens including security, prosperity, and tranquility.

This World government should have a tribunal to settle legal disputes among the nations. The decision of the tribunal will be final. Lesser courts will hear lesser cases. International cases will be heard by the world court. Strife will be settled this way avoiding war. This assembly should be formed by individuals chosen by the legislatures and nobles of all the counties of the world.

Reducing the world's armaments is a good first step toward world peace. Weapons of war can be converted to constructive goods. Once a peace treaty is signed by all nations, the tremendous resources diverted to produce weapons can be used for useful purposes. Each nation will need police forces to keep order, and also the world will need an international police force to maintain the free flow of trade worldwide. Then poverty will disappear, and knowledge will abound. Then nations can concentrate on the well-being of its people. Nations will work closely with neighboring countries.

A meeting of all the nations of the world must be called to create world peace through the formation of a world government. They must agree to be friendly to each other. If one nation breaks this peace, all nations must confront this nation. All nations must agree to disarm except for the forces necessary to maintain the security and order of each country.

Governments are not honest because they act or fail to act for one set of reasons and cite another set of reasons as the rationale for it all. Most governments deliberately mislead their citizens into thinking the government is doing what's best for their citizens. If a government tells a big enough lie, it will more likely be accepted as truth. Citizens are not informed about how politicians came to power, nor any of the actions they have done or will do to stay in power.

Politics, as practiced today, is the art of saying in just the right way only what needs to be said to reach a goal. This excludes truth. Politicians use the self-interest of people, the basis of most people's actions, to convince them their self-interests are the politicians' self-interests. This is the reason governments give goods and services to their citizens.

The problem in giving goods and services to citizens is the citizens become dependent on the government. Independence of citizens should be promoted allowing their exercise of personal power, creativity, and ingenuity, granting them their dignity. They should know they can provide for themselves.

A happy medium between making citizens dependent and not helping those in need must be found. We need not overlegislate to help people survive. Morality and equality cannot be legislated. Laws must reflect who we are. We as humans must elevate our consciousness to treat each other with respect.

Unfortunately, most laws are constructed by those in power to tell those who are not in power how they should live. Most laws provide the most powerful with tools to protect their vested interests. The ideal is to allow the citizens to govern themselves. Over legislation stifles greatness. In advanced societies, few laws are needed. Once we learn to care for each other, few laws will be needed. Ideally, few laws establishing limits would be enacted.

Advanced cultures live in communities. They've abandoned cities and nations. Cities have crowded conditions, eliminating the unity of a community. We, on the other hand, think it is beneficial to move to big cities. We don't see the disadvantages for us. Small communities provide communion.

Advanced cultures have abandoned the idea of nations because it works against the idea we are all One. In our history, we have divided ourselves into nations for reasons of security and survival. This division has produced insecurity and challenges to survival. The solution is to join in one nation thus producing security and survival because everyone is working together, not against each other.

The trend through history has been toward unity and away from separation. This is because the ultimate truth is unity and is an evolutionary trend. Evolution is a process and is a process we can control. We get to choose the principle we will use to guide the process.

Advanced cultures have chosen the principle of unity to guide the evolutionary process. Then they devise political, social, economic, and spiritual devices to support this principle.

True power comes from God. Humans can utilize this power as long as love is not denied, and there is no belief in separation from God. Humans may delegate surrogate power to governments, religions, businesses, people in authority, the environment, the education of our children, and forces external to themselves. As long as these surrogate powers function as intended and reflect the values and beliefs as those granting the power, they can be useful. Otherwise, there is corruption and problems. This corruption is usually implemented by force, mandatory conformity, suppression of rights, and dishonesty. When the surrogate power uses dishonesty and force to convey the idea it is the real power, then we have an example of the surrogate power trying to sweep back the ocean with a broom. Humans can always declare their sovereign rights and remove the surrogate power if they chose.

Any despot who continually abuses or damages others or property must be stopped. Allowing the abuse to continue teaches the despot nothing. Loving a despot doesn't mean allowing them to do as they please. But we don't have to return a hurt for a hurt. Just stop the hurting. Sometimes war is the only way to deal with a despot even though we want peace.

Government leaders have used and continue to use the history of a country to manipulate citizens to continue this history. Governments and people are not their histories. If we continue to live now as we have lived in the past, there will be nothing new. One of the great calamities humans have fostered upon themselves is trying to perpetuate the past. Life should be allowed to select the future. To find the future, we should allow the past to die. Trying to perpetuate the past makes change difficult and new ideas automatically wrong.

Societies not ruled by the powerful, produce an accurate history not designed to show the rulers in a favorable light and allowing for the easy correction of past mistakes. Mistakes are not repeated. What the world needs now is an accurate world history. History at its best is a close approximation of the truth, and at its worst is an outright lie. Don't believe everything read in a history book.

Nations have been founded on great principles. But when these principles are used to manipulate large populations, it is time for a change. The change may be painful or graceful. The American Revolution is an example of a painful change.

In relationships with others, we should restrict our actions to non-damaging actions on our part. If we wish to do something another doesn't, then we should be open and clear about our desires and work for a win-win compromise. If this is not possible, then as Shakespeare said, "To thine own self-be true, and it must follow, as the night the day, thou canst not then be false to any man." Betrayal of self so as not to betray another, is still betrayal. Then make the highest choice for ourselves where our choice is the best for all. This applies to nations equally as well to individuals.

The Application of Government

Governments were created by humans to regulate human activity to produce goodness and ensure fairness. The problem is morality cannot be legislated. Governments can't tell citizens to love one another.

Primitive societies like ours need laws, rules and regulations, to regulate the interactions of humans. Advanced societies don't need laws because each person regulates himself or herself. Laws are not needed where people love their neighbors as themselves, and they love themselves. But societies, where there are no laws, are only practical where advanced beings live. For the time being, some level of government will be needed. Governments must provide laws because humans see themselves as separate from each other and act accordingly.

When we see ourselves as One, we will be responsible for each other. As we treat the least of the members of our society better, we evolve to higher levels. Governments can provide a service to allow its citizens to be the most productive possible. They can ensure the survival of all. This guarantees the greatness of its members. There are enough resources on the Earth to supply the needs of all. The challenge is to find the balance between helping too much or too little. A rule of thumb useful in deciding how much help to provide is to determine if the citizens are enlarged or reduced by the help.

The most important help to be given to anyone is to let them know they are the Son of God. Sometimes it's best to just leave them alone and empower them to help themselves.

The worst help is help where dependence is continued instead of rapid independence. Don't allow anyone to continue dependence in the name of compassion. This is compulsion. It would be taking responsibility for a person to build up self-worth. The goal is to make a person needing help stronger, empowered, and self-sufficient.

Many government programs, to justify their existence and perpetuate themselves, often make their clients weaker rather than stronger. A solution would be to put a limit on assistance. This provides help when needed but prevents addiction and dependence. This promotes self-reliance. Governments know help is power. By helping many people, governments get support from many people.

Tom Moore in his newsletter, *The Gentle Way News,* July 14, 2012, said presently, there are two polar views about assisting the less fortunate, one being allowing us to fend for ourselves, and the other being governments should supply everything, both being unrealistic for today. For now, those who can't care for themselves will need to be cared for by governments. To pay for this happy medium, governments will eliminate loopholes through a fair tax system. As time goes by, dictators will be eliminated, then governments by the people and not special interests will prevail, followed by governments combining to govern regionally, and finally, there will be just one world government by the people for themselves. People can be politically conservative and still help those in need. This is a long-term change covering hundreds of years.

Laws come in two forms; natural laws and unnatural laws. Natural laws are self-evident and are easy to understand why we should follow them. Unnatural laws are difficult to understand and must be explained to show why we should follow them. In the past politicians and the clergy would explain unnatural laws. The more politics and religions fail; the more explanation is given. Truth needs no explanation. It is self-evident.

Political activism, like spiritual activism, is based on love, and not on anger or hatred. It is not an attempt to embarrass or make wrong. It is a pure attempt to change the present for a new reality based on new ideas about who we are. All spirituality is really political because we must be the truth.

Governments are artificial institutions created to control our behavior. When we live as One, awareness, honesty, and responsibility will guide the actions and activities of our governmental bureaucracy.

We create governments because we feel weak, subservient, limited, and guilty. We think governments are necessary to protect us and ensure our wellbeing and we are willing to be submissive to these entities.

Since the basis of any government is the consciousness of the citizens, if Christ Consciousness were fully developed in the citizens of any country, then any action taken by anyone would be for the good of all.

Over the years, we have developed a very complex way of living. This is a difficult way to live. Simpler is easier and more abundant. One way of simpler is to have advisory bodies to provide some guidance for the government. The members of these boards would be selected by the people. There would be no laws, rules, or regulations. People would live their lives cooperating with the Divine. This type of living will be found in the future.

Everything in the Universe is connected, interdependent, interactive, and interwoven into life; in a word, One. Our only hope is to base our governments, our laws, and our politics on this truth.

Some sacred scriptures put it this way:

"So Moses hearkened to the voice of his father in law, and did all that he had said. And Moses chose able men out of all Israel, and made them heads over the people, rulers of thousands, rulers of hundreds, rulers of fifties, and rulers of tens. And they judged the people at all seasons: the hard causes they brought unto Moses, but every small matter they judged themselves" (Exodus 18:24-26).

"And he said unto them, The kings of the Gentiles exercise lordship over them; and they that exercise authority upon them are called benefactors. But ye shall not be so: but he that is greatest among you, let him be as the younger; and he that is chief, as he that doth serve" (Luke 22:25-26).

"But Peter and the apostles answered, "We must obey God rather than men" (Acts 5:29).

"And the multitude of them that believed were of one heart and of one soul: neither said any of them that ought of the things which he possessed was his own; but they had all things common. And with great power gave the apostles witness of the resurrection of the Lord Jesus: and great grace was upon them all. Neither was there any among them that lacked: for as many as were possessors of lands or houses sold them, and brought the prices of the things that were sold, And laid them down at the apostles' feet: and distribution was made unto every man according as he had need" (Acts 32:35).

Summary

Governments should be an expression of our spirituality, but not an expression of any religion. Our cultural values should impact the political process, and as we evolve this impact must allow governments to change. Our beliefs are a problem because they are imperfect. As they change we must change our governments. It is in our best interests to facilitate the evolution of our beliefs.

The goal of our governments should be to provide a harmonious, happy, and peaceful life for all our citizens thereby affirming Life. We the people are responsible for this. Our politicians should do our bidding. They should be co-operative with each other in working for win-win solutions for the problems facing our governments. This work should be based on love and should not attempt to embarrass or make anyone appear wrong. It should facilitate our evolution based on new ideas about who we are. Our politicians should do this with awareness, honesty, and responsibility.

Unbridled nationalism must be controlled. We may be citizens of a community, state, and nation, but foremost we are citizens of the world. Eventually,, this fact should lead to the formation of one government ruling the whole world comprised of the many nations as member states. It should have an executive branch to run the day to day activities of government, a legislative branch to enact laws as necessary and having representatives from each nation-state based on population, and a judicial branch to settle legal issues between the nation states and thus ensure peace. The incredible result of this one act will provide huge amounts of money to end starvation, cloth the needy, provide housing for the poor, care for the elderly, and provide health care for everyone further producing additional savings because this would end crime, create new jobs, and reduce governments even more. Eventually, taxes would be eliminated because the governments would be funded from ten percent donations by the people of the world. This government would ensure the equal availability of all the Earth's resources to all the citizens of the world. We being One Organism, one government makes sense. All our political, social, economic, and spiritual structures should reflect our unity. We are all powerful, and if we say it will be this way, it will be this way.

Governments need to become totally transparent and honest with its citizens. When the governments assist citizens, the goal should be for the citizens to become totally independent of government help. And the overall goal of all governments should be to facilitate the evolution of all citizens to become self-governing in the sense of not needing laws to control our activities, and thus eliminating the need for laws. Now we need laws to protect us from ourselves because we see ourselves as separate, and it will be this way for a long time until we see ourselves as One. We as citizens must learn to care for each other and learn to enlarge our definition of the group of people we love and care for to include everyone. When this happens, we will have peace indeed and not just judicial peace produced by a one-world government.

Life is all about change and trying to maintain the status quo is futile. Embrace change, but guide change for our evolution. Devastating disasters will occur in the future resulting in the deaths of many and the displacement of millions. Cities will be abandoned in the future for the communion of small communities.

Conservatives tend to want capitalism, and liberals tend to want socialism as their forms of government. Instead of fighting over the correct form to use, why not choose the best from all forms of government? Call it something new like idealism. The final form of government would have individual freedom and self-responsibility with respect for everyone. Societies based on love have more freedom, sharing, connecting, and smaller governments. Any action by the government would be for the good of all. Because governing is so complex requiring knowledge for many diverse fields, advisory boards should be formed to provide the necessary information to make decisions. Eventually, there would be no laws, rules, or regulations. We will love others as ourselves, and we will love ourselves, and we will be self-governing.

The ideal government will elect leaders without any campaigning, who will decide how to run the government without the influence of special interests and base all decisions on what is best for all the citizens. This government will ensure the needs of all the people, such as food, clothing, shelter, healthcare, and education, are supplied. It will ensure opportunities are available to all to achieve their highest ideas of who they are without prejudice for whom and what they are or any beliefs they hold.

Law and the Penal System

On June 22, 2012, Jerry Sandusky was found guilty in a Pennsylvania court for breaking the laws related to the sexual interaction between an adult and a child. In the world of illusions, he is guilty. A Pennsylvania governor signed into law a bill making him and thousands of others guilty. Another Pennsylvania governor in the future may sign another bill repealing this law making him and thousands of others innocent. In the world of illusions, legally, guilt or innocents depends on a signature. We decide who is guilty and who is innocent and for what actions. And these decisions have changed over time and from place to place. In some places prostitution is legal, and in other places it's illegal. In some times and places, it was OK to kill Jews, but not always.

In God's World, Jerry Sandusky is innocent. He was just acting out his part in the play we call Life in the World of Illusions. Actors are never guilty of killing another actor as part of a play because the murder was only an illusion and never happened. God knows this.

When we deal with psychopathic killers, how should we deal with them? Are we trying to punish or rehabilitate the criminal, or prevent future crimes? Are our choices fostering more attacks or improving society? In the long run, what is the best way to deal with this problem?

In the past, all criminals were being punished. The penal system is just that, it penalizes. It takes the idea from the Old Testament of an eye for an eye and applies it to crimes. It is a reflection on a society where there is little forgiveness. But as our society evolves, and becomes more forgiving, we will change the penal system to a rehabilitation system. Our realization we are all One will change the way we treat criminals.

At this stage of our spiritual evolution, we need laws to protect ourselves from ourselves. There are some individuals, such as Charles Manson, who promised to kill again if released from jail. Eventually, we will reach a stage where we will need no laws. There will be no jails for criminals. There will be no criminals. But for now, we need our criminal justice system.

The system itself could and should be changed. If we are all One, and we are, what we do to another we do to ourselves. And as mentioned above, we are all innocent. Therefore, punishment is not appropriate. "Penal" should be removed from the penal system. A better phrase would be Protection and Rehabilitation System. People should only be treated by this system to rehabilitate them and to protect society from violent predators. As time goes by, even these two reasons to treat a person for crimes will fade as we evolve spiritually, and crimes will cease to exist.

Morals

Our belief God needs us to behave in a certain way is the basis of morality. Morals must be based on some rock-solid basis, otherwise, they are valueless. They must have some authority behind them. From earliest times the authority has been God. At least God has been claimed as the source of morals. Early civilizations mixed religion and politics to use God to support their laws. God was used as the source of authority rulers used to control the behavior of their subjects. Today we call these rules morals. Most civil codes started as religious codes. No matter if it was one God, or many gods, early ideas of right and wrong came from the civilization's understanding of what their God or gods wanted. Imagine what would have happened if they believed their Deity was without need. Instead, humans have used God to hand down rule after rule.

Our morals are what we believe has been given us by a Being with power, wisdom, and authority greater than ours. This also applies to countries who do not believe in God. These countries take their morals from their ancestors of another time when the ancestors believed in gods.

Worldwide, there are millions of people who have codes of laws said to be given by God for them to follow. These people believe God's law should govern civil society. There are countries where what is understood to be God's law is the civil law.

All civil codes and moral codes are based on the religious beliefs of most of the citizens of a country. To give our morals authority, millions of us use what we believe to be God's law. These same people believe God's law came from some scripture. It is the supreme authority for their morals and laws. But what if the source is not accurate?

There are many laws stated in sacred scripture that make no sense to us now and probably never did. Some examples are we should not cut the hair on our heads or trim the corners of our beards, and if we touch a dead body we are unclean for seven days, and no work may be done on the Sabbath, and any couple is unclean after engaging in sexual intercourse. There are enough of these laws to fill a book.

Our moral values are based on laws from sacred scriptures where we have picked some laws to use and some laws to ignore depending on our mental state at the time, our culture, and current circumstances. We have chosen to ignore laws in our Holy Scriptures when they don't work for us. The truth is our morals have no standards except what works and what doesn't.

As exhibited by our actions, we have decided God's Word in our sacred books cannot be followed to the letter because it is fallible. We are basing our morality on scriptural laws that make no sense if we take them as a whole. These scriptures contradict themselves, within and among themselves. We are forced to select what to believe just to make them sensible.

We can't say we're doing this because that would make us relativists. We want to believe we have the absolute right laws to follow. But in the end, we must decide what's right and wrong. We can't rely on our laws or our idea of our God's laws. We must decide because it's impossible to apply our laws and our God's laws as a whole, indiscriminately, applied absolutely, literally, and without flexibility, and without appearing foolish. It's impossible for them to function this way. Many of our religious laws should be ignored. It is not a good idea to use them as the basis of our moral codes.

We have decided what works to reach our goals is the correct path to follow. We just won't admit it. And we can't agree on what our goals for being, doing, and having for all of us are.

Morals change from time to time and culture to culture, making them dangerous. The reason they change is because they are based on fallacious beliefs. When we find a moral tenant that doesn't work, we change it without changing the supporting belief. We are changing our beliefs when we change our morals. We like to think we don't change our beliefs even though we change our morals, so in the end, we are hypocrites. An example of this in action is we believe God wants us to be honest. Then we go and cheat on our taxes.

We have no beliefs even though we like to think we do. Deep down we know what we are doing and become self-righteous. Our righteousness is killing us. We label all functional errors sins. This leads to judgment, and then to justification. Using judgments of people or nations we justify how we respond to their actions. We say we were morally compelled to respond as we did. We execute criminals for murder using the eye for an eye passage in the Bible to justify our actions. It's not about safety. Life imprisonment would keep the public safe. It's really about revenge.

Functionality

Another way to look at actions is to determine if they are functional. Do they work or not? Eliminate morals. Now our response has a totally different context. This would be a major paradigm shift. It would eliminate our cycle of violence, destruction, and death. This cycle will never end until we see things differently.

Let's examine the death penalty for functionality. Does the death penalty even things? Yes. Does the death penalty deter other murders? No. Statistics prove this. A society using violence to end violence only perpetuates violence.

Thoughts, words, or deeds either succeed or fail to get us to our goals. If they succeed, they are a correct or a right choice. If they fail, they are an incorrect or a wrong choice. Wrong is not a moral failure or transgression of God's will. We just couldn't reach our goals. By removing moral authority from our choices, we remove the possibility of invoking the Word of God, or spiritual mandate to enforce laws on personal behavior.

Do we really want a world of peace? The way to get there is to closely examine what works to get us there and what fails. Currently, we are not doing this, or we would act differently. This means we really don't want peace. To get to peace then, we must do what leads to peace.

Life functions. When life's functionality is threatened, it adjusts or adapts to allow it to continue to function. Looking at a single species in Life, when life situations threaten its existence, it adapts by changing so it can continue to live. When Life adapts, it demonstrates the third Life Principle: sustainability, with functionality and adaptability being the first two. Life is sustainable because it adapts its functionality.

Our culture tries to mimic adaptability by applying justice to adjust conflicting claims fairly by handing out rewards and punishments. Unfortunately, our justice system is flawed. A major flaw is the rich and powerful can unduly affect the decisions of the system in their favor. At the other end of the spectrum are the poor, weak, and downtrodden who receive little justice.

Our justice system needs to be changed so it works better. Seeking to "right a wrong" usually involves a punishment somewhere. This is because wrong is thought of as a moral failure instead of a functional goof.

When seeking to make something work after a goof, we would just make a correction or an adjustment. When we make a functional misstep, we should be allowed to experience the consequences of our actions, but not punishments. Experiencing consequences allow us to know behavior adjustments are necessary.

The Ten Commandments

Laws relating to crime should be kept simple. The Ten Commandments is a good example of this simplicity. Crime destroys unity and needs to be addressed. Endless lists of right and wrong are not productive. Learning to forgive is more important.

Let's take a closer look at the Ten Commandments. It's an old but not the oldest morality code. These laws were not meant to be used as a basis for judgment, but to support life and to heal damaged areas of life.

The first is, "Thou shalt have no other gods before me." This is all about elevating God, who is love, and us by extension, and creating unity for all. We were created by God, the prime cause, and God is who we are, and through God, we create everything in our lives. Unity is the source of all blessings. Separation produces all our problems. Good examples of separation in action are war and criminal activity. Division advocates resist change. Unity is our basis in God, and as time passes in this world, unity will evolve into greater potential. It all starts by recognizing there is only one God, then choosing correct priorities, and finally producing true unity.

The second is, "Thou shalt not make unto thee any graven image or any likeness of anything that is in heaven above, or that is in the earth beneath, or that is in the water under the earth." This has to do with misunderstanding what God is. We should not think of God as being comprised of lower concepts, words, doctrine, substances, myths, construction, or objects. Ideas of a jealous or vengeful God fall into this category. God is Love. Love in all its forms powers the Universe, and It should be honored as such. God cannot be defined, and should not be conceptualized, or symbolized using anything transitory or finite.

The third is, "Thou shalt not take the name of the LORD thy God in vain; for the LORD will not hold him guiltless that taketh his name in vain." This teaches us how to improve our connection with life. God's name is Love. Love should not be devalued, used falsely, misused, tarnished, misrepresented, or disbelieved. Faking love or invoking love for anything not supporting life will diminish our impact on life and increase our suffering.

The fourth is, "Remember the Sabbath day, to keep it holy." This is a time of rest, a time to take a break from daily activities, and commune with God. The thought behind the commandment is respect, starting with God, continuing with all of life, and extending through the designs of creation to the entire Universe. Take time to appreciate the Creator and the created. The day of the week utilized for this purpose doesn't matter if it is accepted by a large enough population to make it a commonly accepted day to rest.

The fifth is, "Honour thy father and thy mother: that thy days may be long upon the land which the LORD thy God giveth thee." This actually means honoring all who preceded us. We should respect what past generations have done for us, to lift us to where we are. This provides a basis for moving forward. Brotherhood and prosperity are gained best through living and working together, including prior generations. Denying and judging our history will cause us to repeat it.

The sixth is, "Thou shalt not kill." Anyone who adopts a destructive lifestyle is a problem for everything and themselves. The opposite lifestyle where anyone consciously takes part in expansion empowers themselves with riches. To nullify the intent, the innate ability, the desire, the idea, or the love of another intending to stop this life force of another is to commit the act of murder. When our interests infringe on others, there is an impulse to kill because of fear. Co-operation with each other to find a win-win solution is a better approach. Sharing will open up tremendous possibilities for all concerned. And there are many more possible solutions other than violence and hostility to choose from. Working together in unity is the ultimate solution.

The seventh is, "Thou shalt not commit adultery." The union of two or more for any relationship, bond, or purpose produces a joining within God. Any marriage should start with pure, relevant, and honest ingredients. The greatest manifestation of kindness and tenderness in the world is found in a loving and pure marriage. Adultery is about being dishonest, and deceitful or a joining for any reason other than love. A marriage based on convenience, money, or social advantage, is adulterated from the start, and may later produce infidelity. There are many different types of marriage, but the greatest marriage is the union of God and mankind.

The eighth is, "Thou shalt not steal." This is all about respecting a person and their property. When we respect the property of someone else, we are demonstrating our love for each other. Stealing is a violation of this respect. Although everything belongs to God, we get to act as stewards of things entrusted into our care to facilitate our own creations. Greed is also stealing. Give to each his own; to God, God's; to the Earth, the Earth's; to our brother or sister, theirs; to ourselves give what belongs to us.

Because we don't know who we are, we don't know what we own. To secure what we think we own, we have established boundaries and legal documents for our protection. When we know who we are, we will know what we own.

The ninth is, "Thou shalt not bear false witness against thy neighbour." Don't lie about a neighbor. The essence of honesty is a love of reality. Deception separates us from God. Honesty is the basis of wisdom and intelligence. We don't need to be brutally honest to speak the truth. Honesty is based on reality and carries with it comfort, support, and harmony. When speaking our truth, we can be kind and gentle and exhibit tolerance and compassion toward the beliefs of others. The truth can be conveyed many ways, and still be conveyed. Frankness is not necessary.

And the tenth is, "Thou shalt not covet." The truth in this lies in not seeking our fulfillment in the material world. We should execute our purpose in life with a love for our inner accomplishments without comparing ourselves with anyone. There is nothing greater than executing our purpose in life as the child of God we are.

The trick is to realize Life is a process. We should enjoy the process because Life and the process are never-ending. We all are scattered along the spectrum of the process, with some just starting, and some just finishing. When we finish we get to start another project. We may be just starting, but we can still rejoice with those finishing. For our own benefit, we should keep our eyes on the goal, and enjoy the process to get there. This is all practical advice to help us avoid pain and suffering.

Here's another perspective on the Ten Commandments. They don't exist. God does not command. There is only One Thing, God, so who would God command. And why would God want to command? Everything God wants exists, so commanding is unnecessary. And if God issued any commands, wouldn't they immediately be executed? And if God wanted something badly enough to command it into existence, wouldn't God insist it is created immediately? What ruler or king would be kept waiting?

The Ten Commandments are really Ten Commitments. They are promises to let us know we have found God when these changes have taken place within us:

The first is, we will love God with all our heart, mind, and spirit, with no competitors with God.

The second is, we will not use God's name in vain, because we can't. We will know our power is enabled by God, and God always answers. We will use this power reverently.

The third is, we will set aside a day to spend with God, to pause for a while from the illusions of this world, and to know who we are.

The fourth is, we will honor our parents because they gave us life, and we will honor our creator, God, and we will honor everyone.

The fifth is, we will not willfully kill without justification. While it's impossible to end anyone's life, their life in the illusion may appear to end. We will reverence all Life.

The sixth is, we will not be dishonest or deceitful in our love relationships. Adultery is all about dishonesty and deceit.

The seventh is, we will not take what is not ours.

The eighth is, we will speak only the truth.

The ninth is, we will not covet our neighbor's spouse for all are our spouses.

The tenth is, we will not covet our neighbor's things, for we share all things.

These two perspectives are different than commonly accepted, leaving them looking less like a code of law. Once we learn to care for each other, few laws will be needed.

The Will of God and Death

Death is the greatest experience anyone can have because once we experience it, we will know there is only Life forever. Every event is permitted by God and therefore is an act of God. God is responsible for everything in Life. In the Absolute World where God resides, there is only Love. In the relative Physical World where we now reside, there are opposites such as good and evil, but even they are illusions and don't exist.

When we "die", we will know we are only goodness and light. We are Love. Because we now think we are something else, we judge everyone including ourselves. But God will not judge anyone. Since we judge, we don't understand a God Who won't.

Our theologies make sense only when we view life as a test to determine our worthiness before God, or God is believed to be so egotistical, God is constantly demanding attention, adoration, appreciation, and affection, and will spare no violence to get it, or God is vengeful and jealous, and therefore possessing the wrath of God.

But life is a process to remember who we are. God has no ego or need. God is unconditional in love, peaceful, joyous, and passionate in ecstasy.

No death is untimely. Everything happening is perfect just as it is. There are no accidents. When someone "dies" they experience the greatest love, joy, peace, and freedom. This is a great experience.

Events and experiences are just events and experiences. They provide opportunities for us to decide how we will treat them. We draw them to ourselves individually and collectively. They are not "works of the devil," "punishments from God," or "rewards from Heaven." We create these events to experience who we are, and who we are, are beings capable of doing greater things than we do now.

Everything happening is the will of God. Nothing can happen against the will of God. Everything happening is our will since we are One with God, and everything happening is happening perfectly. No one can decide an event for someone else without their permission. No one is murdered without their consent. Because we are all One, any event is a co-created event with the co-operation and consent of all involved. Only if we are separate from each other could one individual affect another without their consent.

We cause our own deaths no matter the circumstances. We cannot be forced to die if we don't want to.

As a society, we have said it's OK to kill someone against their will such as in war or as an execution for a crime, but it's not OK to assist someone who wants to die. This is hypocritical.

We are One. We are not separate. What we do, we do in concert with everyone. We co-create everything together. There are no victims or villains. We have all decided together what will be expressed in life.

It is not possible to kill someone. It is not possible to kill ourselves or anyone or anything else. However, it is possible to end life as experienced with a body. This ending of life as a body is treated by society in a convoluted manner. Suicide, assisted death, and murder are treated as crimes while death by cigarettes is not. They all result in the death of a body. It's all a matter of time. Cigarettes and a whole host of other chemicals produce a slow death. This is OK for society. But a quick death is not. In the case of assisted death where the death is to end suffering, it is considered inhumane, while allowing the person to continue to suffer is considered humane. Looking closely at this, it is easy to see this is backward.

All of life in the Physical World is an illusion. There is no pain when this life is seen as an illusion. When we realize "death" is an illusion, being part of life in the Physical World, it can be enjoyed. The statement, "O death, where is thy sting?" has new meaning.

We create the illusion, including the illusion of "death." We have lived before the illusion and will continue to live after the illusion, so, there is no "death."

No one ever dies. We just change shapes. What we call "death" is a joyful experience. "Death" allows the soul to experience its normal state, total freedom, limitless, and the blissful and sublime feeling of Oneness.

The laws of the land make killing a moral crime. But using execution as a punishment compounds the problem. The murderer only attacked himself, since we are all One. The correct solution is to "turn the other cheek," knowing this. Failure to "turn the other cheek" knowing the attacker is only attacking himself, will prolong any solution. By hating another, the other is attached to us for as long as the hatred exists.

We have used physical pain to punish children and adults. We have used the ultimate physical pain, death, to prevent people from killing people. We use the same energy creating a problem to try to solve the problem. We repeat actions we want to be stopped to stop them. We demonstrate this behavior for our children even though we don't want them to copy our actions. These are not rational actions.

The number one principle of enlightened civilizations is unity. All life is sacred. In enlightened civilizations, no one would think of taking the life of another for any reason.

When we live based on the truth of who we are, meaning Love, then laws, rules, and regulations are unnecessary. For those living without this truth, we need laws for protection, and even then laws are not always adequate.

St. Augustine said, "Love and do what you will." If we live in Love, laws are unnecessary.

Protection of human life is very important. It is appropriate to protect human life from attack. Killing as punishment, retribution, or to settle petty differences is not appropriate. Killing another human to settle an argument is absurd. Killing to please God is the peak of hypocrisy and blasphemy.

Governments have decided it is appropriate to kill to achieve a political goal. Religions have decided it is appropriate to kill to spread, maintain, and enforce adherence to their doctrines. Societies have decided it is appropriate to kill as a form of punishment for certain crimes. Are these ideas correct? And why are they correct, if they are correct? We are defining ourselves by our answers.

The Basis of Law

Love is the law, and so for a law to be valid, it must be rooted in love.

All laws should be based on love and truth. The summation of all valid law is to love God with our whole being and to love our neighbor as ourselves. Truth is found in all things.

Morality, many times, is used to control instead of leading to Oneness and lifting humans up. True morality and ethical principles are based on honesty, love, and what works, and are found within and cannot be enforced from outside, nor can they be legislated.

Respect, dedication, and discipline are the foundation for personal responsibility, self-determination, and ethics.

The purpose of the law is to support life and heal problems. Law should not be used as a reason to judge and should be based on love.

Justice is fair play and the golden rule all rolled into one. Justice is a balance maintained by giving and taking. It leads to a healthy person or a healthy planet and all things in between. It produces a fair price for goods and services.

The correct application of justice is through forgiveness. The experiences of this world are based on illusions and forgiveness is appropriate because it's impossible to know everything connected to an event, and because at times those judging lack good will. However, forgiveness doesn't mean we should allow destructive actions or senseless behavior to continue. There are times when a person or nation must be restrained because the person or nation is abusing others and refuses to stop.

Justice is fairness without revenge and is defined as no one losing. Justice is a way of living, not an act of punishment after an act. It is an action, not a reaction. It is not a way to even the score. We demonstrate our definition of justice by the way we experience and create life. God will not judge us after we die, as we have imagined God administering our idea of justice.

Crimes are more common where there is an injustice. When people are treated unjustly, and corrections cannot be made, desperate people will use desperate measures to correct the situation and crimes result. But when we as a society treat everyone justly, there is no fertile ground for crime.

Mercy allows for individual and societal growth and the neutralization of future harm. Mercy doesn't know vengeance, doesn't know self-justification, knows justice, sees all as right and none as wrong, and doesn't dominate anyone.

Brotherhood will flourish when guilt and unworthiness are seen as groundless and condemnation and punishment are discarded. Any destruction needs to be prevented, and offenders need to be restrained and corrected to teach responsibility. The goal of correction should be to restore brotherhood to its fullest. Everyone should be welcomed into the brotherhood of humans without qualification or reservation. This is unconditional love in action.

When judgment ends, unity can begin and there will be peace on earth. To get there, cause positive changes to occur.

The three basic truths are We are all One Thing, there is plenty for everyone, and doing is not important, we only have to be. If we practiced these truths, we would treat others as ourselves, share the entire world with everyone, and solve all our problems by being, for example, create justice by being just.

It all comes down to trust. Do we trust ourselves and others? Lack of trust will lead to laws inhibiting humans doing what they want. Trust will lead to believing God has created natural laws allowing us to do as we please producing man-made laws affirming our freedom.

Individuals, governments, and religions have resorted to revenge and punishment when their blame and judgment have failed to change the world.

The old belief of separation where we have right and wrong, good and bad, crime and punishment, and everlasting rewards and everlasting damnation has not solved our problems. Judgment day does not exist. Condemnation and punishment are only done by ourselves to us. God does not judge, condemn, or punish. The new message We are All One will change the world to end suffering, torture, and killing.

If we are One, who could be the victim or the villain, or the victor or the loser, or the attacker or the attacked, or the murderer or the murdered, or the predator or the prey.

There are no villains or victims. Only perfection exists. Nothing happens by chance nor is anything a mistake. Perfect Souls forget who they are to come to Earth to experience life. It may appear they do imperfect things, but everything is done for a reason. There are no mistakes in life, and there are no accidents. All events are miracles providing us with the context to experience life and to announce to the world who we are. Nothing happens against God's will. Therefore, condemnation is inappropriate.

Freedom is the nature of the soul. Freedom is the nature of Life. Anything reducing, restricting, impinging upon, or eliminating freedom is working against Life. In advanced societies, freedom is a fact. Ironically, freedom is what God is, and free will is God's greatest gift, but both are severely restricted by religions and governments.

Expressions of freedom include the human rights of personal liberty, equality under the law, and fair trials, equality of men and women, and freedom of beliefs.

It is difficult to keep promises. First, most people don't know what they are doing in any situation, and it is difficult to act consistently in all situations. Life is constantly changing. Second, most people can't predict the future, so a promise cannot be made truthfully. Third, a person's truth evolves and changes over time eventually producing a conflict between what was promised and what the person's current truth is.

Therefore, when confronted with whether to keep a promise or not, remember the highest betrayal is a betrayal of ourselves even if it is an effort to prevent the betraying of another.

People are constantly changing. No one should expect anyone to keep a promise. No one should be forced to keep their word because they didn't want to or felt they couldn't. Forcing anyone to do something they don't want to do is an aberration of free will.

Forcing others to keep a promise inflects injury both ways. People doing what they felt they were forced to do, does more damage than people freely living their lives. Granting freedom to others removes the danger. Granting others freedom grants us freedom. Acceptance is important here.

Humans should be allowed to change viewpoints, mind, or heart. Legal documents, agreements, and loyalty should not be used to maintain conformity. Such restrictions restrict creation. The place of least restriction is love. We should love God with all our hearts and our neighbors as ourselves.

Force solves nothing, and revenge injures the one seeking revenge. We only hurt ourselves when we seek revenge. Whatever is done is past and the past cannot be undone. Don't waste time trying to change what can't be changed. There is only the present. The solution is to forgive. Forgiveness prevents disease and frees from the bondage of hate, lack, and limitation.

Anger is never justified. There is no reason to attack. Everyone should be forgiven. Revenge is never necessary. Everything in the world is an illusion, a dream, having no basis in reality. We are only asked to pardon where pardon is justified. Since everything in the Physical World is an illusion, there is no transgression. Penalties, least of all capital punishment, are not justified.

All are innocent. Right and wrong do not exist. They are philosophical extremes in our value system. They are not constants but change over time.

Ending Crime

Suffering is caused by ignorance. Asylums, reformatories, and prisons could be closed if we knew the truth.

We all create the conditions necessary to produce the desire to steal or rape. Our beliefs have created the conditions making rape possible. The solution starts when we see within ourselves the causes of rape and robbery.

We can end starvation, provide dignity and opportunity for the poor to allow them to provide for themselves. We can end prejudice. We can end sexual taboos and restrictions fostering rape. We can help everyone enjoy the wonder of sexual energy properly channeled. We can do all this and more.

Any person who continually abuses or damages others or property must be stopped. Allowing the abuse to continue teaches the abuser nothing. Loving a person doesn't mean allowing them to do as they please. But we don't have to return a hurt for a hurt. Just stop the hurting.

When someone makes a mistake, and a mistake is an action by someone unevolved, they should be provided with the opportunity to correct their action and to evolve. One type of mistake is called a crime. Our civilization has chosen to deal with this type of mistake by punishing the person who made the mistake. Now we have prisons full of people who have made mistakes. The evolutionary state of each person is not the same. And to protect society from some people, they need to be put in prison. In time all people will evolve to the point where this will not be necessary. But as much as possible, we should allow people who commit crimes the opportunity to correct their actions and evolve to a higher state.

Advanced beings have no laws as we know it. They live by three principles: awareness, honesty, and responsibility. This leads to an understanding that what works for the whole group works best for the individual because the whole group is the individual. We are all One. When someone does something that does not work, they are not arrested and put in jail, but given the opportunity to become aware of all the outcomes of what they did, honestly, assess their role in the events, and take responsibility for the outcomes. Then they can correct, change, or heal as necessary.

God will judge no one. God knows all are innocent. We who see less than God does may fail to see the innocence. If we experience judgment, we will know judgment does not come from love. In our society, judgment is accepted and expected. It's part of our judicial system. We can declare someone to be guilty or innocent. For a long time, we have judged ourselves and each other. Judgment implies we are less than perfect or holy. It implies we still need to evolve to perfection. In truth, God sees us as perfect and loveable for we were created of love and love is what we are.

We are all deserving of constant praise. In our illusional world we have inverted this thought to the point we think we should never praise ourselves and sparingly praise others. We think we are imperfect and worthy of condemnation. Condemnation is used as proof we may be damaged.

This is an illusion. God is Everything, the most powerful, and the Supreme Being. Because this is true, God can't be hurt. Being a part of God, the same applies to us.

Advanced societies judge no one and declare no one guilty of anything. All connected to any incident can decide what they want to do because of it. Nothing is done to anyone. Punishment is incomprehensible to them. If we are all One, and we are, even if someone hurt another, to hurt in return is to hurt the self twice. Once was enough. It's like slapping the right hand when it hits the left hand with a hammer. Judgment is a product of a society who sees each of us as separate.

It is impossible to judge anyone because that person no longer exists. We are constantly changing from moment to moment. The person who did something a moment ago no longer exists. We are constantly creating ourselves anew in each moment. This self-creation never ends.

A criminal is not forgiven so he can return to more crime, but so he may return to God. No matter the offense, God accepts us as we are. Past decisions are not who we really are.

To get to a totally loving society, grant everyone the freedom to do anything. On the surface, this sounds like we're opening ourselves to chaos. This would be true if we are evil beings. If we are good beings, then we're not fostering chaos. Every action has a natural consequence. Because we believe we are evil, many times actions are given punishments. Our society is too impatient to allow consequences to play out their natural course.

Dealing with Offences Against the Law

Unfortunately, prisons are also used to restrain those who have mental illnesses. Mental illness is a health issue and should be addressed differently. Drug addiction and alcoholism are also health issues and should be addressed as health problems. None of those suffering from these problems belong in prison. Providing plants and pets to residents of mental hospitals and minimum-security prisons are important therapeutic aids.

Why do we punish? We say to change behavior. But it's more like retribution, an attempt to get even, and a way to punish. Retribution will not create the society we want. Little is learned from punishment. Punishment judges the person to be wrong and produces artificial outcomes by imposing from the outside a different value system. Consequences are better teachers. They produce natural outcomes because they are experienced on the inside by the Self, and the Self-determines their action did not work to produce the desired outcome.

Punishments don't work because someone else is doing it to the offender. Consequences work because the offender realizes she/he is doing it to herself/himself.

Loving fully means we forgive any wrong behavior. In reality, there is no wrong behavior. Totally loving means we will allow each mature person total freedom to act as they wish.

Can anyone be free while imprisoning another? Freedom can only be achieved when no one is imprisoned. We are made free by releasing.

Many believe God will punish us if we break one of God's laws. This is not true. They also believe we have a moral responsibility and authority to punish each other for breaking

God's laws, something we don't have. Punishment is not appropriate or an effective remedy for improper behavior.

The love, compassion, wisdom, forgiveness, intention, and purpose of God are large enough to encompass the most heinous crime and criminal. Forgiveness is human, unconditional love is Divine.

The penal system should hold offenders who commit acts of violence such as rape accountable. This makes a positive statement about how individuals in our society should treat one another. This is where we are now. Sometime in the future, there will be no rape or other violent acts upon one another.

Once we as a society develop compassion for offenders and want to help them, we will have demonstrated we are maturing. To help offenders to heal, they must be engaged in a non-judgmental manner that allows them to share their emotions freely. They must be willing to take responsibility for the offense to heal, but they must be allowed to do this freely. Then they must be lead past self-hatred by discovering the why of the event.

Compassion and unconditional love is the natural state of existence and should be extended to everyone including criminals and terrorists. Victims and villains alike are worthy of our compassion. People who commit unspeakable acts against another, are really confused, and frustrated, and are experiencing pain and self-hatred. They are emotionally diseased. There is no bad, and evil is a product of fear. Criminals are victims of their self-hatred, pain, fear, and limitations. By changing from a mindset of fear to trust, anyone can be changed from a villain to loving person.

Unfortunately, criminals and terrorists are treated with disrespect and little or no opportunity to receive help for their condition. This allows criminals and terrorists to multiply and continue to be a problem. Our world is not dealing with the root cause of the problem.

This is not an us versus them situation, for we are all One. The totality of us all has produced these problems. Even villains are victims.

A totally self-aware person would never harm anyone. Most people today are not self-aware, so we need laws and prisons to protect us from ourselves. If everyone were self-aware of our magnificence, then we wouldn't need rules, regulations, laws, jails or hospitals.

Today, we judge and condemn criminals, not only in this life but in the afterlife. We lack the compassion to see them as the natural result of the reality we have created. In the future when we each can look into the eyes of our worst enemy and see ourselves, then the world will be transformed. To get there, we each need to work on ourselves in our own way to see the world differently from the way our societies have said it is. Each of us influences the Whole.

Putting law offenders in prison is a short-term solution, and it doesn't solve the underlying problems, and the problems will only continue and get worse. Our solution has been to build more prisons and enlarge the court system. Criminals are a symptom of an underlying problem we need to solve. The solution is to develop within each of us an understanding we are all magnificent creatures who are loved, respected, appreciated, and unified with the Whole, and to develop joyful and happy people. We will eventually know when we injure another person, we are injuring ourselves.

Here's what sacred scriptures say:

"He who seeking his own happiness does not punish or kill beings who also long for happiness, will find happiness after death" (Dhammapada 132).

"In the kingdom the multiplication of prohibitive enactments increases the poverty of the people; the more implements to add to their profit that the people have, the greater disorder is there in the state and clan; the more acts of crafty dexterity that men possess, the more do strange contrivances appear; the more display there is of legislation, the more thieves and robbers there are" (Tao Te Ching 57).

"And if a man shall open a pit, or if a man shall dig a pit, and not cover it, and an ox or an ass fall therein; The owner of the pit shall make it good, and give money unto the owner of them; and the dead beast shall be his. And if one man's ox hurt another's, that he die; then they shall sell the live ox, and divide the money of it; and the dead ox also they shall divide. Or if it be known that the ox hath used to push in time past, and his owner hath not kept him in; he shall surely pay ox for ox; and the dead shall be his own" (Exodus 21:33-36).

"And I charged your judges at that time, saying, Hear the causes between your brethren, and judge righteously between every man and his brother, and the stranger that is with him" (Deuteronomy 1:16).

"And said to the judges, Take heed what ye do: for ye judge not for man, but for the LORD, who is with you in the judgment. Wherefore now let the fear of the LORD be upon you; take heed and do it: for there is no iniquity with the LORD our God, nor respect of persons, nor taking of gifts" (2 Chronicles 19:6-7).

"In those days there was no king in Israel: every man did that which was right in his own eyes" (Judges 21:25).

"Defend weak people and orphans. Protect the rights of the oppressed and the poor" (Psalms 82:3).

"Thus saith the LORD; Execute ye judgment and righteousness, and deliver the spoiled out of the hand of the oppressor: and do no wrong, do no violence to the stranger, the fatherless, nor the widow, neither shed innocent blood in this place" (Jeremiah 22:3).

"But I say unto you, That ye resist not evil: but whosoever shall smite thee on thy right cheek, turn to him the other also. And if any man will sue thee at the law, and take away thy coat, let him have thy cloke also" (Matthew 5:39-40).

"JUDGE NOT, that ye be not judged. For with what judgement ye judge, ye shall be judged: and with what measuer ye mete, it shall be measured to you again" (Matthew 7:1-2).

"Then said Jesus unto him, Put up again thy sword into his place: for all they that take the sword shall perish with the sword" (Matthew 26:52). This infers violence produces violence. Violence can only be conquered by love. The spiral of violence after violence can only be stopped by replacing violence with love.

"Judge not, and ye shall not be judged: condemn not, and ye shall not be condemned: forgive, and ye shall be forgiven" (Luke 6:37).

"Therefore if thine enemy hunger, feed him; if he thirst, give him drink: for in so doing thou shalt heap coals of fire on his head. Be not overcome of evil, but overcome evil with good" (Romans 12:20-21).

"It is not for thee in anything to judge of their motives, nor for them in anything to judge of thee" (Sura 6:52).

Other Thoughts

When we are making decisions such as how to deal with this murderer, or this rapist, or this terrorist, or this child molester, remember this person is us. Remember also, no one can be harmed. No one was murdered. No one was raped. No one was terrorized. No child was molested. Everything in life is an illusion. Just as in a play, each part was selected by the actor or as in life, by the individual. There are no victims or villains.

However, anything destructive is working against Life. Destructive individuals should be allowed to experience the results of their actions and be allowed to make any corrections they wish to make.

Our young delinquents are not delinquents by nature. They are neglected and they know it, and so they take their anger out on society. The solution is to provide them with loving attention.

Here are some thoughts on abuse:

Everything is One Thing. In life, the biggest illusion is separation. It appears we are separate from everyone and everything, but, we are connected to everyone and everything. Because we are connected to everyone, what we do to anyone we do to ourselves. What someone does to another person, she or he does it to herself or himself. When an abuser abuses someone, she or he is abusing herself or himself. So, by allowing an abuser to abuse someone, the abuser is being allowed to continue to abuse herself or himself. This is not a healthy situation and should be stopped for both the abuser and the abused. The abuse can be physical, mental, moral, or spiritual. And abuse can be done by a person, group, corporation, religion, or government.

One reason we incarnate is to experience everything. This includes being abused. Until we learn to stand up and stop the abuse, the abuse will continue until we learn to control it. Now the abuser should not be vilified, because before we were born, the abuser and abused agreed to the relationship so the abused could experience abuse. In other lifetimes, the abused was the abuser. The abuser is only supplying a service. One very important point about life: it's just a simulation.

To a person being abused it certainly doesn't feel like a simulation. The abused feels all kinds of pain and emotional turmoil. Since the plans for the abuse were washed from memory before birth, to tell someone they asked to experience it would further traumatize them. The best thing to do when we're abused is to first stop the abuse and then forgive.

We can't be harmed, even though our bodies may die. Death is an illusion. There is no death. We will always continue to live. All of life is an illusion, including abuse. Sometimes we play the bad guys, and sometimes we play the good guys. We are all actors in each other's plays to provide the experience we each want. In the end, the "goodness" and the "badness" average out to zero. Because of this and the fact life is only an illusion anyway, it is inappropriate to judge anyone, and the spiritual writings say so. It's impossible to make a fair judgment about any situation, because we never know all there is to know about it.

There are a spiritual side and a practical side to every situation. It's nice to allow everyone to do whatever they choose to do, but if a mass murderer is running around, from a practical perspective, the mass murderer must be stopped, and society protected. Whatever works in any situation is the way to go. As with everything in life, we are constantly evolving. From a practical perspective, we can't go from today's mass incarceration to incarcerating no one. Over time we will get there, but for now, we must protect society by incarcerating violent criminals. And we should try to rehabilitate them, not punish them, as best as we can.

Economics and World Hunger

Once upon a time, two humans swapped one thing for another and trade was initiated. Since then there have been all kinds of variations on this theme. Eventually, precious metals were accepted instead of goods or services, and then coins were used. It took a while, but in time we realized we could assign a value to anything, and paper money was introduced. Today we use bank accounts to keep track of our accumulated cash and use plastic and electronics to transfer this cash to others. Ownership is an important part of the equation, with ownership being traded in an exchange. We have even devised ways to spend money we don't have by utilizing different forms of credit. We see ourselves as separate and feel the need to compensate "others" for the goods and services we receive. Our present system is based on the false assumption we are separate. There are many ways to construct an economic system, and we will devise others in the future.

Our definitions of "life" and "better" need correction. Better is not bigger, and more money, more power, more sex, and more stuff. Life is not the period between birth and death. A corrected definition of better is a grander experience and a greater expression of our state of being. A corrected definition of life is an eternal, sustained, never-ending process of being.

A better life is not collecting as much stuff as possible. Yet collecting stuff is what drives most people. If we don't care for things, it's easy to let them go. Now it is not wrong or bad, wrong and bad don't exist anyway, to enjoy the things of this world, but the time will come when we will find spiritual things more interesting and satisfying. A better life is an abundant life of happiness. The one who dies with the most toys is not the winner, but the one who had the happiest life.

The Problem

Some people fight for survival each day. Some have the basics of survival and try just to get ahead. These two groups make up most of the people on Earth. Another much smaller group has all it could ever ask for, and yet many in this group ask for more and hold tightly to what they have. Then there is the last and smallest group of all. The members of this group don't need material things. For them, spiritual truth, reality, and experience are most important. Their goal is to know God, fulfill self, and express truth. This struggle is a process of self-discovery, of growth, and of being. Instead of concerns of the body, they focus on concerns of the soul. For them, greatness is measured by spiritual progress. For them, the definition of success is not coveting, acquiring, protecting, and increasing in worldly possession, but in developing their spirituality.

Presently, our social, religious, political, and economic systems are primitive. We consider them the best, because we don't know of, nor can we think of better systems. We resist change or improvements involving any loss of power or wealth even if these would help the vast part of the world's population.

What is needed is a huge change in consciousness, awareness, and respect for all of life, and a greater understanding of the unity of everything.

Equality of opportunity for all should be guaranteed, and not equality in fact. To provide equal opportunity, each person will be provided with the basic needs and the opportunity for advancement.

Advanced cultures share everything with everyone. Our culture is not advanced. Notice we don't share. Advanced cultures share all of their planet's resources with everyone equally. No one person or country owns a natural resource even if it is located on land they occupy.

We as humans must live as a community for us to experience Holy Communion with God and to know God. Advanced societies never fail to share with others and their economic systems are not based on supply and demand. Our present system does not provide for the common good. We don't share the common good with everyone. Advanced societies don't have personal possessive words in their languages, like my and mine.

Giving and receiving are the same. We can only give something to ourselves because we are all a part of One Thing. There is no one else.

We have created an illusion by saying we need money to buy food to prevent starvation. This is insanity.

Ownership is sharing. Since we are all One, if one of us owns something, we all share it. And we own everything. This is true in the Spiritual World. In the Physical World, ownership is used to separate and retards sharing.

The use of fire in our past is an example of the benefits of living as one big community. Fire provided heat, light, and energy for industry. By sharing the flames of fire with others, we did not diminish our quantity of fire, but we increased the amount of fire and provided security for all of us in the event our fire went out by producing other sources of fire.

By living as one big community, quality of life for all is assured when each of us survives, and the quality of life for each is guaranteed by the whole surviving. We each add to each other's survival. Sharing not only fire, but the truth, liberty, honor, the right to exercise free will, food, technology, knowledge, beliefs, and ourselves, benefits us all.

For us, the concept of scarcity changed all this. Then it was every person for themselves leading to greed, strife, and war. Scarcity is a real problem in some non-important areas, but not related to human survival.

How we as a world community treat the nourishment of each of our members says a lot about how advanced we are as a civilization. Allowing for starvation casts us as a primitive society. Advanced societies nurture each member by supplying economic and biological needs, and through thought, emotion, play, work, celebration, and worship. Structures should be implemented to support and allow the growth of its members. Look at how we nurture others and how others nurture us. And examine the support cycle found in nature. Then we can nurture based on our values. What is nurtured will increase based on its nature. Do what is appropriate and logical. For example, nature operates so effortlessly in one of its nurturing cycles where plants provide oxygen for animals, and animals provide carbon dioxide for plants. The world's economic interdependence is observable. When one part of the world is in need, the whole world is in need.

Our interdependence can be illustrated by looking at the millions of people, animals, and plants we depend on just so, we can have a drink of milk. First, we depend on the cows. Then there is the whole support package for the cows, including the plants producing the food for the cows, the farmer who harvests the food, feeds and cares for the cows, and the veterinarian and health support network. The equipment the farmer uses is manufactured by workers using parts from other manufacturing plants. The raw materials for the farm equipment components must be extracted from the earth by other workers using equipment from other factories. There are the driver and tank truck used to transport the milk to the milk plant for processing. The tank truck and all its components must be manufactured somewhere by other workers. The fuel used in all the equipment in this network is produced by a whole other manufacturing industry with equipment produced by an army of workers. Then there are the workers in the milk processing plant with their own equipment produced by other industries. The packaging material must be produced by other industries with some of the raw material coming from trees necessitating the harvesting of trees by loggers and involving the manufacturing of logging equipment. The trees are then processed at a pulp mill by many workers involving the use of other equipment that is produced by others. Finally, the milk is transported by other workers to the store where it available for purchase. These transport vehicles must be manufactured by other workers using other equipment. The store must be built by contractors using construction materials produced by other industries. There are the store workers, and the refrigerator units requiring manufacturing facilities and workers. The store then is supplied with electricity produced by an industry supported by other industries and raw materials. This electricity is needed by all levels of this network to power computers from still another industry. The computers require computer programmers and computer networks. Also, is how the milk is purchased. If coins are used, there is the whole branch of extracting the minerals from the Earth, the smelting, the minting, and the transportation of the coins. If paper money is used, there is everything involved with its production. If electronic transfer is used, such as credit cards or debit cards, there are all the people, manufacturing, electrical connections, and management necessary to make this possible. This is only a brief outline of what is involved just to allow us the opportunity to drink a glass of milk, illustrating the vast network necessary.

We can protect human life from calamities but refuse because of greed. Pain, injury, and death could be avoided by simple safety measures. Human life is sacrificed for money.

Work should be the basis for exchange based on its value to others. We shouldn't sell ourselves, our time, or our being. The basis of our economy should be the perceiving and creating of values. Workers should be compensated for values produced rather than based on time spent working. This will stimulate initiative, imagination, and creativity. For example, a janitor who cleans offices should be paid based on the number of offices cleaned, and not by the hour.

True profit is not gained at the expense of someone else. Inflation is caused by increasing the forward movement of monetary exchange faster than debts can appear. This creates the illusion of profits. Inflation is a symptom of a force-based culture. It speeds the decline of poor nations and is concealed in rich ones. This forward movement is maintained by technology, production, expansion, and human energy to produce the illusion of profit.

Inflation is not generated by economies based on compression. The economies based on compression work easier and more efficiently producing more leisure time. Compression works by using organizational efficiencies, learning new skills, and attracting and utilizing the help of others. Our economy should be based on perceiving and creating values.

Expansion can be expedited by cooperating to further the interests of everyone. Look for win-win. Competing businesses would have more success by cooperating. Sharing technology would spur the collective expansion. Sharing would produce more business possibilities than any could service. The purpose of life is to expand. By supporting expansion, we support life. To prevent the expansion of someone is to kill. Someone's expansion does not come at anyone's expense. Anyone opposing expansion is opposing life and is opposing themselves.

A fair price exists for all goods and services. Paying too little is just as inappropriate as paying too much. Both are inappropriate. By giving justice, we will receive justice. In all exchanges, we are all really exchanging love, even though it may appear we are exchanging money for goods or services. What's really happening is we are exchanging friendship, trust, and values building justice. Without justice, there is no trust. Without trust, there is no civilization.

By treating everyone justly, we're not putting ourselves at a disadvantage. We are opening our special advantages. To utilize these advantages, we must seek fairness. Would we rather work for and buy from a company who was open and friendly or one who was nasty to both workers and clients?

A panacea we believe in is money will cure any problem. Just throw enough money at it and the problem is gone. Money and our financial institutions have been overwhelmed by problems based on this belief. We seek answers where we think there will be answers. There are no panaceas in life, and money is not the solution to all our problems.

In today's world, sharing has taken on a large corporation form. We believe helping people must be done through giving money to large organizations, or through government. This has deprived us of the simple act of sharing.

Everything is shared by advanced cultures. We are enriched by giving to others because we are giving to ourselves. Advanced cultures share everything equitably. In these cultures, it is possible only to share. Withholding is not possible. Their economies are not based on supply and demand. The system of supply and demand does not allow a win to be experienced by all.

Advanced cultures have nothing to compare to our ownership. To them, being in the presence of another is to be in the presence of God. So, who would withhold anything from God? Or another way to look at it, who would withhold what is God's from any part of God? Failure to follow this principle creates all the discord on Earth.

Those who practice moderation, the basis of the new economy, will inherit the world. The ideal practice of moderation will be in a spirit of abundance while sharing with love. Buy with money, service, or any other way, only what we love.

Solutions

Communism is a workable system if freedom is guaranteed. The versions used in Russia, China, and Cuba were flawed because freedom was greatly restricted.

Communism also failed because their adage, "To each according to his needs; from each according to his abilities," was applied to goods, services, and capital, when it should have been applied to safety, security, and daily sacred experience. They also had the problem of providing this in a large nation when it's easier to provide in a smaller community.

Capitalism and socialism both have good points. The trick is to combine the advantages while eliminating the disadvantages of each. The final combination will include the individual freedom and the responsibility people feel for themselves from capitalism with the recognition of the inherent worthiness of each person from socialism. This will combine individual freedom with caring for others. We will find when this happens we will want to contribute to society because it brings us joy and a meaningful life. Societies based on values of the heart share with each other. Such societies have more freedom, sharing, and connecting, and utilize smaller governments. Now we have laws to protect and regulate our societies, but eventually, each person will be self-regulating.

The words capitalism, socialism, and communism carry varying degrees of emotional baggage with them. Whatever system or combination of systems works the best, is the system we should use. Call it idealism to remove the emotional baggage. As Shakespeare said, "A rose by any other name would smell as sweet," or in this case, a workable economic system by any name would still work well. The solution is to find a system based on what works to lead us to our goals.

Everything we do, we do for ourselves. There is only One of us, so there is no one else to do it for.

Moderation and mobility make life work with freedom and growth and make use of the minimum structure necessary, i.e. institutions, corporations, or governments.

Moderation in all things is the way to live. Moderation in wealth, physical comforts, what we eat, mental activities, work, and recreation is the standard economy of heaven. Excess is to be avoided. Excess is excess if it is eating too much, accumulating too much wealth, working too much, suffering too much, receiving too much punishment, experiencing too much grief, controlling too much, or experiencing too many physical pleasures. An excess of personal denial leads to poverty. This is not ideal.

Sharing will take on new meaning when it is realized everything we share will be multiplied and is the basis of what we receive.

Excess and scarcity both illustrate a problem of understanding true ownership. Love is true ownership. Endless wealth is available when love is honored. Dishonoring love leads to scarcity. Spending rent money on trivial, compulsive, or fleeting things are dishonoring love.

When someone else's rights are respected, sharing occurs naturally when needed. Property has become a separating barrier because of lack of respect. Some have too much, and some have too little with no way to balance the differences. Respect, wisdom, and trust are needed.

Economics should be based on what is real. Governments, businesses, institutions, religions, and social constructions provide for the best economy when they are as simple as possible. Life should be spent on personal health and productive living. To decide what to discard and what to keep, use this test: what would happen if we eliminated or simplified this system. What works is the way to go. The transition from the complex structures of today to the simple of the future will require some time. The complex structures not supporting life will collapse first.

Real profit benefits everyone and should be sought whether it is material or spiritual. It is unworthy of guilt. It takes nothing from others. It produces new values, and energies for others. It lowers prices and inflation, invigorates workers, because of an increase of joy and morale. When leading a group for profit, the supervisor should provide direction and service to make the worker's job easier, and not for dominance. Real profit energizes and enriches the economy for everyone. There is never any extreme or widespread poverty. False profits are merely the moving of money around mostly to secure positions of power.

Expansion and compression are cyclical events for all things. When one is out of symmetry with the other, the health of the organism or institution will fail. The Roman Empire collapsed because its force-based economy was over-extended. In our migration to spiritually based systems, it is possible to succeed without major disruptions. But if major disruptions occur before the migration is complete, there will be an economic, political, and social collapse. Expansion should not be pursued to the exclusion of compression.

The experience we have had receiving and spending money has been great. Money is neither good nor bad. But judgments by society cast money as evil and filthy. This belief money is evil causes us to work at jobs we hate and do for free what we love. Our perverted ideas about money have caused all kinds of financial problems for us.

Spiritualistic capitalism is doing with love what we would do while serving the world and earning an income. When we live as One, the world economy will be built around the concepts of awareness, honesty, and responsibility. These concepts will guide all buying, trading, selling. Our economy reveals our spirituality.

The Universe lacks need. Need would only be needed for a certain outcome. The Universe requires no certain outcome. It is the outcome. Everything exists inside God. There is nothing outside of God. God is Everything. We have enough for everyone to be happy. We just must change our belief from separation to unity consciousness and our economy based on "every man for himself" to the "highest good for all."

We do have enough of everything we need to be happy. Unfortunately, we don't believe it. Because we believe there are shortages, we established the concept of ownership to ensure we get what we need and to keep it forever, so others can't have it. All this is for security reasons and to ensure our happiness. We are secure being immortal, and we don't need things to be happy because being Love, we are happiness itself.

Some of the major fallacies about life leading us away from peace are we are separate from each other, things needed for human happiness are limited, we must compete for this limited supply, some of us are better than others, and killing is appropriate to resolve differences. These fallacies have and continue to create a world of anger, violence, loss, sorrow, and terror. Our beliefs are the source of all of this. The solution is to change our beliefs. Other means such as political or economic will not solve these problems.

In our world of illusions, a gift appears to make the giver poorer by the gift given, and the receiver richer by the gift received. Insufficiency and limits are implied. In the world of finance, the gift, i.e. loan, is given with the expectation of receiving back more than given in the form of interest with the total gift plus interest paid in return. The receiver pays back more than received for the short-term loan. This kind of thinking permeates our world.

A true gift includes no loss. It's impossible for one to gain at the expense of another. A gift isn't given this way. True gifts never produce a loss, because it is creation, producing only increase. Giving and receiving are the same thing. Since we are all One, all our gifts are gifts to ourselves.

Greed leads to imagings of scarcity. Scarcity leads to fear. Fear leads to all negative emotions.

The healthiest economy has a lot of exchanging of goods and services. Fluid economies prevent structures from dominating. Free exchange prevents hunger, unemployment, and allows all worthy ideas to be productive.

The supply for every need is found within. Everyone must cooperate to produce a higher form of manifesting our desires.

We believe our abundance is the result of the production of goods and services, and if we don't produce goods and services, we will have scarcity. It's something to be earned. In reality, abundance appears after we believe in abundance. Our beliefs and ideas of abundance produce it in our experience. Our beliefs in shortages of everything perpetuates these conditions.

God created a world of abundance not requiring any work on our part. People who benefit from charity or welfare are resented for living on the work of others because of a belief in scarcity. When we believe in abundance, there will be no resentment. Gratitude for God's abundance permeated early civilization as exemplified by returning ten percent to God as a tithe. Charity and welfare are attempts to share.

Our belief in separation and disunity causes the experience of lack of abundance. The solution is to experience life and active unity with love and exhilaration.

Gratitude leads to abundance because it is not based on scarcity but on sharing. All systems based on scarcity, acquisition, hoarding, and greed must be eliminated.

Thousands starve each year, not because there is not enough food to feed everyone, but because we have not decided to prevent starvation.

The rich and powerful in the richest nations are now exploiting the poor in other nations because the rich can't do it in their own countries anymore. The owners of the mills in these other nations work with the governments of the poor to allow their employees to be abused by unfair labor practices. Government leaders have been killed for opposing this exploitation. This struggle between the rich and powerful and those much less fortunate will continue until the love of fellow man replaces the love of money.

Our socioeconomic system discriminates against groups of people such as women. We fear if all of us received the same amount of compensation, we would lose the incentive to work. This is not true. We would happily work to enjoy the feeling of accomplishment and creativity.

Advanced cultures have no understanding of work. Their daily activities are doing what they love to do. This is their highest expression of who they are. Menial labor doesn't exist. Those tasks required for a culture to exist are the most highly rewarded. This is self-fulfillment at its greatest. Words such as drudgery, overtime, pressure, and phrases such as getting ahead, rising to the top, and being successful have no meaning for them. Failure does not exist. For them achieving is doing what brings value. The goal is not fame and fortune. They value what produces a benefit for all. Our society honors and pays sports players and movie stars more than teachers and ministers. Advanced cultures do what works. They also have no poor and destitute. No one starves.

To do this, they apply the principles of We are all One, and there is enough. They have a deep understanding of the relatedness of everything. The natural resources are not destroyed or wasted, producing plenty for everyone.

We, on the other hand, have a strong belief in insufficiency. This belief is the source of all worry, all competition, all jealousy, all anger, all conflict, and all killing in our world.

We believe there is not enough of love, money, food, clothing, shelter, time, good ideas, us, or anything. Because we believe this, we do what we think we need to do to get what we think we need. One moment in the Spirit World and we will know there is enough of everything. God never says no.

90% of the entire world's misery is caused by the belief in insufficiency and the belief in separation. Think of it! Just by changing our beliefs to there is enough for everyone, and we are all One, we could reduce the world's misery by 90%.

To get started, we could act as if we were all One. Think of everyone we meet as us having a different experience. Then we could act as if there was enough for everyone and enough of everything. We would not have to worry about anything, and we could share what we have with the world. We have everything.

First, know God, and then all our desires will be abundantly supplied.

Compassion can be used as an instrument for power and control. Helping someone in need through compassion is a loving thing to do. Continually helping someone to make them dependent on us is unloving. It's a power and control action. It deprives the needy of the power to re-create their lives. It makes them dysfunctional, and the relationship with them dysfunctional.

Beware we don't fall into the trap of constantly trying to supply the needs of others. This leads to resentment on both sides. If we fall into the illusion of anyone being needy, and then try to supply all their needs, we deprive them of the power to supply their own needs.

All of us will experience lack at some time. It may start as a desire for wholeness and completion leading to a search for growth and experience. Poverty may be experienced as a deficiency of material goods, love, safety, or emotional well-being. Poverty may be experienced as any deficiency. Poverty is usually experienced as a lack of physical materials plus a feeling of being unrecognized, unappreciated, deserted, and ignored. Poverty truly wounds the soul. It will be abolished when we all realize enough is truly enough. Poverty is not punishment. Poverty is relative. The poor in a rich country are richer than the poor in a poor country. What we think determines if we experience abundance or lack. If we have feelings of gratitude and fulfillment, we experience abundance no matter how poor we are. Poverty or wealth is an inner state of mind. If we have feelings of gratitude and fulfillment, we experience abundance no matter how poor we are.

Helping the poor is not just about aiding them with the necessities of life, but more importantly about helping them develop a deep sense of empowerment and self-esteem. The poor have to overcome poverty consciousness. Continually giving them food will only make them dependent on the handout.

The first step to helping the poor is to help them believe they can rise above poverty. This involves believing in themselves. Someone who has faith and trust in themselves to rise above poverty physically, psychologically, and spiritually can provide a living example of how it's done.

Healing our poverty consciousness can be done by reminding ourselves we have inner worth, and we are all inherently equal. We are by nature kind, pure, and worthy. We are light and love. Knowing we are Divine frees us from any social label. Each of us has incomparable value. Social strata are artificial constructs having no meaning in ultimate reality. We are all Divine Souls connected to God. The best help we can give to those dwelling in poverty is to let them know they are powerful spiritual beings capable of doing anything. This knowledge will empower them to create miracles and attract changes and opportunities transforming their lives.

Beliefs about being undeserving of abundance produce poverty, while our society instills in us a sense of undeserving. We raise our children to follow our model of decorum and to repress and doubt their own emotions. Religions teach us we are undeserving, we should mistrust our emotions, and disbelieve the Universe was created for our benefit. But we are more than deserving. We need to change our beliefs from undeserving to deserving. God loves us with unconditional love, and we are innocent and beautiful just as we are. The Universe was meant to provide for us an abundant and joyful life. Only we can prevent an abundant and joyful life from happening.

The first step is to recognize we have beliefs of unworthiness. Some are obvious, such as religious dogma, but others not so much. These are just beliefs, and we can change them. We can believe we are worthy of all good things.

The second step is to rid ourselves of these false ideas, from the mind, and from our emotions and feelings. Dealing with emotional habits is difficult and will take some time.

As we change ourselves, society will change producing a world where we respect ourselves and others. What we believe creates the world we experience. If we're experiencing poverty, we can change our beliefs to experience abundance. Transforming our experience from poverty and the feeling of powerlessness to the experience of abundance also produces a feeling of how powerful we really are.

When we face an economic crisis, we must act together, and cooperate globally, to solve the crisis. The solution is about getting back to basics and recognizing what really matters. We are aware things must change. Part of the solution is about living simpler, moving away from the image of wealth and status, and projecting honestly who we are and engaging in activities we love to do. Another part of the solution is recognizing our divine nature and our unity with all living things. We must break with current society limitations and express our heartfelt longings and visions. We are Divine Beings and we can change the world for the better and avert disaster. We must walk our own path, believing in ourselves, and contribute to the transformation of the world in our own unique way.

When we feel our divinity, we will experience abundance. We may or may not have many material things. Possessing many material things is not necessary to experience abundance. We will have our emotional and physical needs provided for, and surround ourselves with beauty. We will create our soul's desires, providing us with more than any material thing can.

The world is the way it is because we want it to be this way. If we wanted to change it to something else, the world would change to what we desired. Whatever humanity has inflicted on humanity, humanity can undo.

Our monetary system is not necessary. We have created the system, and we have decided what is valuable. We have decided certain pieces of paper are worth $1 while others are worth $100. We have decided certain pieces of metal are worth one cent and others are worth $1. Instead of bartering to get what we want, we have devised a system where money is used as an intermediator to pay for goods and services.

At some future time, we will decide love, i.e. light energy, is the most valuable substance, a material we all have equally, in unlimited amounts. Instead of using currency, credit cards, debit cards, or other means of payment in exchange for goods and services, payment will be made immediately with love because the constant flow of energy feels so good.

In the business world, as well as our personal lives, granting others the freedom to change what they promised, prevents danger, and grants the business freedom. Currently, our society is based on force, the force of law, and at extremes, armed force. Our cultural ethic makes this mandatory. If we changed our cultural ethic to the understanding we are all One, it would no longer be necessary. Hurting part of ourselves, hurts us all, and using force hurts someone.

With the new ethic, agreements would change. Being unable to give something of value in exchange for something else of value would not be required. Giving and sharing would not be withheld because a just return could not be provided. Giving and sharing would be automatic. Today's contracts are about exchanging goods and services for monetary compensation. The new ethic would be about giving goods and services regardless of whether an exchange takes place. When we see ourselves as One, we realize when we give to another, we give to ourselves. And the receiving is multiplied seven times. The highest quality giving produces the highest quality getting. The more we cause others to amass, the more we will amass, without effort, without contracts, without agreements, without bargaining, without negotiating, and without the force of courts and lawsuits.

To produce a world where the basic needs of everyone would be provided for and opportunities for advancement would be available to all, two shifts should occur. First, a unified world government would be created based on the model of the USA government with three branches of government: executive, legislative, and judicial. The judicial branch would resolve international disputes, and the executive branch would have control of peacekeeping forces to enforce the laws enacted by a representative legislative branch. The legislative branch would be composed of two chambers: one with two representatives from each nation, and one with the number of representatives from each nation in proportion to the nation's population. All the nation's militaries would be disbanded, but each nation would be allowed to maintain a peacekeeping police force. The world government would maintain and control the world's military forces for keeping the peace. Each nation would have the right to call up its own militia and have the right to secede from the world government by a vote of its people.

The second shift would be a spiritual change.

These shifts would produce a peaceful resolution to all disputes, end poverty, starvation, and mass exploitation of people and resources, stop the destruction of the Earth, end the need for bigger, better, and more, provide an equal opportunity for all to reach their highest expression of themselves, and end limitation and discrimination. The redistribution of wealth would not be required, but the redistribution of resources would voluntarily occur. The world's resources belong to everyone, not just the rich and powerful. Everyone would receive a proper education with an open opportunity to apply the education in a field they enjoy. Healthcare would be guaranteed to all as needed. Adequate shelter, clothing, and food would be guaranteed. Basic needs would be provided guaranteeing basic dignities. Unconditional love would guarantee all of this.

The open market would decide the amount of compensation each earns for their endeavors. There would be a minimum wage. Everyone would have equal opportunity to develop themselves. This would produce some who are richer than others, but all would be enriched through the joy of doing what they love. But the amount that could be earned would be limited. The gap between rich and poor is inordinate and creates much suffering, world instability, and disharmony. This has been a problem down through time. A spiritual and practical solution leading to a worldwide attitude to solve this problem is required. To prevent a huge gap forming between the super-rich and the poorest on Earth, there would be an upper limit placed on income. The arbitrary upper limit would be agreed to by everyone. Anything earned above this figure would be donated to the world charitable trust in the donor's name. Everyone would know who the donors are. Donors would have a say in how sixty percent of the money is used. The other forty percent would be used in legislated programs by the world federation. Each person will donate ten percent of their income to the government. Initially, it would be in the form of a tax till the shift in consciousness takes place and taxes would turn to donations.

The elimination of the mass production of weapons of war would be enough to supply the basic needs of the world. The ten percent donation would elevate the entire world's population to new levels of dignity and abundance. The contributions from earnings above the established ceiling on earnings would end jealousy and social anger and the whole system would produce unheard of opportunities and satisfaction of the world's population.

This upper limit on income would be an indication of the shift of consciousness of the people of the world showing the need to accumulate great wealth, and the accumulation of things are no longer their understanding of the highest purpose of life. It also reflects the understanding the concentration of wealth is the largest single factor producing the most persistent social, and political problems in the world.

In general, the wealthiest people try to increase their wealth and power by restricting the opportunities of others. They do this through unfair labor practices, exploiting the world's poor, controlling public policy, and government programs to ensure the vast majority of the world's population remain regulated, controlled, and submissive. This is accomplished through social systems, and institutions the rich have created. And the rich resist any efforts to change these structures. Any economic and political effort to provide true opportunity that provides genuine dignity to everyone is staunchly resisted. The rich would keep the world's population poor and powerless, preventing them from impacting the system.

People are not open about money. A person's wealth and financial dealings are considered private matters. Transparency is lacking in the way we handle money. Openness and transparency of all money transactions of everyone would transform the world and produce fairness, honesty, and the goal of producing the best for the collective.

It is possible to hide money and use it without others knowing how much money is involved or how it is used. This produces inequalities. For example, two people could be paid different amounts for doing the exact same job. This is economic discrimination.

A solution is to publish the exact compensation each worker receives. Going further, publish the amount of money each person and company receives, holds, and how each uses its money. This would produce a revolution! The world population would demand the end to the extraordinarily disproportionate distribution of wealth, and how it is gained.

Transparency produces appropriate behavior. Sunshine Laws are an example of this in action. One way to do this would be to eliminate all currency throughout the world, both paper and metal. Replace it with a new totally transparent monetary system. All transactions would be visible, traceable, and accountable. The new system would give credits for goods and services produced, and debits for goods and services used. All transactions would be covered including interest earned, wages and salaries, tips, lottery winnings, inheritances, and gifts. Credits would be needed to buy anything. This would be the only currency. All records would be open to everyone. Each would know more about everyone and everything. Consumers would know the costs to corporations to produce products and their price. Imagine a price tag including the cost of production along with the price for the product. This would produce more competition, reduced prices, and increase fair trade.

All records for each person, government or business would be open to inspection at any time. There would be no secrets or private matters.

Each person could voluntarily donate ten percent of their income to the government each year; no income taxes to pay or complicated forms to fill out. But everyone would know who is donating their ten percent and who is not. It would be simple and very visible. It would eliminate corruption, unfairness, and inequities.

Because our current system is based on maneuvering to get the best advantage in every situation and the advancement of those best able to do this, the world would never agree to this. Suppressing transparency is diametrically opposite to a society where the goal is the survival, benefit, equality and good life of the collective, and a totally visible society.

In the past, "primitive" societies enjoyed cradle-to-grave security. These societies cared for themselves by caring for each individual. They shared all the food, and if one of the members was sick, it concerned everyone. Wealth was measured in terms of security. The sharing made money unnecessary, and hoarding was unthinkable. Each member took responsibility for everyone.

Nations have been founded on great principles. But when these principles are used to manipulate large populations, it is time for a change. The change may be painful or graceful. The American Revolution is an example of a painful change.

We are now at a point in time when changes of gigantic proportions will occur. To survive these changes, favor life, love, personal integrity, and community. Earth changes will shift populations. The displacement of huge numbers of people will lead to changes in economic systems.

Sacred scriptures have this to say:

"Contentedness [is] the best [of] riches" (Dhammapada 204).

"He who is satisfied with his lot is rich" (Tao Te Ching 33).

"And God said, Behold, I have given you every herb bearing seed, which is upon the face of all the earth, and every tree, in the which is the fruit of a tree yielding seed; to you it shall be for meat. And to every beast of the earth, and to every fowl of the air, and to every thing that creepeth upon the earth, wherein there is life, I have given every green herb for meat: and it was so" (Genesis 1:29-30). God provides abundance.

"For all the earth is mine [God's]" (Exodus 19:5).

"If thou lend money to any of my people that is poor by thee, thou shalt not be to him as an usurer, neither shalt thou lay upon him usury" (Exodus 22:25). Usury is loaning money at high-interest rates.

"And when ye reap the harvest of your land, thou shalt not wholly reap the corers of the field, neither shalt thou gather the gleanings of thy harvest. And thou shalt not glean thy vineyard, neither shalt thou gather every grape of thy vineyard; thou shalt leave them for the poor and stranger: I am the Lord your God" (Leviticus 19:9-10). This is charity in another time.

"And the LORD spake unto Moses in mount Sinai, saying, Speak unto the children of Israel, and say unto them, When ye come into the land which I give you, then shall the land keep a sabbath unto the LORD. Six years thou shalt sow thy field, and six years thou shalt prune thy vineyard, and gather in the fruit thereof; But in the seventh year shall be a sabbath of rest unto the land, a sabbath for the LORD: thou shalt neither sow thy field, nor prune thy vineyard. That which groweth of its own accord of thy harvest thou shalt not reap, neither gather the grapes of thy vine undressed: for it is a year of rest unto the land. And the sabbath of the land shall be meat for you; for thee, and for thy servant, and for thy maid, and for thy hired servant, and for thy stranger that sojourneth with thee, And for thy cattle, and for the beast that are in thy land, shall all the increase thereof be meat" (Leviticus 25:1-7). Not only does this practice make the land more productive in the long run, but it instills the idea of abundance.

"In the year of this jubile ye shall return every man unto his possession" (Leviticus 25:13). Every fifty years was a year of jubilee where any land sold was to be returned to the family of the original owner. This is one solution three thousand years ago for the problem of wealth being concentrated in the hands of fewer and fewer people over time.

"If there be among you a poor man of one of thy brethren within any of thy gates in thy land which the LORD thy God giveth thee, thou shalt not harden thine heart, nor shut thine hand from thy poor brother: But thou shalt open thine hand wide unto him, and shalt surely lend him sufficient for his need, in that which he wanteth" (Deuteronomy 15:7-8).

"For the poor shall never cease out of the land: therefore I command thee, saying, Thou shalt open thine hand wide unto thy brother, to thy poor, and to thy needy, in thy land" (Deuteronomy 15:11).

"When thou cuttest down thine harvest in thy field, and hast forgot a sheaf in the fielde, thou shalt not go again to fetch it; it shall be for the stranger, for the fatherless, and for the widow: that the Lord thy God may bless thee in all the work of thine hands When thou beatest thine olive tree, thou shalt not go over the boughs again: it shall be for the stranger, for the fatherless, and for the widow. When thou gatherest the grapes of thy vineyard, thou shalt not glean it afterward: it shall be for the stranger, for the fatherless, and for the widow" (Deuteronomy 24:19-21).

"Honour the LORD with thy substance, and with the firstfruits of all thine increase: So shall thy barns be filled with plenty, and thy presses shall burst out with new wine" (Proverbs 3:9-10). This instills the idea of abundance.

"Moreover the profit of the earth is for all" (Ecclesiastes 5:9). This is sharing.

"He that loveth silver shall not be satisfied with silver; nor he that loveth abundance with increase" (Ecclesiastes 5:10). This is lack of satisfaction with material wealth.

"Therefore all things whatsoever ye would that men should do to you, do ye even so to them: for this is the law and the prophets" (Matthew 7:12).

"Who then is a faithful and wise servant, whom his lord hath made ruler over his household, to give them meat in due season? Blessed is that servant, whom his lord when he cometh shall find so doing" (Matthew 24:45-46). Blessed are the faithful stewards in caring for the resources entrusted into their hands.

"And the Lord said, Who then is that faithful and wise steward, whom his lord shall make ruler over his household, to give them their portion of meat in due season" (Luke 12:42)?

"When they were filled, he said unto his disciples, Gather up the fragments that remain, that nothing be lost" (John 6:12). This demonstrates conservation and abundance.

"For the earth is the Lord's, and the fulness thereof" (1 Corinthians 10:26).

"God will bring usury to nought" (Sura 2:277).

"And the good that ye shall give in alms shall redound unto yourselves; and ye shall not give but as seeking the face of God; and whatever good thing ye shall have given in alms, shall be repaid you, and ye shall not be wronged. There are among you the poor, who being shut up to fighting for the cause of God, have it not in their power to strike out into the earth for riches. Those who know them not, think them rich because of their modesty. By this their token thou shalt know them–they ask not of men with importunity: and of whatever good thing ye shall give them in alms, of a truth God will take knowledge" (Sura 2:274).

"Be good to parents, and to kindred, and to orphans, and to the poor, and to a neighbour, whether kinsman or new-comer, and to a fellow traveller, and to the wayfarer, and to the slaves whom your right hands hold" (Sura 4:40).

"And to him who is of kin render his due, and also to the poor and to the wayfarer; yet waste not wastefully" (Sura 17:28).

"To him who is of kin to thee give his due, and to the poor and to the wayfarer: this will be best for those who seek the face of God; and with them it shall be well" (Sura 30:37).

Summary

In a United Nations University study from 2006, 1% of the world's population owned 40% of the world's wealth. In the same study, 10% of the world's population owned 85% of the world's assets. This inequality must be addressed.

Our world is one of interdependence. We do indeed depend on each other. A calamity in one part of the world affects us all.

We are all responsible for our neighbors. What we fail to do for our neighbors, we fail to do for ourselves. Giving should be a way of life. Giving and receiving are the same. What we give to others, we give to ourselves, and the gift is multiplied when we get it back. The new economic system to replace our current system will involve a change of belief and attitude. An improved attitude would include moderation in all things including income and contentedness with income and possessions. The world was set up for our benefit and to provide abundance, so we are all deserving. We must believe abundance is available for us all, and we deserve all blessings. Love should be the basis of everything. Give in love. Love everyone. Love ourselves. Be the Love we are.

A new economic system must improve our quality of life and reflect our unity. It must be based on abundance. There should be a guaranteed minimum income for everyone and an absolute maximum income any person can acquire. A new fair tax structure is needed. Everyone should be guaranteed enough food and clothing, adequate shelter, healthcare, education, and an opportunity to excel. The system should empower the poor, not make them dependent on the system, but enable them to leave the ranks of the poor. Those living in poverty must change the way they see themselves. They must see advancement as possible for them and deserved. The system should be open and transparent. All the resources of the Earth should be shared by all. The system should be simple and based on what works. Cycles of expansion and contraction are normal and should be anticipated. Prices should be fair, not too low or too high. The price of production should be listed on the price tag along with the price. All this will require change, and time for the change to take place, but eventually, we will get there.

Education and Raising Our Young

The most important thing we can do as a society is to raise and educate our children properly. 'Abdu'l-Baha said the greatest service to God is to educate our children. The education of our children is indispensable and obligatory.

Everyone should be provided with a good education. Ignorance moves civilization backward and encourages prejudice. Some nations lack the resources to provide an education for all its citizens now. It is recommended women and girls be educated first in this situation because mothers will transfer the information the fastest. World citizenship should be a part of every child's education.

In the past and present, education has been used to indoctrinate children with fables about our past and how life works. The system has been used to prevent change and the introduction of new ideas. Few educational systems teach the students how to think and reason for themselves, and to decide what is true and correct for themselves. Today the errors of one generation are passed on to the next this way. Our children are imprinted with copies of our beliefs whether the beliefs are true or not. We deny the horrible treatment of our young.

Present educational systems, both in schools and at home, pass down the errors of the past to the present crop of students so they can pass the errors down to their children.

A proper educational system can save us from ourselves. It can cut the passage of prejudices, and preconceived ideas from parent to child. Because of today's educational systems, we can't solve conflicts without violence, live without fear, act unselfishly, and love unconditionally. We've failed after thousands of years of trying. But we've successfully taught our children to be martyrs by blowing themselves to pieces to kill others. We've successfully passed our prejudices to our children. Certainly, if we choose to do so, we can teach them to love unconditionally.

We have believed in the panacea of education. This belief has drawn all kinds of problems to education absent earlier. When we call something a panacea; we think it can solve all our problems. Because of this, we have ineffectively applied education as a solution for problems requiring other solutions. Education can do great things for our society, but it's not a panacea.

Otterbein Dressler said in his book, *Parking on the Other Fellow's Nickel,* fear of passing a grade or test should not be part of education, and education should lead the student to learn.

Our educational systems demonstrate our spirituality and should stimulate interest and joy in learning. Education should involve creativity, and originality while fostering a desire to conquer adversity and improve the self. Making a game of education and using humor will improve learning. Students should not be graded, but feedback on the student's progress in an attempt to motivate to higher performance is important. They work best when they want to learn. They should be allowed time to decide what to learn.

Above all else, we should teach our children they are each unique, with each having a marvelous body. Each child has the potential to become a wonder of science, literature, art, or music. They have unlimited potential. If we teach our children this way, when they become adults, it will be inconceivable to them to injure another uniquely marvelous being.

Our world problems exist because we have not allowed our schools to teach unconditional love and that Love is all there is.

Our children haven't been told they are spiritual beings using bodies to navigate this world, nor do we treat them as such.

It is not possible to raise children to live peaceful lives by allowing them to watch depictions full of rage and violence through TV programs or video games.

The time is coming when we will see each baby as wanted and as a benefit for us all. Each new child will be told and shown they are wanted, appreciated, valued, and loved. Their education will be a shared process for we will learn from each other. They are masters just as we are. The educational system of the future will be based on love and worth. It will be a sharing as among equals.

Teaching is a constant activity occurring all the time. The teacher and the learners are one and the same. All teaching is learning. An example for teachers to follow is to maintain a professional distance from their students to allow them space to freely express themselves among other students. It's best for teachers not to be hovering over their students all the time.

In the future, children will be taught they are not their bodies, and time is an illusion. They will be aware of the wisdom of older citizens.

Critical Thinking

Education is not the passing on of the accumulated knowledge of our society. Wisdom as knowledge applied is what education is all about. Children should be taught how to think, not what to think. They should be taught how to arrive at their own truth. Knowledge should be used as a tool to teach thinking. Knowledge can be forgotten, but wisdom never is.

Today, the major emphasis of education is on knowledge with little on critical thinking, problem-solving, and logic. Society fears the changes a new generation of skillful thinkers will bring, even though many of the "facts" taught today are fiction. The child should be allowed to arrive at its own truths. Our history books teach our children to see the world as we would like them to see it, from our point of view, biased at best, and outright lies at worst. History is written by the group in charge, with other groups such as women, blacks, and other minorities left in a less favorable light. History is written to justify what happened not to tell what really happened.

Programs developing abilities and skills in children are treated as less important than knowledge by today's society. Abilities and skills are more important.

Where children are taught critical thinking and problem-solving skills instead of memorized facts, past actions, even if justified, are carefully examined. Face value is not accepted.

Teachers, where critical thinking is important, explain all the facts surrounding an event. The views of historians on all sides would be examined. All points of view are considered. The students would be asked to examine all points of view and draw conclusions about the event. How would they solve similar problems? Is there a better way?

Today's societies fear such an education would have their children doing what they did differently thus making them wrong.

One of our responsibilities is to filter all violence and war from our societies' beliefs and pass only the positive parts on to our children. This starts with removing all thoughts and feelings of violence from ourselves. One thing everyone can do is to remove all horror, violence, and hatred from the TV programs, videos, movies, computer games, and other sources children are exposed to. In general, TV is not a useful tool for raising children. We must carefully select only the best material to fill the minds of our children. Even our conversations with our children should be the finest possible to nurture their inner feelings of love and peace.

If we want to stop our children from growing up killing each other, we must spend quality time with them by becoming involved with them, their teachers, and their friends. We must show with our lives our stand for peace. We must insist movie makers, TV producers, video game companies, and all other image venues create non-violent stories. Images do teach and influence our children. We must insist all things used for violence are unavailable to our children, and all violence is eliminated from our lives. This is most important because our children will imitate us.

When correcting a child, spanking a child for hurting another child only teaches the child violence is the way those in control correct problems. Criticizing and punishing will not alter their behavior, but it will lower self-esteem. It can stop the behavior at times, but it is not the ultimate solution. There are many ways to alter unwanted behavior including allowing the child to experience the consequences of their behavior and explaining how the child can be helpful.

Certainly, we can think of ways other than startling them, scaring them, or hurting them to instruct them. Throughout our history, we have used physical pain as a punishment for children and adults. We kill people to stop people from killing people. The actions we model will influence our children to follow in our footsteps. If we demonstrate violence, so will our children.

Education has made it difficult to have a peaceful world and especially schools associated with religions. They teach a limited view of the world, limiting the intellectual development of the students, and are basically used to indoctrinate children.

Creativity and Core Concepts

Memorization is used in most schools to duplicate the lives of the parents in lives of the children. Then the children will have the same knowledge base, understandings, beliefs, and thoughts, and act as their parents.

Education should focus on creation, not duplication. It should teach children how to experience Everything as One and Themselves as the Creator, Source, and Authority of their lives. This kind of education would awaken, free, expand, and release the students' minds to experience Everything as One.

In the early years of education, students will learn the core concepts of unity with everything, no one can make a mistake or fail at anything because it's impossible, all creations are perfect just as they are, creating is their purpose in life, there are consequences to their actions, help and love others without harming them, there is enough of everything to make everyone happy, and life is eternal with no judgement, condemnation, or punishment ever.

Students will learn to create their experiences in life by thinking, saying, and doing them into existence. Life is our greatest teacher. We evolve by the choices we make.

Learning facts is not important in education. Learning to read, to write, and to do mathematics is only necessary to learn other more important concepts such as reconciliation, recreation, and reunification. Students will be awed by life by increasing their sensitivity, awareness, understanding, compassion, acceptance, celebration, and appreciation of life. Reading, writing, and mathematics will be taught as tools to create the grandest vision we ever had about who we are. Children will be highly motivated to master these tools when they experience the joy and fun of creating.

Educations foundation should be to teach how to create a new world with new definitions about who we are as individuals, societies, and citizens of the Earth.

Today students don't understand the relevance of what they are being taught and consequently resist what schools are trying to teach. Children learn fastest when they understand the reason for learning something. Schools must get students to see everything is connected to life and must supply the why of learning first to motivate students to learn. The trick is to use something of interest to the student to teach the tools of life. A good way to do this is to ask what the student wants to learn today. If a student is interested in cats, reading would be a good place to start to find out more about cats. Later the student could write a story about cats and use numbers to keep track of all the cats and figure out the costs of buying cats. Core values, such as we are all One, would also be incorporated into the lesson. Facts, concepts, and formulas would be used to reach some goal desired by the student. The imagination of the teacher is very important.

Learning unorthodox abilities not taught in today's schools such as psychic abilities, manifestation abilities, and meditation will happen in the future. Psychic abilities are abilities we all have and learning to develop them is just as natural as learning to develop our physical abilities to compete in sports.

The process of teaching should be about getting wisdom out of a student, not put wisdom into a student. The teacher need not know the wisdom, just how to extract it from the student. It all involves creating a learning environment. Buildings are not necessary. In fact, the whole process would be better without our traditional schools.

Learning centers, on the internet and elsewhere, based on the interests of the students should replace schools. Students of all ages, all genders, all races, and all cultures or backgrounds will participate in learning. The synergy of the diversity will stimulate learning at unbelievable rates. A unique and personalized learning experience will be provided to each student.

Education of our young should start by:
1. Treating them as the spirits they are, who are using a body to live in this world. Supply each child with a sense of unlimitedness.
2. Introducing them to the world gently and carefully. Spanking at birth is unnecessary. Separation from the mother immediately after birth is callous. Images of violence should be replaced with images of love for newborns. Be careful what newborns are allowed to experience because they remember everything.
3. Teaching children they have nothing to be ashamed or embarrassed about their bodies and bodily functions. Allow children to explore and pleasure their bodies.
4. Allowing children to progress through the educational process at their own rate. Allow no competition, and reward none as best. Performance should not be graded.
5. Teaching the joy of dance, music, and art. The mysteries of fairy tales and wonders of life should be covered.
6. Teaching logic, critical thinking, problem-solving, and creation using school facilities and the students' deepest inner knowing. Present methods of

memorizing societies' rules and conclusions have demonstrated they have prevented the evolution the world's population.

7. Teaching the core concepts of awareness, honesty, and responsibility. Reading, writing, and mathematics would revolve around these concepts. They would be embedded in the reading material, would be part of writing exercises, and would be part of math problems. Computational skills are the basic tools for life. True wisdom knows how to reason and understand what exists and what works.

In advanced societies, the desired behavior is modeled by adults. It's do as I say and as I do. Awareness, honesty, and responsibility are modeled by all adults and easily acquired by children. During learning time children get to decide what they want to learn, and when they want to learn it. Motivation is thus at its highest.

For humanity to make great strides in our evolution, we must teach our children certain life principles. This isn't about academic subjects, it's about the core concepts of awareness, honesty, and responsibility. Included in these core concepts are transparency, sharing, freedom, unlimited self-expression, the joyful celebration of sex, the bonding of humans, and our diversity while being One.

A world auxiliary language known by everyone would help facilitate communications among the various parts of the world. World citizenship and the Oneness of humanity should be a part of everyone's education. Teaching these principles will prepare the world for the changes required for peace.

Now schools provide answers. It would be better if they asked questions. What are the meaning and the implications of being honest for example? Children should be encouraged to discover and create these answers for themselves.

Information about past discoveries, observations, decisions, and choices should be presented as information, and not as correct information. Students should be allowed to decide for themselves what is true and correct. Everything from the past should be questioned. What does the student think about past information?

Students from earliest ages should be encouraged to examine, explore, apply, functionalize, and question past values. The goal is instilling wisdom, the ability to reason given any set of data, and skill development. The new curriculum will be based on this.

Teaching Principles

Here are some principles for educating our children:
1. We need nothing exterior to ourselves to be happy. No person, place, or thing is needed. Happiness is found within and we are sufficient unto ourselves.
2. No one ever fails. Each attempt is a success. Success is achieved by our every attempt. All attempts are worthwhile.
3. We are One with all things, people, and God.
4. Our world is full of abundance. There is plenty for everyone. When we share the most, we receive the most. Gathering the most is counterproductive.
5. God blesses everyone alike. No one needs to compete with anyone to have anything or to have a dignified and satisfied life.
6. No one will be judged by God. Everyone is perfect in the eyes of God. There is no need to get things right, improve performance, or change anything to impress God.
7. Consequences and punishment are two different things. We will experience the consequences of our actions but will never be punished for anything we do. There is no death. God condemns no one.
8. The greatest gift anyone can give is unconditional love. Love has no conditions. Tell all children they will never lose our love or God's love for them.
9. All children are special, but none are superior to another. Anyone claiming superiority over another lacks an understanding of who the other person is. A

person who acknowledges their path is not a better way, just another way is a great healer.
10. Children can do anything. Ignorance is an illusion and the illusion can be eliminated. The only need anyone has is to be shown Who They Are.
11. We must teach our children these things by the way we live our lives. Our children will emulate our actions.

We can restore respect for life by teaching our children the Universe is a Living System, and our Earth is alive, and we are all part of this System. Our children should be taught we are all One with each other and One with God. Children taught this will, as adults, revere life to hold it as the most important value. They will see life everywhere from one end of the Universe to the other.

We should frame our instruction with words like "Until now," or "Up to this point, our society has believed." For example, in science, the teacher could say, "Up to this point our scientists believe the fastest anyone can travel is the speed of light." Present knowledge should be tentative in nature allowing for the possibility of change. Down through history, our knowledge has changed as we got more accurate information, and so it will continue. In fact, the speed of light is not a limit.

Teaching today is difficult because our textbooks are full of distortions, and incomplete and untrue information. The information presented in classrooms should be presented as present-day understandings, and not the final truth. Students should be encouraged to dig deeper and listen to their inner understandings of what is so. Teachers should allow the students to freely express new ideas. Discussions could be framed with asking the students, "What if there is additional information about a current understanding. What are some possibilities?"

Teachers can go within for help in teaching, and then model this for the students. This will guide anyone to the highest benefits, and greatest choices. The students will learn these quiet times are essential and will give them strength, certainty, and intuitive knowing. One challenge for teachers is to stay as up-to-date on current information as possible and be willing to accept new information and new perceptions, and the implications of these new understandings. This is a constant learning experience for teachers. In the field of science, there will be radical changes in our understandings. This is a huge, never-ending job.

Students should be allowed to feel safe to express any idea and to be ahead of the times. Openness should be encouraged. This is a learning opportunity for both student and teacher. Students may at times recount their psychic experiences, and this is to be encouraged. Social and educational beliefs should be allowed to change as clearer understandings emerge. Education is the extracting of truth from the student's inner source. Some of this information may be new undiscovered understandings going counter to present day "knowledge." Filling students with information from textbooks as we do today is much less productive because the textbooks contain inaccuracies. For some rudimentary subject this is acceptable, but not for most.

Mothers can start the educational process while the baby is still in the womb by talking to the baby about the purposes it wishes to convey to the world through its life. Fathers should likewise be involved because a balance of male and female principles is important to the development of any child. Both should foster a structure of love and curiosity in the child. Children can bring great satisfaction to a couple, but children are never property or a possession. Within the framework of spiritual responsibility and joyful love, provide unlimited opportunities for growth. Provide a caring attitude before and after birth. Be especially gentle in the beginning and later lovingly provide for the child's welfare. The parents may not always allow the child to do as it wishes if they truly love the child, and children must be taught to respect the rights of others.

Children must be taught their beliefs will impact their view of life and reality. They must know God is a loving spirit who does not make life difficult for us, and the choices we all make come to pass sooner or later. Our persistent negative thoughts produce all the difficulties we experience in life. When all children know this, it will be easier to have peace.

What we need now is trust, the cornerstone of love. Do not fear. We have nothing to fear, including fear itself. Love is more powerful than fear. Children should be taught to love and trust God, and judge no one including themselves. This is for our own safety because focused loving thoughts will overcome any problem. God is not some external being, but totally envelopes us, and lives within each of us. We can experience God, and our experience can be intuitive, very personal, and very profound. Children must be taught they are lovable, they are loved by God, and they are worthy of God's love. They totally control their will and attitude, and nothing else can, and God is constantly expressing through their lives. They can allow God to guide their experience in each moment of time. Teach our children they are free to create almost anything they choose.

All education must instill a sense of responsibility and love in the students for the world. Education must motivate the students to strive to improve the world and to impact humanity positively with their lives. All of society must be involved in this part of education. By our lives, we should be an example of love and kindness for our children. When our children are old enough we should meditate together. We and our children can do almost anything we set our minds to do. We can choose to consciously direct what we experience.

Our children should know God is everywhere, and we are all a part of the Creator, and we all form the mind of God on Earth. We are Love, just as God is Love, with our own mind and word to create. What we create produces our future.

Raising our children is a group effort. All facets of our society must be involved including the parents, relatives, teachers, school administrators, governments, and religions. Children must be taught loving responsibility with no threats of punishment. God's law is unconditional love, and all our actions should be based on love. Any action without love produces pain.

We must teach our children God does not punish. What we create or cause others to experience will return to us. This is the law of cause and effect. If we punish others, we will experience the punishment. If we send love into the lives of others, we will experience love. So, we should do unto others what we would like to experience.

Peace is the only necessary curriculum. One by one we must agree to choose and implement peace. We must become peace, teach peace, join for peace, and demand peace at the local level of government, the national level of government and the international level of government.

Each child comes here with a purpose, and our job as teachers is to assist each child in finding their purpose in life. Love and respect are our tools for this job, and we should guide them by using strong ethical principles such as compassion and care for all living creatures. Children must be prepared for their future as caregivers and stewards of Earth. They must be taught our interdependence with all of life, and these relationships must be respected and maintained. Our abuse of the Earth must be reversed. They must be prepared to meet similar appearing humans from elsewhere in our galaxy. Our ideas about other life forms in the Universe must change from fear to acceptance. The life forms depicted on *Star Trek* is a sampling of some of the life forms found in other parts of the Universe.

Teachers

Teachers of all kinds should elevate their own consciousness through meditation and the use of divine principles, so we can teach from an elevated level consciousness and wisdom. Teachers have a high calling and must be held to high standards. Only a violence-free person is qualified to teach.

Typically, in the past, parents were responsible for raising their children, a difficult job for anyone. In the future, each community will raise our children.

Young parents are not prepared to be parents, and they know it. They lack life experience being just parented themselves. They are still learning with unanswered questions. They don't know who they are and are still trying to define themselves while recovering from the blotched job their parents did. They are not able to help a new life discover who they are. These young parents then fail their children and themselves in trying to define themselves. The wisdom, patience, understanding, and love necessary to be great parents are gained after the parenting years have passed.

People who produce children should not raise children, because they are not mature enough to do it. Childbearing is best done by those with young strong bodies. Child raising is best done by those with well-developed and strong minds.

We have made the child bearers responsible for raising their children. This thought is so strong we say the children they produce are theirs as if they owned them. This automatically produces a problem with sex. The young are told not to engage in sex until they are ready for the responsibility of raising any children they may produce. This creates a taboo about one of life's greatest experiences, a taboo ignored by the young because it's unnatural. If a young couple produces a child, both parents may be put in a very stressful situation greatly impacting their future negatively. They will be expected to support the child and care for it. This may radically change future plans both may have had. When our elders are responsible for the raising of our children, this stress is removed, and the young couple can develop to their full potential.

It is natural to copulate as soon as the young feel the urge to do so. By age 15 the young are racing toward copulation with adults trying to stop it. Adults have used all manner of reasons to stop this natural process, causing the young to believe their own sexuality is unnatural.

Adults, because of their own training, think it is unnatural and can't use the correct terms for sexual body parts. Adults instill in children from little on up that sexual body parts are bad, dirty, and embarrassing. By the time the children become teenagers, they realize this is not correct. Then the teenagers are told about the possibility of pregnancy from sexual activity, and they get the feeling sexual activity is wrong. This creates all kinds of confusion and mayhem in our society. When we mess with anything natural we can expect this. Our society has produced sexual embarrassment, repression, and shame leading to sexual inhibition, dysfunction, and violence. In any society, embarrassment produces inhibition, repression produces dysfunction, and shame produces violence when everyone instinctively knows shame has no place in connection with sex.

We, humans, are totally conflicted. What is bad about something that feels so good? Eventually, when we realize sex is good, we have become angry with parents for repressing us, religions for shaming us, members of the opposite sex for daring us, and society at large for controlling us. Moreover, we become angry with ourselves for being inhibited by all of this.

This anger produces the monumental acts of violence seen in every area of our society from statues to movies. The most beautiful acts of love have also been cheapened by this anger. This is all the result of requiring anyone who has a child to raise it.

This is our idea of how things should work. But we could have a paradigm shift and make the whole community, especially the elders, responsible for raising our children. The elders could pass on to our children our wisdom, teachings, and traditions. In societies where producing offspring at a young age is allowed because the elders will raise the babies, sexual repression, rape, deviance, and dysfunction are missing.

In our society, children are thought of as property, personal possessions of the parents and therefore the parents are responsible to care for their possessions. This idea of ownership of spouses and children is the cause of many of society's problems.

Parents are not emotionally ready to raise their offspring. Even parents in their 30's and 40's are not mature enough to raise children and shouldn't be expected to do so. Up to at least age 50, people should be learning their truth. After age 50 they can begin to pass on their truth to our children. Then they will realize the truth is not a constant, but always change.

In the grand scheme of things, the elders, those over 50 with those over 60 being better equipped, were meant to raise children. They know about truth and life, and what is important and what is not, and what integrity, honesty, loyalty, friendship, and love mean. In the future with people living much longer than today, the elders will be around for a long time. Retiring at seventy will seem ridicules. All the wisdom, experience, and expertise should not be wasted.

The way this might work, children would be placed in the care of respected elders. Parents would visit and be with their children as much as they wished. They could live with them if they wanted to, but the responsibility for the care and raising of the children would stay with the elders. They would provide the education and values for the children. The entire community would provide the physical, social, and spiritual needs of the children.

This will not work now because of the way we have structured our society. Elders have been marginalized and pushed aside. They are resented, and their power has been removed. Elders are not allowed to contribute. They are forced to retire when they have the most to contribute. Elders have been removed from parenting, politics, economics, and religion. Our society favors the young.

Families have been split, and small communities have been disassembled in favor of big cities. In these big cities, there are fewer tribes, clans, or groups whose members will take responsibility for the good of the whole. Our society is a society of individuals instead of groups. Because we have individualized and focused on youth, we have lost much of our richness and resources. This has produced a society poor emotionally and psychologically and depleted of its resources.

The solution is to first realize this is a problem. We must learn to recognize what is so. We must learn to recognize the truth when we see it. Second, we must build community and extended families. Third, we must honor our elders and put them to work. It will take time to make these radical changes. We will have to proceed step by step till we make the changes.

In the future, the elders will supervise and organize the education of the children, in addition to overseeing the housing, feeding, and care for them. The elders will provide the children with understanding, patience, love, and wisdom. The future of the entire species is dependent on the proper raising of our children.

Children feel no shame or guilt until they are told they have done something shameful, or worthy of guilt. The more shame and guilt a society heaps upon its children, or anyone else, the more primitive it is.

Advanced cultures have no competition in sports, business, or elsewhere. If someone loses, everyone loses. Watching someone lose is not considered entertainment. In our societies, one advances at the expense of someone else.

We are entrusted with the care of the soul of each child born into the world. Even though the soul of each child is a powerful spiritual being, they enter the world as a vulnerable baby. Each baby needs our care and unconditional love to allow it to mature in this world feeling safe and welcome. All parents feel a deep sense of responsibility for their offspring regardless of their life circumstances. There are no accidents or coincidences. All events have meaning and were planned, even the entry of a child into the world.

For parents, the greatest punishment for their children is withholding love. Withholding love has been used to control and direct children's behaviors from the beginning of time. And they have told their children God withholds God's love. But true love never withholds itself.

The fastest way to lead children to maturity is to give them the opportunity to make as many decisions as possible as soon as possible. Love releases. Release children to make their own decisions. Let go of any expectations, requirements, rules, and regulations we may have for them. Restrictions indicate restricted love.

When providing freedom of choice, also provide all the information we have to assist them in making decisions to get them to where they want to go and live a happy life. Share our wisdom and information freely, but don't require them to follow our advice. Love them regardless of their choices. Love them especially if they make what we think are poor choices. Children, especially young children, are not always aware of danger. The freedom we grant them must be tempered by our knowledge of what is safe for them.

As teens grow into men and women, a primary goal of theirs is to project an image to impress others. Society can influence these teens to project an image not in alignment with the desires of the soul. This inner turmoil will eventually produce fear and depression. The solution is to get them to talk about their insecurities and fears and impress upon them they are more important than their accomplishments. Expressing their deepest darkest thoughts in the presence of non-judgment will set them free. Society can also help by allowing each individual the freedom to grow and develop into the individual their soul desires.

Tom Moore in his January 20, 2012 newsletter, *The Gentle Way News*, says old systems of education will be replaced with more natural ways. Education will concentrate on a student's interests and abilities and will become more individual. Groups of students will study together because of similar interests.

His July 21, 2012 newsletter says, the internet will be a big influence on education with students self-educating themselves through its use.

His December 13, 2014 newsletter says, students will be tested to determine their interests, and their education will be tailored to their interests. Skull caps will be used to download information into their brains, saving time. This will allow the students to spend more time on their interests.

Sacred texts have this to say about education:

"Love learning" (Confucius, Analects 8:13).

"Train up a child in the way he should go: and when he is old, he will not depart from it" (Proverbs 22:6).

"My son, attend to my words; incline thine ear unto my sayings. Let them not depart from thine eyes; keep them in the midst of thine heart. For they are life unto those that find them, and health to all their flesh. Keep thy heart with all diligence; for out of it are the issues of life" (Proverbs 4:20-23).

"And, ye fathers, provoke not your children to wrath: but bring them up in the nurture and admonition of the Lord" (Ephesians 6:4).

"If any of you lack wisdom, let him ask of God, that giveth to all men liberally, and upbraideth not; and it shall be given him" (James 1:5).

Summary

Raising and educating our children is the holiest, sacred, and important task our society has to do. It is a task our communities must do utilizing our older citizens as the directors of the process. This is a major social shift and it will take time to become implemented. We must first establish local communities to provide a framework for this, and then engage our elders to provide the service.

The elders would be responsible for caring, housing, feeding, educating, passing on our values, and for providing understanding, patience, wisdom, and unconditional love. Each child would be given the opportunity to receive all the education they wanted. Initially, in communities with limited resources, girls and women would be educated first. Education would be joyful and interesting.

Each child would be taught they are powerful spiritual beings with unlimited potential using a human body to navigate Earth, and they would be treated as equals with the teachers. Children would not be exposed to violence in any form, including books, video games, movies, TV, discipline, and the way the people live their lives who meet them. The whole purpose of education would be to teach them how to think and solve problems using logic, and critical thinking. Grading would not be a part of the process, although feedback would be collected to guide learning. The "why" of what they were being taught would be answered. They would be taught to create their lives in a new and unique way, and not just duplicate past lives.

In the early years of education, students will learn the core concepts of unity with everything, no mistakes or failure can happen because this is impossible, all creations are perfect just as they are, creating is their purpose in life, there are consequences to their actions, help and love others without harming them, there is enough of everything to make everyone happy, and life is eternal with no judgement, condemnation, or punishment ever. Other core concepts are awareness, honesty, and responsibility. Included in these core concepts are transparency, sharing, freedom, unlimited self-expression, the joyful celebration of sex, the bonding of humans, and our diversity while being One. Reading, writing, and arithmetic would be used to teach these. The joy of dance, music, art, fairy tales, and the wonders of life would also be taught. History and science would be taught as information, not as the truth. All of us would teach the young with the way we live our lives. The children would be made aware they are all citizens of the world, and to facilitate communication, all would be taught an auxiliary language in addition to their native language.

School buildings as we know them will not be necessary because of the use of the internet and other forms of communication. Students will set their own pace and choose what they want to study.

If we raise and educate our children properly, our world and everything in it will be transformed in unimaginable ways. All areas of society will be transformed, and life will evolve without limits. We will enjoy heaven here on Earth.

Earth and the Environment

Earth is a magnificent, very complex living "body", with wonderful purification systems. But we can and do overwhelm these systems. We are One with the Earth, spiritually, and our bodies are intimately connected to the Earth's ecosystems. If we poison the Earth, we poison our bodies. If we put poisons into the air, we will breathe them. If we put poisons in our water, we will drink them. If we put poisons on the soil, we will eat them. The poisons may be in small quantities and not produce instant death, but over time our health will suffer.

The Earth has many resources we all use. In protecting the Earth, it is counterproductive to stop using these resources. For us to live on the earth, each time we eat, something has to die, either a plant or animal, and we need many other resources for clothing and shelter. To explore the Universe, our destiny, we will need to use a variety of resources. To protect the Earth, we must use these resources wisely, and without any pollution. A big step forward will be when we discover unlimited supplies of energy not based on fossil fuels through future technology discoveries. This will greatly reduce our air pollution, as well as be an economic boon because the price of goods and services will be reduced by present-day energy costs. We must learn to love and appreciate our Mother Earth for the home She provides for us.

"They too who, delighting in the welfare of all nature, serve me [Krishna] in my incorruptible, ineffable, and invisible form;

all-pervading, and incomprehensible, dwelling on high, fixed and immovable, with subdued passions and mind, equal-minded to all around, shall also, come unto me" (Bhagavad Gita 12:2-3).

The Problem

Our impact on the Earth is huge. The FAO (Food and Agriculture Organization, a branch of United Nations) in 2011 estimated that the global loss of productive land through erosion is 12-17 million acres per year. The UN Environment Program in 2010 estimated 150 to 200 species of plants and animals become extinct each day, a rate 1,000 times the normal rate of the past. The FAO estimates in the decade prior to 2010, there was a net loss of 13 million acres of rainforest each year. The World Health Organization estimated 7,000,000 deaths were the result of air pollution in 2012. The Blacksmith Institute estimates 125,000,000 people are at risk from toxic chemicals in 2012. NASA (National Aeronautics and Space Administration) estimates trees and phytoplankton produce most of the oxygen produced today, both sources being negatively impacted by us humans.

We deny we are abusing our natural resources.

The passage in Genesis giving humans dominion over nature actually gave humans the power to command in love all nature and creation to adapt to us.

We have chosen to systematically destroy the Earth. This causes the Earth to respond by producing powerful hurricanes and other disasters. This has been our choice. But we may choose to stop destroying the rain forests, to stop destroying the ozone layer protecting Earth, and to stop destroying our ecosystem. We may choose differently. We may choose to work with Nature, not against it.

God will do nothing for us we can do for ourselves. It's our fault, and we can correct it.

It is possible to save the Earth and ourselves by extension even though major damage has occurred. But a wide scale change of attitudes and efforts must be implemented, and soon.

Soil erosion has depleted the amount of soil needed to grow our food worldwide. We have abandoned or shortened the practice of alternating fields for growing crops. By the use of chemicals, we are growing more and more food on the less fertile soil. This accelerates erosion, produces soil with less nutritional value, and produces food with toxic residues of these chemicals. In the long run, these residues will cause illness. The use of any chemicals in agriculture is unnecessary. Nothing can out produce Mother Nature. Using chemicals in agriculture will increase the amount of food produced but doing so reduces the nutritional value of the food produced while incorporating toxins into the food.

In general, most citizens of Earth want more, bigger, and better. Little thought is given to the impact this has on the Earth and its inhabitants. Can we learn to say enough is enough?

We have not been good stewards of our natural resources. This demonstrates we believe (or don't understand, or care) the environment, natural resources, and our ecology provide us with no benefits. We have demonstrated we don't share the world's resources. 20% of the world's population utilizes 80% of the world's resources. There is plenty for everyone if we stop squandering them on the privileged few. We can use the resources, just don't abuse them. Living as if we were all One, and there were enough for everyone would change this.

We have demonstrated our indifference to the Earth's environment in many ways. Cutting down hundreds of thousands of trees to produce a Sunday paper does have a negative effect on the Earth and everything on it. Polluting our atmosphere with all kinds of impurities does have a negative effect on the Earth and everything on it. Using fossil fuels instead of solar energy does have a negative effect on the Earth and everything on it.

We pollute our environment, misuse politics, abuse economies, misunderstand spiritual truth, create inappropriate mental constructions, produce flawed social conventions, and misbehave, all moving humanity toward extinction.

We act this way because we think we are separate from Everything, and not a collective. We know things go better when we as separate beings cooperate with each other. But when we think us or our group's survival is on the line, we try to save ourselves or our group at the expense of others. This mentality works against the collective.

Currently, we deny the dangerous materials we've placed in our atmosphere are a problem, even in the face of proof. All this is an attempt to protect special interests. It would cost companies a lot of money, and it would inconvenience many people.

Our perspective should shift from what's best for the individual to what's best for all humans. If putting poisons in the air benefits a company economically, but poisons all the people on Earth, or even only one person, or one life form, it is detrimental to everyone and everything. Our definition of the self must be increased to include everything.

To develop advanced technologies without advanced thinking is suicide. If some promising new technology makes life much easier for us but ends up exterminating us from off the face of the Earth, what good are the benefits for us? The extermination part should be anticipated before the new technology is implemented. Advanced technologies can wipe us from the face of the Earth if we don't develop an appreciation for all of life and the fact we are all One. Appreciation and respect for everything is advance thinking.

Other worlds in the Universe are able to control their weather, so we too will learn to do it by what we place between ourselves and the sun.

As we learn more about how the Universe works, it becomes easier to destroy our world. The mechanics of the Universe works perfectly, but by messing with it inappropriately, we can create disastrous results. There are many ways to destroy the world; nuclear weapons, destruction of our ecosystem, cloning and genetic engineering without sufficient care, and relying on medicines to replace the body's own defenses. The technology we created to help us, could end up killing us. We now have the technology, and we know how to use it to destroy the world.

The System

Studying the "parts" of the Earth will not lead to an understanding of the Earth. Science's approach to understanding complex systems like the Earth is to examine the parts in order to understand the whole. Using analytical and deductive reasoning, science has constructed its model of our Universe being composed of rigid, inert structures with a dissipation of energy. We will eventually learn there is only an intricate pattern surrounded by a huge organization of life lacking any parts, being just One Organism. The Earth is more than the sum of its parts. It is a system of relationships. Studying the ecology of the Earth is the way to understand the Earth. Every living thing has value to the whole. There is merit in studying the various parts of the Earth, just to understand the trees and animals for example. But to understand the Earth, we must look at the big picture.

The Universe has closed systems leading to death, and open systems leading to life. A balance is needed between the two overlapping systems. Closed systems involve most inorganic matter. Open systems involve the living part of the Universe and everything in the Universe is alive including dark energy and dark matter. The closed systems tend toward disorder and loss of energy. Open systems, move toward order and more energy. By changing our perspective from separate objects to the relationships of the united whole, we will be able to utilize the power of life. This comes from caring - caring for each other, the Earth, and the Universe.

The foundation of life is simplicity. Based on this foundation, life becomes more complex with ever wider possibilities.

Whales are a very ancient race and are great beings deserving of our respect. Dolphins are highly evolved beings who embody joy, laughter, and harmony, and spiritually enrich our world. Both deserve our protection because of the blessings they bring to the world.

Animals have knowledge and wisdom and are a benefit to humans. They deserve our respect and should be treated as equals. Losing our superior attitude toward them is a good place to start. Loving animals aids our evolution. Animals being a part of God, as we are, are made of the same stuff as we are.

Ownership is our society's way to mimic sustainability. We declare ownership of everything we wish to sustain. Things we claim we own are our bodies, our mates, our children, and many other things. Ownership of these people is expressed in the way we deal with them. The same is true with the land. The Earth is divided into parcels for ownership. This ownership includes the resources under the surface and the space above the surface. Ownership may also be held by our representatives, such as governments and industries.

We have gone to war over what we consider we own. But the truth is it is impossible to own anything. We are only stewards of everything we have in our care. We have no ownership of any possessions; we only have things in our care. We are stewards for a limited time, and the things we have for safekeeping are to be sustained. Saying we own something and the item belongs to only us is nonfunctional for any period of time.

We possess nothing forever. We may possess something, but that doesn't mean we own it. Ownership is a defensive social convention based on the fallacy there is not enough of what is needed to be happy.

We do have enough of everything we need to be happy. Unfortunately, we don't believe it. Because we believe there are shortages, we declare we own things to ensure we get what we need and to keep it forever, so others can't have it. All this is for security reasons and ensure our happiness. Our belief we have rights through ownership we don't intrinsically have has harmed our psyche and our species.

Life will continue. When faced with a threat, it will adapt to continue. This adaptation may not be to our liking or comfort. If we want life to continue in the form we are accustomed to, we must change or face the changes Life forces on us as it adapts.

Trees know nothing of death. They only know energy in form. In this regard, they are like rocks, possessing the energy of life. We are One with the trees and can communicate with them. If we have a need for wood, we can ask the trees and they will provide it. The Life energy in the trees is in us. Honor the forms of the trees every day, whether tree or wood. Experience our Oneness with them. The same applies to synthetics. Synthetics are inorganic but still made of the same stuff as us.

The lesson from over-population of the World is our need to have a love for the environment or it will not sustain us. We have been saying, we are unworthy of our environment. Overpopulation of the Earth is disrespect for the environment. We consider ourselves separate from the environment. We think the environment is something to be conquered and changed to please ourselves. We must learn the value of each person, each individual animal, and each individual plant, and stop dismantling our ecosystem. Destroying the Earth, or the birds, flowers, grain, or animals on the Earth only destroys us.

Advanced cultures, such as those on other planets in the Universe, don't live in houses or buildings unless the environment becomes inhospitable. They live in the natural environment, just as wild animals do here, and create, control, and maintain their environment. Advanced cultures know they are a part of and mutually dependent on their environment. They would never damage or destroy the environment supporting them.

What we do is dependent on who we think we are and what we wish to accomplish. We cannot be good stewards of the Earth's resources by acting as if these resources are unlimited.

We are now in the midst of an ecological crisis. We must act together, and cooperate globally, to solve this crisis. The solution is about getting back to basics and recognizing the value of all human, plant and animal life. Our planet, and us by extension, is endangered by our treatment of the Earth.

We are aware things must change. Part of the solution is about living simpler, moving away from the image of wealth and status, and projecting honestly who we are and engaging in activities we love to do. Another part of the solution is recognizing our divine nature and our unity with all living things. We must break with current society limitations and express our heartfelt longings and visions. We are Divine

Beings and we can change the world for the better and avert disaster. We must each walk our own path, believing in ourselves, and contributing to the transformation of the world in our own unique way.

All our problems arise from our fundamental beliefs about how life works, and solutions are not forthcoming because any proposed solutions are based on the same beliefs causing the problems in the first place. Only if we change our beliefs about life can we correct our past mistakes. The two most important beliefs are we are One Organism, and there is enough of what we need to be happy.

Our oceans ability to produce oxygen is impaired because of millions of acres of dead zones caused by nutrient pollution of our streams, and our forests ability to produce oxygen is being reduced because of forest conversion to other uses, including the most important forests, the rainforests. Forests provide additional benefits including removing carbon dioxide from the air and pumping water vapor into the air providing rainwater downwind of the forests. The ability of our environment to produce oxygen, reduce carbon dioxide, and provide water vapor for rain is being imperiled. The raining of heavy metals and acid rain from air pollution on our forests have killed large numbers of trees. The atmospheric concentration of carbon dioxide has increased from burning fossil fuels, contributing to global warming.

We have a history of exhausting our forests for wood for fuel and building materials and of exhausting our crop land of productive soil. The forests of Lebanon, Mesopotamia, Greece, Rome, China, and other places were all destroyed leading to the collapse of these civilizations. The United States was headed down the same road until coal, oil, and barbed wire came along to spare the forests. The cropland was also destroyed by Mesopotamia, Greece, Rome, China and other places.

The Epic of Gilgamesh records the earliest desertification caused by the destruction of forests. Lebanon was 90% forested at one time and was reduced to 7% over a period of 1,500 years, resulting in an 80% reduction of rain downwind. This turned millions of acres of the Fertile Crescent to scrubland or desert.

The vast forests along the Tigris and Euphrates were removed increasing siltation of cropland and irrigation canals and reducing downwind rainfall.

The Greeks started clearing large tracts of forest land in the thirteenth century BC. By 600 BC, Greece was a wasteland, with denuded eroding hillsides filling rivers and irrigated cropland with silt. An effort was made to plant olive trees to hold the soil, but it was too late, leading to the decline of the civilization.

By 200 BC, Rome had wiped out its own forests. The lack of wood to smelt silver caused a monetary crisis. Roman's cropland was decimated about the same time, and there was reduced rainfall because of the elimination of forestland. There were food shortages. Rome was forced to expand to use the resources of countries around the Mediterranean Sea. When the destruction of forests and depletion of soil was complete, Rome collapsed.

Wood was the primary source of fuel and building materials up to the time of the Civil War in the United States. Then coal filled in as the main source of fuel, followed by oil, sparing the forests. Rail fences for agriculture used tremendous amounts of wood until barbed wire came along and again helped spare the forests.

We will each have a different experience of the same event because of our ideas about how life works. An ancient person seeing someone killed by lightning would assume a deity kill this person for some offense. Today most of us would think the person had bad luck or used poor judgment to receive the effects of a natural phenomenon. The difference is the difference between our thoughts about the event.

Different times, different cultures have different stories, beliefs, myths, paradigms, or ideas about how life works. Some of these work and some of these don't work. In the past, every transformation of a culture, whether it worked or not, started with a new idea about how life worked and what was possible. This freedom of thought allows us to change our societies and the world by changing our ideas about how life works.

Societies are groups of people who have similar ideas about how life works. These beliefs are not necessarily absolute, real, or true, but they affect how the societies experience life and can be healthy or toxic, life-affirming or life destroying. These ideas and beliefs can be changed to improve life and solve our problems.

Some of our ideas about how life works, while providing us with "wealth" and comfort, are also leading our culture to its collapse. One such idea is we are separate from our world, including the minerals, plants, and animals. We think we are superior to all these and we have the right to utilize these resources as we see fit. A second destructive idea is we have been given a Devine directive to govern and control the Earth and everything on it. A more enlightened way to view these two ideas is to feel we have the responsibility to care for the Earth and all the plants, animals, and resources on it. Cooperation with the Earth and everything on it is our destiny. All of life and everything is life, is sacred. Competition at times is necessary, and killing at times is necessary, such as when we eat. We are all connected to the Earth and everything on it.

According to anthropologists, when comparing "primitive" societies, and "modern" societies, the "primitive" humans generally have more relaxed lives, less poverty, little crime, and healthier diets and lives, including less psychological disorders. As a group, these "primitive" societies are more cooperative and more respectful of others, are better stewards of our natural resources, and enjoy better equality among individuals, sexes, and nature than the "modern" societies.

"Modern" societies are hierarchically organized producing a concentration of power and wealth at the top and a class of have-nots. This hierarchical organization presupposes nature is similarly organized with humans at the top and allows us to damage and destroy the rest of the "inferior" world. We have exceeded a sustainable population, have polluted the air, have made our food unfit for consumption, and have created conditions for the development of deadly microbes. Based on history, similar "modern" societies of the past have risen to dominate for a relatively short span of time only to eventually collapse.

"Primitive" societies have no concept of "more is better" and find "greed is good" insane. Failing to share food with a hungry person is obscene. For "primitive" societies security is wealth, not goods and services. These societies work to get each person to the "enough point" so each can then fulfill their lives with their own interests. They provide security, safety, and the framework for daily spiritual experience. The people in "primitive societies are spiritually, mentally, emotionally, and physically stronger than members of "modern" societies. This is true wealth.

The Jews had a system of land Sabbaths. Every seven years there was a year-long Sabbath for the land where no crops were planted, thus allowing the land to rest and restore its fertility. This provided a means for sustainable agriculture over three thousand years ago.

We have a society based on war. We waged war on poverty with people still starving, war on illiteracy with people still unable to read, war on drugs with addition still rampant, war on insects producing an increase in insect crop losses, war on germs producing new and virulent forms of lethal bacteria, and war on each other producing obscene amounts of death and destruction. It's the idea we must strive, compete, and strain to gain an objective. What opposes us must be obliterated, eliminated, destroyed, or killed.

Competition by plants among themselves for sunlight, and competition by animals for food does not include the extermination of other species with whom they're competing, with rare exceptions. Cooperative competition, not extermination, is what works. Organic gardening is an example of this in action where insects and weeds are not exterminated but allowed to compete. Some of the most successful insects and diseases are those who don't kill their pry. If they kill their host, they have just lost a source of food, and if they exterminate a species, they may end up exterminating themselves.

An advantage of organic gardening is the elimination of toxic chemicals from the food. If zinc or calcium are absent from the soil, they will be absent in the food consumed. Whatever chemicals are added to plants will become a part of the food consumed, as illustrated by the radioactive material found in plants downwind of Chernobyl.

Solutions

Decentralization of electrical power, food, and water supplies, while seemingly uneconomical, has an organizational structure more stable than centralized sources. When centralized, those controlling these supplies benefit economically, while the customers are kept dependent. When these important commodities are locally produced, the people in the local community are freer and more independent.

Conservation is a way of living for self-preservation and allows those who practice it to succeed in life. It does not waste resources. It is a way of living efficiently.

We tend to love our cities and can't imagine life any other way. But think about this setup. We are dependent on trucks to bring our food to our supermarkets. If there was an interruption in the food being delivered, we would then have to compete with our neighbors, and large numbers of them, for the limited food supply available. This also applies if the water supply were interrupted. Self-sufficient communities have a history of surviving.

Big corporations have corrupted us into thinking life is all about consumption. The commercials we get everywhere suggest we need more of everything, or newer replacements, or the latest improved model, or something more to improve our social status. We are told we all need a better car, a bigger more impressive house, and all the while fearing the loss of our jobs. All this has cost us the awe and wonder of life and of this world.

Eventually, fossil fuels will be replaced with something else. But if we haven't changed our beliefs, we will continue on our merry way overpopulating Earth, destroying other species, consuming more resources, fighting more wars against other humans and other species, and all this eventually leading to our collapse as a society.

It needn't be this way. Anthropologists and psychologist tell us we are naturally compassionate and loving. We instinctively seek the divine. The present social sickness has produced a dysfunctional society where damaged humans are violent. We can heal ourselves, and for our own benefit, we should.

We have been blind to what is going on in the world. We need to sit up and pay attention to our surroundings, be alert, alive, aware, and conscious of what is going on. See what is true. See divinity in everything.

Work with oil now to transfer to a new source of energy before we run out of oil. Conserve oil for other uses, because it is important for many industrial processes, and it provides many useful products.

Advanced cultures share everything with everyone. Our culture is not advanced. Notice we don't share. Advanced cultures share all of their planet's resources with everyone equally. No one person or country owns a natural resource even if it is located on land they occupy. The whole ecosystem, including the inhabitants, is thought of, by these advanced cultures, as a whole system, not composed of many parts to eliminate, destroy, or eradicate. They know doing so would damage the whole system. They do nothing to damage any part of the system. This makes each part of the system important - each plant, each animal, and each person.

Our culture has subjugated the needs of most species to the desires of the richest and most powerful humans. And this will continue until we see this is not in our best interest.

Advanced cultures ensure the needs of all parts of the system are met. But the needs of some parts are less than others. Trees, as an example, have fewer needs than humans. Trees produce oxygen, needed by humans, and humans produce carbon dioxide, needed by trees. Eliminating one puts the survival of the other in jeopardy. Eliminating rainforests is putting human survival in jeopardy. For our culture to advance, it must raise its consciousness from a mindset of exploitation to a mindset of respect for all of life and the Earth itself.

It should be noted the elimination of rainforests is not forest management, but land conversion, where land is converted from a rainforest to agricultural land use. Another issue is forest exploitation where little regard is given to forest reproduction or the sustainability of the cutting practices applied to forests. Proper forest management's primary objectives are to sustain the forest and ensure the forest reproduces itself to continue as a productive forest. Forest management aimed at sustaining our forests is important to supply us with wood as a raw material and trees as a source of oxygen for us.

Advanced cultures are guided by the principles of We are all One, and everything is interrelated. No one owns anything, but all are stewards of whatever is in their care. They love, embrace, and care for things. The land would never be harmed by them because they know to do so would harm themselves. Advanced cultures don't pollute the air, water, or land. They don't apply chemicals to plants that are then absorbed by plants and later ingested by themselves. They don't poison themselves. Psychologically, they don't worry, hate, experience rage, jealousy, panic, shame, or guilt. They would do nothing to damage themselves or another. Their definition of self includes everyone. Because of these practices, they live a lot, lot longer than we do.

To live long, we must stop polluting our air, water, and land, and never eat plants contaminated by chemicals. This is suicide.

Our free will allows us to fill our position of caretakers of the Earth and everything on it, or not. So far, we have not lived up to our assignment. Life on Earth was created to be interdependent and symbiotic. We should have cooperative and mutually beneficial relationships with plants, animals, and the minerals on Earth.

Honor the Earth. Be good stewards of the Earth's resources and protect the environment. Renew and share the Earth's resources.

Tom Moore in his May 10, 2014 newsletter, *The Gentle Way News*, said the oceans are rising now and will rise two feet in the next four years plus or minus. In his July 6, 2013 newsletter he said major earthquakes will result in the deaths of millions of people soon.

Sacred scriptures have this to say:

"Knowing them, a wise man should not act sinfully towards earth, nor cause others to act so, nor allow others to act so... Knowing them, a wise man should not act sinfully towards water, nor cause others to act so, nor allow others to act so." (Akaranga Sutra I.1.2-I.1.3).

"And the LORD God took the man, and put him into the garden of Eden to dress it and to keep it" (Genesis 2:15).

"And Abraham planted a grove in Beersheba, and called there on the name of the LORD, the everlasting God" (Genesis 21:33).

"And six years thou shalt sow thy land, and shalt gather in the fruits thereof: But the seventh year thou shalt let it rest and lie still; that the poor of thy people may eat: and what they leave the beasts of the field shall eat. In like manner thou shalt deal with thy vineyard, and with thy oliveyard" (Exodus 23:10-11).

"Thou shalt not let thy cattle gender with a diverse kind" (Leviticus 19:19).

"Speak unto the children of Israel, and say unto them, When ye come into the land which I give you, then shall the land keep a Sabbath unto the Lord. Six years thou shalt sow thy field, and six years thou shalt prune thy vineyard, and gather in the fruit thereof; But in the seventh year shall be a Sabbath of rest unto the land, a Sabbath for the Lord; thou shalt neither sow thy field, nor prune thy vineyard" (Leviticus 25:2-4).

"When thou shalt besiege a city a long time, in making war against it to take it, thou shalt not destroy the trees thereof by forcing an axe against them: for thou mayest eat of them, and thou shalt not cut them down (for the tree of the field is man's life) to employ them in the siege" (Deuteronomy 20:19).

"But ask now the beasts, and they shall teach thee; and the fowls of the air, and they shall tell thee" (Job 12:7).

"The earth is the LORD'S, and the fullness thereof; the world, and they that dwell therein" (Psalm 24:1).

"Even the cypress trees rejoice over you [king of Babylon], and the cedars of Lebanon, saying, 'Since you were laid low, no tree cutter comes up against us'" (Isaiah 14:8). In the past, when civilizations crumbled, the Earth had a chance to heal itself, and forests returned to cut-over areas.

"When the poor and needy seek water, and there is none, and their tongue faileth for thirst, I the LORD will hear them, I the God of Israel will not forsake them. I will open rivers in high places, and fountains in the midst of the valleys: I will make the wilderness a pool of water, and the dry land springs of water. I will plant in the wilderness the cedar, the shittah tree, and the myrtle, and the oil tree; I will set in the desert the fir tree, and the pine, and the box tree together" (Isaiah 41:17-19). We have decimated the world's forests, and wrecked the world's ecosystems, but if we change our ways, the Earth can heal itself.

"Seemeth it a small thing unto you to have eaten up the good pasture, but ye must tread down with your feet the residue of your pastures? and to have drunk of the deep waters, but ye must foul the residue with your feet" (Ezekiel 32:18).

"O LORD, to thee will I cry: for the fire hath devoured the pastures of the wilderness, and the flame hath burned all the trees of the field. The beasts of the field cry also unto thee: for the rivers of waters are dried up, and the fire hath devoured the pastures of the wilderness" (Joel 1:19-20). Fire is a part of the ecosystem, and field and forest are renewed by it.

"And the Lord said, Who then is that faithful and wise steward, whom his lord shall make ruler over his household, to give them their portion of meat in due season? Blessed is that servant, whom his lord when he cometh shall find so doing. Of a truth I say unto you, that he will make him ruler over all that he hath" (Luke 12:42-44). We are blessed if we are good stewards.

"When they were filled, he said unto his disciples, Gather up the fragments that remain, that nothing be lost" (John 6:12). This is an act of conversation.

"We are members of one another" (Ephesians 4:25).

"For I have learned, in whatsoever state I am, therewith to be content" (Philippians 4:11).

"And above all these things put on charity, which is the bond of perfectness" (Colossians 3:14). Love binds us all together in perfect unity.

"Cause not disorders in the earth" (Sura 2:10).

"No kind of beast is there on earth nor fowl that flieth with its wings, but is a folk like you" (Sura 6:38). We are all part of the web of life.

"And it is He who hath made you the successors of others on the earth, and hath raised some of you above others by various grades, that he may prove you by his gifts" (Sura 6:165). This speaks of us as being stewards.

"And God sendeth down water from Heaven, and by it giveth life to the Earth after it hath been dead: verily, in this is a sign to those who hearken" (Sura 16:67). This deals with stewardship of water.

"Seek not to commit excesses on the earth" (Sura 28:77).

"Destruction hath appeared by land and by sea on account of what men's hands have wrought, that it might make them taste somewhat of the fruit of their doings" (Sura 30:40). What we do to the Earth, we do to ourselves.

"And it pleaseth God that he hath given all these things unto man; for unto this end were they made to be used, with judgment, not to excess, neither by extortion" (Doctrine and Covenants 59:20).

Summary

We deny we are damaging the Earth and we deny damaging the Earth is a problem. But we have done much damage to the Earth and continue to damage the Earth, including polluting the air we breathe, the water we drink, and the soil supplying us with food. We are converting rainforests to farmland, and mismanaging other forests, never mind the tremendous good trees do for us. And our population continues to grow even though it is so large it puts a strain on our resources. Another problem is the Earth's resources are unequally shared.

The consumer mindset we have contributes to the problem. We want more, more of everything when there are many things we don't really need. Our resources are squandered on excess. We have made things our god, and accumulating things our goal. This is a shallow meaningless life. We ignore the weightier more important things of life such as love, and communion with others, our planet, and God.

The problem is in destroying the Earth, we are destroying ourselves. Our destroying of forests, and polluting our seas resulting in the death of phytoplankton is reducing the production of oxygen and reducing the conversion of carbon dioxide to plant material. Carried to the nth degree, we will die from lack of oxygen. When we pollute the Earth, we are polluting ourselves. Carried to the nth degree, we will poison ourselves to death in short order. Seeing the Earth as an ecosystem with everything interconnected will show the connection between our polluting and our death.

Now the Earth is adapting to the abuse we have done to it to ensure its sustainability. Many will die from severe storms. Millions will be displaced and killed because of earthquakes, and millions more will be displaced as a result of the oceans rising. Islands will disappear, and shorelines will recede. We will have to find new homes and jobs for millions of people.

The solution is to change our beliefs about how life works. What we believe in now is not working. Learning contentment is a good first step, but the most important beliefs we can have are to believe we are all One, and we are all interrelated with each other and our environment, and there is enough for everyone. All of life is important, and revering life is an important way to live. A new definition of wealth is needed to move us from "things," and "the one who dies with the most toys wins" attitude, to wealth as security, love, joy, and peace. The Earth's resources are limited, but there is enough for everyone. Conservation will spread them farther. Sharing should be an activity everyone engages in and again will spread the resources farther. We must stop polluting in all its forms, and if we're smart, we won't harm anyone, or anything, or the Earth.

Ownership is an illusion having no basis in fact. We are stewards of all we possess and making prudent decisions about caring for these possessions is an intelligent way to live. This includes taking responsibility for everything in our care and taking responsibility for caring for the Earth. We must be careful with new technologies or we could end up destroying ourselves.

Agricultural practices must change. Our food is now contaminated with chemical residues from present-day farming practices, and too much of our valuable soil is eroding. We should rely on Mother Nature more, and organic farming is an example of this in action. Decentralizing our food supply by forming local communities where food is grown locally can help ensure a good supply of healthy food. Transportation costs are reduced, and the redundancy of food production helps ensure our survival if food production fails in one community. These local communities could also declare independence from big utilities and corporations.

We will have clean air, a blossoming productive Earth, loved and nurtured by all of us, protected minerals, plants and animals, and all of us joining together in love. We are all powerful, and if we change, the world will change. It's up to us to make the change.

The Future and Implementation

Someday we will live as One. Someday we will be tolerant of everyone. Someday we will accept each as a part of ourselves. Someday illness will be a thing of the past. Someday we will control the weather allowing us to live without clothes or houses. Someday we will move with the speed of thought from one place to another. Someday we will communicate through thoughts. Someday the whole world will be one country. Someday each student will study what he or she wants to study most. Someday education will be under the direction of our elders. Someday religions will realize there are many paths to God, and no one can fail to reach God. Someday each person will govern themselves without the need for laws. Someday we will respect and reverence the Earth and everything about it. Someday no one will lack for food or educational opportunities. Someday we will be fully honest and open with each other. Someday we will have world peace. Someday we will love ourselves, our fellow humans, and God to the maximum. Someday we will include everyone and exclude none.

Today is not this someday. But someday. How will we get there? This is the all-important question. Two things would solve about 90% of our problems; living transparently and living as One.

We are not here to fix anything, but we can change the world to make life more fun, happier, and last a lot longer. We can eliminate guilt, shame, punishment, and revenge. We can provide opportunities, education, food, clothing, and shelter for all. We can eliminate bigotry and prejudice, and we can be accepting, and totally loving of ourselves and everyone.

Changing Our Beliefs

An important change we must make to get to a peaceful future is to change our beliefs. By the very nature of beliefs, this is very difficult for anyone to do. Why would anyone want to change what they believe? Each has invested much in their beliefs, and no one wants to be wrong. The new beliefs must be compelling to entice anyone to change. Beliefs are based on something lacking proof. With proof, beliefs are unnecessary because of knowing. So, why change?

Experience! We have been taught to discount any experience going counter to prevailing doctrine. But our experiences are valid and should be used to prove beliefs. As an example, we may have had the experience of having the same thought at the same time as someone else. This is an indicator of our ability to read other people's minds because of our unity. There are many other "psychic" experiences we have from time to time belying our separation, but we tend to ignore them.

Our current beliefs are based on fallacies, making these beliefs a problem. If our beliefs were based on the truth, there would be little reason to change them. Some of the fallacies our beliefs are based on are:

1. God is needy
2. God may fail to obtain these needs
3. God has separated us from God because we have not given God what God needs.
4. God still wants us to provide these needs from our position of separation.
5. God will damn us if we don't provide these needs.
6. We are separate from each other.
7. We lack enough to provide for our needs to stay happy.

8. We must compete with everyone to obtain our needs.
9. Some of us are better than others.
10. The solution for our differences because of these fallacies is to kill one another.

It is important to see life as we have constructed it is not working. If we can't see this, there is no hope of improvement. Organized religions are based on the first five fallacies above. Nationalism is the result of the second five fallacies above. Organized religion and nationalism have produced constant turmoil on Earth for centuries. Improvements can be made by just looking at these ten fallacies and replacing them with new ideas that work.

Some truths we can use to base our new beliefs on are:

1. We are all One because we are all part of the One and only Thing in existence called God. God is Everything, so God is separate from nothing. Being a part of God, we are not separate from each other.
2. God has everything because God is Everything, so there are no needs or any possible way a need may not be fulfilled for God. Therefore, God requires nothing. Having everything, God needs nothing from us, because we are a part of God. Being a part of God, we have all we need to be happy, and there is no need for competition with others for we have it all.
3. All paths lead to God, because there is only God and our starting, ending, and all points in between are in God. No path is the one true way.
4. God still talks to us and talks to us all the time.
5. God is not subject to the same emotional turmoil and needs as we experience. It is impossible to hurt or damage God so God has no reason for revenge or punishment. God will never obliterate any of us because it would be like obliterating a part of God.
6. No one, past, present, or future is superior to anyone. No religion, group of people, or prophet is superior to any other religion, group of people, or prophet.
7. Right and wrong do not exist. Right and wrong are human constructs having no basis in fact.

8. What works, based on our goals, is the truth. If it works, it's true. If it doesn't, it's false.
9. We are not our bodies. We envelop our bodies and use them to navigate this world.
10. We are eternal without the possibility of judgment and damnation.
11. We are all saviors of the world to bring about an understanding of the truth.
12. Everyone's actions are appropriate in their own eyes because of their understanding of how the world works.
13. We create everything in our world.
14. God gives us free will to live as we choose.
15. Our purpose in life is to produce the greatest imaginable life, a life without limit.
16. Everything in this world is an illusion.
17. We can neither kill anyone nor can we be killed, so killing is an illusion. Killing is not a solution even though we can create the illusion of killing illusional bodies.
18. The only thing in existence is Love.
19. The best way to help anyone is to help them become independent.
20. It is appropriate to solve all disputes peacefully.
21. True wealth is spiritual, not material.
22. Good, bad, or indifferent, everything in the world is for our benefit.
23. Life in this world is all about change.
24. Forgiveness will transform the world even though no one needs forgiveness.
25. Transparency and honesty demonstrate our Unity.
26. Tolerance leads to peace.

There are false beliefs we have used to create our present religious institutions, economic systems, political structures, and educational programs. These false beliefs are wrecking our society and should be replaced with beliefs reflecting reality. We can change our society for the better by deeply examining our religious wisdom and by allowing new expressions of our spirituality to be experienced. We can open ourselves to new ideas, thoughts, and revelations to explore innovative spiritual expressions. The whole of society needs a major renovation based on new beliefs reflecting reality.

To change the world, we must change ourselves. First, we must select ourselves to be an agent of change. Then we must demonstrate our decision with the way we live our lives every moment. We define ourselves with every act we commit, everything we think, everything we say, and everything we do. Our lives lived, demonstrate to the world what we believe about life. And our lives are a very effective influence on the world. If we change ourselves, we will change our world. If we change our inner world, our outer world will change. And little by little the whole world will change. If we don't do it, who will? If we don't do it now, when will we do it?

We must be open to the possibility of humans imagining new ideas about God and Life, big new ideas.

Unity

What is the common good and how do we provide for it? What does it mean to be One, and what are the implications? We appear to be separate, when in fact we are all part of One Organism.

We are all One. We don't think of ourselves as One Thing, but we are. It is in our best interest to live, act, govern, educate, regulate, investigate, and heal ourselves as if we were One Thing. How would we relate to each other knowing we are One? How would we govern, educate, conduct commerce, and deal with ownership if we are One?

If you and I are One, then you are I having a different experience from me, and I am you having a different experience from you. If I kill you, I am killing a part of me. If I put you in jail, I am putting a part of myself in jail. If I allow you to starve, I am allowing a part of me to starve. If I fail to educate you, I am failing to educate a part of me. If I restrict your freedom, I am restricting my freedom. If I fail to love you, I am failing to love myself. If I give you a gift, I am giving a gift to myself. If I love you, I love myself.

Our society is just one of an infinite number of possibilities. It is based on faulty assumptions, the primary false assumption being separation. If we believe we are separate, we will act as we do now. If we believe we are all One, we will try to help our fellow humans knowing we are helping ourselves. We start providing for the common good from the basis of our Unity.

Do we choose to see Life in its true magnificence or as a shriveled-up version? We may choose to see We Are All One. We may choose to see there is only One God who doesn't care what religion we practice or if we practice none. We may choose to see the only thing we need to do is love one another and the world will proceed in a joyful fashion, because of our loving acts for one another. We may choose to see none are superior to any of us. We may choose to see all the Earth's resources belonging to all of us regardless of the resources' locations. We may choose to see no one owns anything or any person. We may choose to see we are free, and nothing will be able to limit our freedom for our freedom will ultimately be expressed. We may choose to see love is unconditional and unlimited and will ultimately be expressed. We may choose to experience joy, our natural state of being, and fully and rapidly experience joy by giving it away.

See God in everyone and praise and appreciate them. Help everyone to see God in each other. End divisions, rivalries, competitions, battles, wars, and killings. Love unconditionally and freely share. Communicate openly and completely. Create all things together. Eliminate all hidden agendas. Love without limit. Withhold nothing. Realize and know we are all One. Whatever is good for anyone is good for us. Whatever is bad for anyone is bad for us. Everything we do for anyone we do for ourselves. Everything we fail to do for another, we fail to do for ourselves. We can live this way.

To guide our evolutionary process from where we are to where we want to go, we should start with the principle of unity, meaning we are all One. Then we build our political, social, economic, and spiritual mechanisms to support this principle.

When there is only one of us, governments, laws, social structures, economic systems, and spiritual institutions are very simple. Advanced cultures are simple. We would act as if we were alone on a deserted island. All aspects of advanced cultures are elegantly simple. Governments would amount to self-government.

Unity is achieved by suspending judgment and ending opposition. Unity produces the experience of One Spirit. Judging and separating because of misunderstandings will not produce unity.

Just imagine each person we meet as a great person. Together we have a huge ability to impact the lives of others because of our unity. We need do nothing to enjoy unity, just appreciate it. We cannot produce unity through control and dominance. We must master ourselves. Unity will spontaneously produce unity and support without limiting or imprisoning.

When it comes to implementing our desires, the use of the separation paradigm will only hinder progress. Thinking in terms of separation limits our potential. Embrace all possibilities even those not wanted but choose the desire of the heart.

To experience a life of love, joy, peace, and freedom, we need only live our lives as if everyone and everything is an extension of ourselves. This is the Golden Rule in action. Treat everyone and everything as if it were a part of us. Don't stereotype people and things, and put them into groups, and say everything in each group is all the same. Each person and thing is unique.

Roger Bacon, English philosopher and Franciscan friar, said, "I believe that humanity shall accept as an axiom for its conduct the principle for which I have laid down my life - the right to investigate. It is the credo of free men - this opportunity to try, this privilege to err, this courage to experiment anew. We scientists of the human spirit shall experiment, experiment, ever experiment. Through centuries of trial and error, through agonies of research…let us experiment with laws and customs, with money systems and governments, until we chart the one true course - until we find the majesty of our proper orbit as the planets above have found theirs....And then at last we shall move all together in the harmony of our spheres under the great impulse of a single creation - one unity, one system, one design."

All sadness and suffering are a direct result of our decision to withdraw from the reality of our unity.

The three basic truths are We are all One Thing, there is plenty for everyone, and doing is not important, we only have to be. If we practiced these truths, we would treat others as ourselves, share the entire world with everyone, and solve all our problems by being, that is, create world peace by being peaceful.

All wisdom for dealing with life can be summed up by doing the following: observe what is true and then do what works.

Building on this, observe we are all One so we will then treat others as ourselves; observe there is enough, so we will then share the whole world with everyone; observe there's nothing we need to do so we will then be the change we want to see in the world and all our problems will disappear. By being love, joy, and peace, love, joy, and peace will spring from our lives.

The old belief of separation where we have right and wrong, good and bad, crime and punishment, and everlasting rewards and everlasting damnation has not solved our problems. Accepting a new idea, We are All One, will change the world by ending suffering, torture, and killing.

This new idea shows our part in the change, making us totally responsible for everything happening in the world. All choices are made by us as a group, and we as a group can change our choices. We are torturing, maiming, and killing only ourselves. What we do to another, we do to ourselves. And it is impossible to do anything to someone without their permission.

We should do for others what we would like done for ourselves because what we do for others, we are doing for ourselves. It is in our best interest to do good for others. This is practical advice that works. If we send love into the lives of others, we will receive love. If we send fear into the lives of others, we will receive fear. We must decide whether we want to love or fear.

Live life in a practical way as if we were all One, lacking separation. What would this mean? How would we live? Make this a part of our inner core and our response to everything in life.

Albert Einstein said, "A person experiences life as something separated from the rest — a kind of optical delusion of consciousness. Our task must be to free ourselves from this self-imposed prison and, through compassion, to find the reality of Oneness."

We are now a worldwide community. Our economies, transportation systems, communication infrastructure, and other systems are interconnected and interdependent. If there's a disruption anywhere in the world, all are affected. We are all One spiritually and materially. We must learn to live and act as One even though we haven't had much experience doing so. To do otherwise will be disastrous.

The most important philosophical idea is Oneness. If adopted, the whole world would change, including our politics, economics, relationships, ideas about careers, parenting, sexuality, conflict resolution, and the purpose of life.

Make choices and decisions based on this idea. Make plans, and strategies as if we were all One. Set earnings goals, employee salary scales, and set sticker prices as if we were all One. Act in the War Room, Board Room and Bedroom as if we were all One. Enter the mosque, the synagogue, the cathedral, and the temple as if we were all One. Live life as if we were all One and our future will be bright indeed.

It is impossible to change the world with military force. People may be subjugated, but not changed. Change only happens when people's beliefs change. For the world to have peace and harmony, we must change our beliefs. Military, economic, or political intervention will not work, because the problem is a spiritual problem.

Presently, our social, religious, political, and economic systems are primitive. We consider them the best, because we don't know of, nor can we think of better systems. We resist change or improvements involving any loss of power or wealth even if these would help the vast part of the world's population.

The only problem is separation. There is only one solution to this problem. What is needed is a huge change in consciousness, awareness, and respect for all of life, and a greater understanding of the Unity of Everything.

We are One with God, our fellow humans, and Everything. Act as if we were One and we will heal our world. This is the answer to our problems. Unity gives power with, not power over. In unity is an inner strength, true power. This power will allow us to do, be, and have anything both as individuals and as a society. This power allows creation. Inner strength does not come from separateness. The idea of separation causes all the dysfunction and suffering in the world. It produces all the class, race, gender, and power struggles. It produces war.

If we created laws, and international agreements based on the concept we are all One, our political, economic, and spiritual reality would change for the positive in ways they could never change based on exclusivist religious teachings. Our exclusivist, elitist, separatist theologies do not work.

The highest interest for humans is self-interest. This is true when the definition of self includes everyone. Solving our problems is easy just by enlarging the definition of the self. Believing we are One with everyone will stop our destructive behaviors. Believing we are One with God will allow us to create a wonderful new world.

Societies move from separateness to unity. Viewing the world as composed of separate things is the bottom of evolution. Viewing the world as One Thing is at the top of evolution. Anything viewed as separate is an illusion. All things viewed as One is the truth.

Solutions

We face a spiritual problem. We have thought the problem was a political, economic, or military problem, but it is not. The problem is our ideas about spirituality.

It all comes down to trust. Do we trust ourselves and others? Lack of trust will lead to laws inhibiting humans doing what they want. Trust will lead to believing God has created natural laws allowing us to do as we please producing man-made laws affirming our freedom.

There is the law of cause and effect, sometimes referred to as we reap what we sow. This makes us responsible for our actions. It also makes us responsible for the condition of the world. Enlarging this idea, by providing for others, we provide for ourselves. By working for world peace, we are working for our own peace. By working for the prosperity of others, we are working for our own prosperity.

Acceptance of everything appearing in life is the highest way of life. It is inclusive and leads to experiencing our unity.

By living as one big community, quality of life for all is assured when each of us survives, and the quality of life for each is guaranteed by the whole surviving. We each add to each other's survival. Sharing not only fire, but food, technology, knowledge, beliefs, and ourselves benefits us all.

For us, the concept of scarcity changed all this. Then it was every person for themselves leading to greed, strife, and war. Scarcity is a real problem in some non-important areas, but not related to human survival.

Because we are all One, there is abundance, for the All is self-sufficient. Because abundance exists, nothing is required because abundance supplies all our needs. Because nothing is required, there is nothing to judge. Because nothing is judged, no one is condemned. This lack of condemnation reveals unconditional love. Since love is unconditional, superiority doesn't exist. Nothing is better than anything else. All love is maximal, lacking degrees. Love can't be quantified.

Life works best if we provide for everyone equality of opportunity and not equality in fact. The natural life force is to express uniqueness. Just as no two snowflakes are the same, no two humans are the same. Freedom of opportunity is produced when survival needs are guaranteed.

All of us humans have the right to participate in life at the highest level in any way we choose if our choice doesn't impinge on the rights and safety of another without regard to our race, gender, nationality, religious persuasion, sexual orientation, or any aspect of our individuality.

We have no control over others, and it is fool hearty to try to control others.

We limit ourselves by accepting reality as being the structures we see instead of seeing life as a flowing stream giving us unlimited potential originating from God.

Freedom is the nature of the soul. Freedom is the nature of God. Freedom is the nature of life. Anything reducing, restricting, impinging upon, or eliminating freedom is working against life. In advanced societies, freedom is a fact.

The most important decision we have ever made about ourselves is the decision to believe we have been born in sin and we are basically evil. Because we create our reality, we have created a world where laws are required to protect us from each other. If we believed we were basically good, few laws would be required. Our present society is freedom limiting. If we restructured our society to believe we are good, our new society would be freedom giving.

To fully love, we must love our selves. To do this, we must believe we are basically good. To fully love, we must be totally free. Limited freedom produces limited joy and limited love. To get to the solution of totally loving, we must allow everyone to do anything.

Life as we have constructed it is hard. When we live a life based on who we are, life becomes easy. We are pure, unlimited, and unconditional love. When we live open, transparent lives, releasing others to live their lives as they please, and granting ourselves the same, life becomes easy and peaceful.

To live in peace, happiness, and provide for a better life for our children, we need to live as One organism, knowing there is enough of everything for everyone to be happy. All we must do is share everything with everyone. Sharing information, truth, liberty, honor, and the right to exercising free will benefits us all. This should be easy since we are all One. Now, a vast amount of wealth is controlled by a very small percent of the Earth's population. This imbalance is not productive. Only we can decide how to implement Oneness. The question is **when** will we live as One?

There is nothing we need to do. It's something we have to be. It's our life lived. It's being who we really are: God. When we act like God, we will be totally joyful, loving, accepting, blessing, and grateful. Live this way intentionally and consciously. Live beneficially. Live life based on the core concepts of awareness, honesty, and responsibility.

Be aware of the probable and possible outcomes of our actions, the causes of our outcomes and why, and what is so and what is occurring and why. We need to watch ourselves living our lives.

Be totally honest everywhere all the time. Be honest about all our actions and outcomes and take full responsibility for them. When we take responsibility for our lives, we demonstrate great maturity and spiritual growth.

Taking responsibility for our actions is problematic now because of its association with guilt. Being responsible means attempting to produce the best outcome possible, and a willingness to remedy any outcome perceived as damaging by someone.

"In those days there was no king in Israel, but every man did that which was right in his own eyes" (Judges 17:6; Judges 21:25).

We need a new way of living. Starting with the basics, we need a new view of God. The view of a God Who is violent, angry, and vindictive has not served us well. It's easily said, If it's OK for God, it's OK for us. The result has been a violent, angry, vindictive way of life here on Earth. All our conventions are faulty if they aren't unlimited, eternal, and free. Changing our ideas about God and life is the first step. All other steps will be based on this step. This step alone will dramatically impact all areas of life in a positive manner.

The second step is almost as important and related to it. We must live as if we were all part of One Thing. We are all One: One with God, and One with each other. What we do to another, we do to ourselves. What we fail to do for another, we fail to do for ourselves. This wisdom is like the Golden Rule, but it gives us a psychological reason to want to treat others as ourselves. If everyone in the world took these two steps, the world would be a totally different place.

Before we can plan, we must define the world of the future we choose to have. It will be difficult to reach a consensus of what this will be. If we like the world the way it is, then changes are unnecessary.

All changes impact on all areas of life. For example, a change in the area of economics will impact on all other areas of life. Changes will be incremental. We won't be able to jump to the final goal without going through many intermediary steps.

There will be massive displacements. Billions of jobs, primarily in the military and allied industries will evaporate and need to be replaced with other fulfilling and productive jobs. This will be a massive shift for the world, and the devil will be in the details. New jobs will be created, and industries can adapt by changing the products they produce.

In making changes, don't take the position of standing against anything. Take a stand for something. For example, don't be against war, but be for peace. Focus on what is chosen for the world. By resisting something, we cause it to persist. Where we focus our attention, energy flows.

Everyone should be guaranteed good nutrition, effective health care, a sound education, adequate shelter, respect, and the freedom to do and be anything they choose if it doesn't impinge on the freedom and safety of others. When each is participating at the highest level of love, no one would want to infringe on the freedom of another. Then it's up to each individual to make the life of his or her dreams.

At first glance, it seems like an impossible task. It appears there are not enough resources to provide this for everyone. This is not true. There are enough resources to make everyone happy. There is enough.

We have the potential to be great both individually and collectively. We have come a long way, but we have the potential to be infinitely greater and it will happen. This is our potential. Can we see it as our destiny?

Spiritual principles produce perspectives, attitudes, and a will to find solutions and implement them to produce the desired outcome. Government leaders would do well to identify these principles.

World peace can only be produced by the general acceptance of our Oneness, leading to the abandonment of every prejudice, and anything used to produce a feeling of superiority over others. The Oneness of humanity is a spiritual principle.

Honesty is the basis of wisdom. We can be honest without being frank. Telling the truth can be done with gentleness, tolerance, and compassion.

What we perceive affects our lives. The world is not what it seems to be. Quantum physics shows our lives are dependent on what we look for in life.

How we perceive ourselves affects how we perceive life. If we think of ourselves as friends we will act one way, and if we think of ourselves as enemies, we act in a totally different manner.

All suffering is shared. All hope is shared. All power is shared. We choose what we wish to experience. If we are suffering at the hands of someone, love the person and their idiosyncrasies as if the person were us, and suffering will be relieved.

Everything inflected on humans by humans is possible to be reversed by humans.

Life has nothing to do with our bodies. It has everything to do with experiencing ourselves as greater and greater versions of ourselves.

The world would be free of aggression, jealousy, insecurity, and competition if all of us were in contact with our source, God.

All structures in life, such as governments, organizations, schools, religions, solar systems, galaxies, and the Universe itself will cease to exist eventually. Everything born in time dies in time. These structures are beneficial if they remain our servants. Structures no longer serve us when they perpetuate lies after being proven false. Holidays no longer serve us when it is only a ritual with no meaning. Governments no longer serve us when they exist only to perpetuate their power over us. Bureaucracy no longer serves us when they cease to serve the public. Businesses no longer serve us when they are buried under paperwork choking production and services. Schools no longer serve us when they fail to teach about the way life really works. When structure is the master it no longer serves us.

Scientific theory must be relaxed to allow innovation. Businesses must relax to allow new goods and services to emerge. We must feel we are participating in governing ourselves to allow responsibility to increase. There must be a feeling of joy in doing the right thing to provide respect for ethics.

Mind structures can be the worst structures of all if internalized. We can create life-altering fantasies. We can choose to believe life extends way past 80 years of age. We can choose to believe rich and poor, and other cast systems do not exist. We are love and nothing else. Love is power, purity of intent, and the core honesty of everything.

When a structure is declining, we should move away from it to avoid pain and suffering. This applies to switching from oil as a major fuel, to any relationship, to any business, government, or religious structure.

Abandon things in life when they decrease, become ineffective, become obsolete, or appear to be dying. Refresh life by following the innovative, the new opportunities, and the new ideas.

Death of people, and death of structures, and the illusion of time will continue if we are servants of structure. As love is infused into the world, inadequate structures will fail. But from this destruction will spring new life.

Solutions should be as simple as possible. Some structure is necessary. There will be a necessity for institutions, organizations, and governments, but they should be kept as simple as possible. Initially, they will need to be more complex, but as we evolve, e.g., as we develop more loving relationships with God and our fellow humans, simpler structures will suffice.

Organizations, governments, corporations, and all structures define boundaries and therefore define separations. This is the antithesis of unity. The goal of the evolution of humans is unity.

Respect the past and lovingly use it as the foundation to build the future. Don't destroy the past and start over.

Each has a right to a full understanding of how life affects himself or herself without having to accept someone else's misunderstandings. There are mysteries about God humans can't understand in this world, but all else is open to understanding.

Practicing unity produces discernment. All things have their time and place, and loving discernment allows all things to have their time and place as appropriate. Disallowance is part of this process.

The true test for any plan of action is first, does it work, second, does it bring understanding to life, and finally, does it raise consciousness and purpose to higher levels.

To achieve great things, do it with simplicity, do it now, do it with innocence, do it with love, do what is necessary without hesitation, do it without unnecessary conditions, do it within our nature, do it by concentrating on what needs fixing, do it by concentrating on the goal, do it by utilizing all available resources, do it by honoring nature, do it by being efficient, do it by adjusting to people and circumstances, and do it by eliminating distractions and focusing on what is valuable.

The type of government used to govern doesn't matter as long as it is fair and supports the needs of humans. The strength of humans is the reality of the unity of all. This strength is demonstrated most during times of disaster.

Seeking comfort and security through governments, businesses, institutions, religions, and social constructions, and miracles through illusions and competence through specialization all leads to separation and the attendant problems we've endured for millennia. Specialization leads to separation and loss of energy. Work activities should be enriched involving other dimensions of the self-leading to growth. Learn new skills or improve existing skills. The solution is living as One. Duties at work should not be repetitious. Robots will do this type of work in the future.

The correct action in any situation can be summed up by saying do what brings out the best in us, all of us, and the situation. It reflects unity, love, life, respect, honesty, justice, and kindness.

Forgiveness moves us from the past and away from the dead and the dying. Forgiveness releases negative attachments. But forgiveness should not have people submitting to repeated abuse. The abuser must be corrected. First, forgive ourselves for dreaming the illusion, and then those around us because they are innocent. This system of forgiveness will heal the world.

It is possible for differences to occur among humans and still maintain harmony. Communication is based on this principle. A common language fosters this harmony. By honoring the differences in another, we honor our own differences.

There are times when it is prudent to ask for help. When faced with a situation where we don't have the knowledge, skills, or financial resources, ask for help. By seeking help, we unite with others to build trust to solve problems multiplying the resources being brought to bear on the difficulty. If we bring the total resources of the world to bear on a problem, there's nothing we can't solve.

We existed before we were born and humbly accepted the opportunity and challenge to come to this world to evolve to greater versions of ourselves and greater versions of civilization, in general, to prove we were worthy candidates for the job, and knowing we would make mistakes. It is the goal of everyone to master life experiences.

God can be found in all spiritual writings, including the Bible. We may ask any question of the infinite and expect an answer. But the answer may appear anywhere, so we must be watchful.

We have all the power and don't know it, and those enjoying power like it this way. Most of the world's personal and national problems and conflicts would be solved if we accepted our unity and established visibility in all areas of our lives. We should see ourselves as One with each other and One with God. Telling the whole truth should be established as the norm in all intercourse among people and nations. Believe only the greatest truth about God.

If we are all One, and we believe it to be so, then it becomes obvious telling the truth is in our own best interest. But fear will be the greatest obstacle to this understanding. If we are going to make this paradigm shift, we will need great determination, great courage, and great wisdom. Unless we make this paradigm shift, it will be impossible to have the utopia we wish for here on Earth. We must see what we do to others we do to ourselves, and what we fail to do for others, we fail to do for ourselves. Their pain or joy is our pain or joy, and our pain or joy is their pain or joy. Wishing, hoping, and thinking of harm for others will bring harm to us.

When we live as One, we will know we are responsible for the experiences of others, because there is only One of us. There is only One Thing expressing as the multitude of us. Because we will know we are One, the world will change from hell to heaven. We will use a global approach, a global perspective, and a global system for everything as we move forward.

Before this change will occur, chaos will be created by those who do not want to change, and who want to end the idea of better, and who want to prevent the acceptance of the reality of our Oneness. There will be the unfounded fears the change will result in each person losing control of their life and losing their personal and national identity. However, ethnic, national, and cultural differences will not disappear. Traditions and heritage will not be dishonored, and families, tribes, and communities will not be disassembled. All these will be strengthened because we will know we can experience all these without causing others to have their experience weakened.

The change will not end our differences, but it will end what divides us. Diversity will be honored, but not divisions.

The great fear is we as an individual will disappear as we produce Oneness. Also feared is Oneness will produce sameness. Neither will happen.

Our belief we must eliminate all competition to preserve ourselves, our race, our religion, and our nation has caused us to kill each other. When we realize we are One, we will know we no longer have to kill each other to survive, and the killing will cease. We will stop killing each other because we will know our survival is guaranteed. We will know there is no other one to kill, and we have been killing ourselves all along. The bottom line is there is only One Thing, us, and we are eternal.

Any action should not be based on fear. It is impossible for us to die, but we may drop our bodies, causing them to die. The emotion of fear attracts the object of the fear. Proceed with positive energy. See everything in life as perfect. We will experience exactly what we have chosen to experience. Don't try to avoid anything when we are told forecasts and predictions. Everything will turn out OK.

We think the way we do things is the best way to do them. By examining the way the world is working, we'll see this is false. Yes, we can do better.

The future will require taking responsibility for everything in our world, including our thoughts, words, and actions, removing the negative and concentrating on the positive, seeking understanding, boldly seeking new ideas instead of conforming to the old, practice love and forgiveness, and be openly honest for all to see. We must work on solutions to problems.

Smile! Celebrate! Enjoy! Treat life as a game to be played. All are winners in the game of life with everything being perfect just as it is.

Is there a better way to live in the face of horrific predictions than to live in a calm, peaceful, serene state? Living so will produce the best possible outcomes.

If we believe we are separate from each other, we worry about retaliation and abandonment. This leads to beliefs in attack and rejection, producing what is taught and learned. We are what we teach. Thought systems are weakened by those who believe otherwise. If we don't agree with thought systems of others, we are perceived as attacking those who do. Each thought system centers on what we believe ourselves to be. If the system is based on truth, truth radiates out from it. Those based on a lie produce deception.

To change a belief system based on a lie to truth, the teacher only has to cause a learner to be motivated to change. This produces a change of mind leading to a change in the thought system.

None of our problems are real and therefore don't need a solution. We are fundamentally perfect. Wherever we go, God goes providing us with joy and peace. We are all very holy. We just need to see things differently to cause all our problems to melt away.

The greatest problem we as a race face is dependence. In general, we don't want to take care of ourselves. This has produced religions telling us what to believe, governments directing our actions, schools instructing us in what to think, economies directing what we should have, and societies telling us what to be.

Because we believe we are dependent, we are oppressed by unreasonable, violent governments, religions, societies, economies, and schools. Not only must we defend ourselves in our schools, we must also educate ourselves.

Lack of interdependence is our second greatest weakness. Interdependence is a reciprocal relationship, while dependence is a habit-forming reliant relationship.

We can be the highest idea we can imagine of who we are. We can take our grandest thoughts and create living realities. We can share our love, compassion, wisdom, and abundance. We can imagine, conceive, and create the magnificent life of our wildest dreams. We can smile, touch, laugh, forgive, and share. We can love life, trust God, and accept each other. We can choose to live as One because we are One.

Love or fear is the basis for all actions and reactions. For us, most of our behavior is based on fear. Our mental constructions and social conventions are designed to protect us from something.

To protect us from God's punishment, we constructed morals. To protect us from being treated unjustly, we constructed justice. To protect us from having our possessions taken from us, we constructed ownership. Unfortunately, none of these constructions protect us over time.

When we replace the fallacies that cause our fears with the truth, our social conventions will change to reflect the truth found in Life principles.

There are three Life Principles buried beneath the three social constructions. Functionality, adaptability, and sustainability are buried under morality, justice, and ownership. These social constructions have produced distorted results because they are built on false ideas about life. Still, they are among our most treasured philosophical, political, and economic ideas.

The solution is to elevate the social conventions from concepts to the Life Principles. We must become more aware of all facets of the process of life. This will be difficult because we refuse to change our beliefs even though keeping these beliefs makes life difficult for us.

Our laws should be based on what works and not moral codes. No mistake should be thought of as a sin. When seeking to make something work after a goof, we would just make a correction or an adjustment. When we make a functional misstep, we should be allowed to experience the consequences of our actions, but not punishments. Experiencing consequences allow us to know behavior adjustments are necessary.

The fastest way to change our beliefs is by moving away from our fallacies. We haven't done anything this courageous for centuries. What is necessary is for everyone to see things in a new way. See what is true, and admit it is true. Eliminate self-righteousness. Notice we are evolving, adapting, and changing the rules as we progress. All this is necessary.

Now, Life is becoming less functional. We must adapt soon if we want Life in its present form to sustain itself. Life will continue. When faced with a threat, it will adapt to continue. This adaptation may not be to our liking or comfort. If we want Life to continue in the form we are accustom to, we must adapt as Life now needs us to adapt. We have the opportunity to create the world of our greatest dreams while discovering the tools to do it.

The major obstacle to creating Heaven here on Earth is overcoming the fear of going against the prevailing beliefs, even though these beliefs are killing us. Most of us want to change but were afraid to say anything. Saying something would acknowledge our present beliefs aren't working.

We have a major choice to make. Do we change our spiritual beliefs, or do we allow our way of life to die? We have already lost our safety and security, and if we want them back, we have to make changes to get them back. This can be done physically with war, or we can do it spiritually by changing our beliefs.

Spiritually, we can believe we are safe and secure. Our perceived loss of safety and security was only an illusion. Based on human terms, we have lost them. Spiritually, it's impossible to lose them.

The road to inner peace spiritually knows we are One with God. Outer peace comes from inner peace. Without inner peace, outer peace is impossible. World peace has not happened because we haven't used the correct tools. We have been trying for world peace by changing our behaviors when only changing our beliefs will work.

World change is not completed by thinking, working, or frantically doing some activity. To change the world, we must be the change. It is something within our being. It is a change of heart. As Mahatma Gandhi said, "Be the change that you wish to see in the world."

Most of us live in fear. This makes us resistant to change even if the way we live now is painful. Often a crisis is needed to cause us to change.

The first step to evolving or improving a situation is to recognize what is and accept it as it is. Then it can be changed. A drug addict must first recognize he or she is a drug addict before he or she can change the situation. Denying something exists eliminates all possibility of changing it. Resisting something causes it to persist. Denying something declares and creates it. Seeing something and accepting its existence allows the possibility of change.

If we accept something, it doesn't mean we are agreeing with it. We are just embracing it. When we bless something, we are sending our best energies to it, and our highest thoughts. Then if we don't agree with it, we can change it. To change something, make a new model to replace the old. Create a new way of doing it. To change the world, we must create a better way. This will require changing our old beliefs and be open enough to examine new ideas about Life and God. New perspectives must be presented for examination.

Beliefs produce our behavior. Our beliefs haven't changed in a long time, so our behaviors haven't changed in a long time. The big belief we haven't changed is our belief in our separation from God and Everything else. And we think life is happening to us and not being created by us.

It all starts with our beliefs about God. If we believe God judges, condemns and punishes we will do the same. If we believe God loves some and hates others, we will do the same. If God can do it, it must be alright for us to do it. If our ideas about God are flawed, our actions will be flawed. The only solution is to be open to the idea we may not understand everything about God there is to know. A new idea about God may change everything we believe about God and how we should treat each other.

We are all a part of God making us Divine. Each of us is a powerful spiritual being, capable of doing anything.

Dr. Amit Goswami said, "Ordinary activism involves changing the world without changing ourselves. Since we are Everything, we must change ourselves to change the world. This is a group project. We must all change at the same time. We must become collectively organized to gain the massive changes available to us."

The bringing about of the changes necessary to elevate humans to a new level will cause the old institutions and power structure to fight back. This will hasten their collapse as the new order arises. This new order will bless all humans.

We can create life anew in every aspect of life including economics, relationships, politics, economics, and religion. Everything.

When a person changes their core beliefs, it is an act of freedom. When people are forced to change, they may outwardly reflect the change, but inwardly, their core beliefs remain intact. When the force is removed, they will revert to their core beliefs. Both parents and tyrants have experienced this.

To evolve to new beliefs, we must create, not become obedient. To facilitate the evolution of humans, we should not try to change the world. We must change ourselves first. This involves being the change. If we are being peaceful, for example, we will notice the people around us being more peaceful. World peace requires a change of heart and attitude of all of us leading to changes in religion, economics, government, education, tolerance, health care, and care of our Earth. It all starts with the heart.

All of existence from sub-atomic particles to universes including all dimensions of reality is interconnected. It can be described as the web of life or an energy matrix, but it all comes down to one thing, Everything is connected. Any change will impact everything.

We can't change the lives of other people. But we have unlimited ability to change our own. By believing we can limit the actions of others, we limit our own actions.

Attention should be given to opportunities appearing as events unfold. Pay attention to great opportunities.

Changes made within are significant and lasting and they indirectly affect the world without. Changes based on discontent, intolerance, and unforgiveness will not last. Changes based on love have lasting value. Add our efforts to these changes. Change within and allow God to take this energy and make the changes on the outside. Be the change. Forget about producing any change on the outside. We can change our heart, mind, attitude, values, and willingness. Areas, where we have progressive influence, are our effects on the world, our companions, our knowledge, our goals, our purposes, our mission in life, our stewardship of resources, our health, our wealth, and our freedom. There also are areas where we can only contribute with the help of others. The final result is what the group produces. The change will be based on the sum of the wills of all involved. This includes things of the environment such as weather, and things of the community such as government.

Mastering external change is through mastering internal change. Change the mind, heart, and soul, and the external will be influenced. People are opposed to change because of fear of losing a sense of self, of losing loved ones, of losing wealth, and of losing reputations.

Change is slow because of lack of agreement on what is so. Group agreement is very powerful. What we agree as a group as being so is what we experience in our lives. The solution is to change ourselves within. Then as our external reality is softened by our internal changes, we can adjust our external reality as far as we can. Then make more internal changes, adjust external reality, and so on. We start by strengthening ourselves internally.

The greatest barrier to understanding and advancement is our acceptance of only what we think we know. This is because we only agree with what agrees with our understanding of the Universe. The solution is to be open to everything we don't believe is true.

When implementing new ideas, we must start first with the ideas firmly fixed in our minds and forget those ideas we don't wish to implement. Thought, word, and deed must all support the goal. We must guard our thoughts to think only what we wish to produce. This requires concentration.

Equally as important are the will, the determination, the self-confidence, and the faith to see it through to the end. This is a test of the will. The objective should be to serve the Whole, rather than to be served.

Change a person's thinking, and we change a person's actions. Historically, those groups who were most successful in changing things changed people's beliefs. To change the world, the beliefs of people must be changed. There are two ways to change a person's beliefs: one is to enlarge their beliefs, and the other is to change their beliefs completely.

Generation after generation we have passed our beliefs along, often in the form of "facts." Unfortunately, most of these "facts" are incorrect. We are not lying to our children intentionally, it's just the "facts" were taught us and we assumed them to be true.

It is noteworthy the biggest offenders in this miseducational process are religious schools. We teach our children of an intolerant God, allowing our own intolerance. We teach our children of an angry God, allowing our own angry behaviors. We teach our children of a vengeful God, allowing our own vengeful behaviors.

Then we send these educated children into battle. It's predictable most soldiers in radical movements are young. These soldiers have been told they are fighting for "a higher cause," "a grander purpose," or "God is on our side." Shouldn't they believe their elders, teachers, or religious leaders? We teach our young not only in our schools but with our very lives. To teach our young the truth, we must change our beliefs. Everything we think, say, and do instructs others. Young people are keen observers and try to learn from everything they sense. Our lives lived are their greatest sources of information. Our thinking, saying, and doing are sensed by them. To change our children's beliefs, we must change our own. If we don't, we will see our children do terrible things and wonder why.

Nations, religions, and societies have been founded on great principles. But when these principles are used to manipulate large populations, it is time for a change. The change may be painful or graceful. The American Revolution is an example of a painful change.

We are now at a point in time when changes of gigantic proportions will occur. To survive these changes, favor life, love, personal integrity, and community. Earth changes and war will shift populations. The displacement of huge numbers of people will lead to massive changes.

Here is a guide to making changes:

A change is appropriate if it:

1. Supports life and the living
2. Produces order from chaos
3. Improves community
4. Produces greater understanding of our responsibility
5. Improves the wellbeing of people

6. Increases consciousness
7. Is sustainable
8. Simplifies external conditions
9. Facilitates the unified experience of God and Humans
10. Inspires, unifies, revitalizes, and facilitates freedom.

We can change the world by changing ourselves. What a great idea! This change would involve changing our ideas, the way we live, and the way we experience each moment of time. Just about every religion in the past down to the present has given us this message. We can save the world by changing ourselves. It all starts with feeling the power of living in the present and realizing the Creator and creation are located there.

"Have we not all one father? hath not one God created us? why do we deal treacherously every man against his brother, by profaning the covenant of our fathers" (Mal 2:10)?

"But the fruit of the Spirit is love, joy, peace, longsuffering, gentleness, goodness, faith, Meekness, temperance: against such there is no law" (Galatians 5:22-23).

"If we could renounce our sageness and discard our wisdom, it would be better for the people a hundredfold. If we could renounce our benevolence and discard our righteousness, the people would again become filial and kindly. If we could renounce our artful contrivances and discard our (scheming for) gain, there would be no thieves nor robbers. Those three methods (of government) thought olden ways in elegance did fail and made these names their want of worth to veil; but simple views, and courses plain and true would selfish ends and many lusts eschew" (Tao Te Ching 19). The 19th verse is saying we should not put our trust in the outward forms of education, religion, and economics, but trust our inner wisdom, know who we are, and live simply to produce a better world.

"In the kingdom the multiplication of prohibitive enactments increases the poverty of the people; the more implements to add to their profit that the people have, the greater disorder is there in the state and clan; the more acts of crafty dexterity that men possess, the more do strange contrivances appear; the more display there is of legislation, the more thieves and robbers there are" (Tao Te Ching 57). This does not speak well for having many of laws.

We have all the answers to all the questions. We know how to solve and deal with all our problems.

To reach our goals, we should work together to get there. We each have to organize our own lives, and collectively we can get there. The steps are:
1. Know we are love, and practice being love.
2. Remove all beliefs harmful to us.
3. Remove all beliefs not supporting our love, and our purpose in life.
4. Correct our minds, bodies, emotions, and lives
5. Embrace God and allow God to empower our lives.

In summary, be love, and align with God.

We each have a job to fulfill. No one else can do it. If we don't do it, it won't get done.

Solutions for problems will not be found at the level where they were created. The solutions will be at a higher level. Be Love to find the solution. Love rules the Universe. When Love is absent, humans use control, a poor substitute. With Love, life is restful. Control is exhausting.

Solving a problem involves the use of the same amount of energy that created the problem but of a different type. A spiritual solution is needed instead of a religious, economic, political, or military solution.

When solving problems, we should find higher ground to view them. The solution will not be found at the level where the problem was created. When we honor God and the individualization of God in each person, finding the higher ground will be easier.

The best way of doing anything is doing what works. If it doesn't work, it's not worth doing.

The rate we evolve or grow wiser, is in proportion to the effort we put into observing what is really happening in our world.

We have the power to create our own extinction in many ways. If we ignore this possibility, it cannot be avoided. By resisting this possibility, we cause it to persist. Only by facing it and dealing with it can we cause it to disappear.

Put God first in our thinking, speaking, action, and reaction, and we will prevent lack, sickness, unhappiness, and disharmony. Go within to God to get guidance for every situation. It is self-destructive to strive and struggle to obtain the good things of life. It is self-destructive for a nation or person to kill, steal, or take anything by force.

The struggle is not necessary. Life should flow, so we can relax and let it unfold. It helps if we appreciate ourselves, and everyone and everything in our lives. It is our duty to be who we are, love life with all our hearts, and utilize our abilities.

We have built walls and prisons with the conditions we have decreed are necessary for our civilization. We must relax these conditions. We should be more tolerant, be open to new ideas, be more forgiving, and increase our curiosity about life.

There will be a need for conditions, but we must strike a balance between these conditions and fair play. This balance can be the difference between war and peace.

Baha'u'llah said, in essence, each age has its own problems to solve. They will be different than the problems of future ages. We should not concern ourselves with future problems but work on our own problems.

When working toward a goal, settle for nothing less than the goal of knowing love solves problems. Honor the right of others to express their free will with their own goals.

Goodwill produces Heaven on Earth. Misdirected and conflicting wills produces Hell on Earth in the natural, social, religious, economic, and political areas of our experience.

There is more going on in life than we are aware of. By being positive, we allow life to flow. If we are negative, we become obstacles preventing life from flowing.

Implementation must be based on appropriateness and logic. Give help to those who are ready to receive the help. If it is inappropriate to do something, don't do it. Invest energy where there is a possibility for success. It is disastrous to give support when it can't be utilized or reciprocated. Trying to manipulate recipients with help is equally disastrous. Be careful where energy is invested. What is chosen will produce the future. It forms the foundation for everything we will have or create.

Never disempower when helping others. There is always a way to empower others with our help. If they wish to be left alone, grant their wish, but be willing to provide the help needed in the future when it is desired. Display all the help available and let those in need choose. True assistance to others will enable them to be better able to cope with their problems.

Survival with dignity should be guaranteed to all. Enough food, shelter, and clothing should be available to all ensuring survival. There is enough for everyone. More may be gained by individual endeavors. Love and compassion would always provide for survival. A world united can provide this.

And this can be done without destroying millions of acres of forest land, destroying the ozone layer, polluting our rivers and streams, or exploiting disadvantaged humans. The solution is a shift of consciousness, to see ourselves as One with God and One with everyone. Nothing in the Universe is separate from anything else. It should form the basis of all laws, politics, and governments. Only one law is required: the law of love where nothing is required, and all is given.

We should pursue our goals knowing failure is impossible. We will need courage, gratitude, ingenuity, faith, charity, and persistence.

As we are an integrated whole with many smaller parts, we must nurture each of these small parts of our physical body, and our heart, mind, and emotions. On a larger scale, social structures and nations must do the same.

Institutions, governments, religions, organizations, and other groups take on a life of their own and strive for self-preservation. This prevents solutions for world hunger, cures for diseases, and other changes to take place. If these problems were solved, whole organizations and businesses would have to close.

It is beneficial to separate organized religion from our governments that create and implement laws. It is also beneficial to combine our cultural values and sacred beliefs with the process of selecting our representatives to the government who write and pass laws, and who decide on the process of enacting laws. Governments should not establish religious doctrines. Religions should not influence governments. No religion can speak for all the people.

As we make decisions about how to live in the future, our decisions should be based on the facts we are One Thing, immortal, and we have unlimited freedom. What we do to one of us, we do to all of us. What we do to our Earth and everything associated with it, we do to ourselves. What we fail to do for one of us, we fail to do for all of us. What we fail to do for our Earth and everything associated with it, we fail to do for ourselves. Any institutions we construct should allow for maximum freedom. Punishment in any form is inappropriate and unjustified.

Because our mindset is based on separation, we now need laws to protect us from ourselves. If our mindset was based on unity and our magnificent selves, we would not need laws because we would treat each one as ourselves. When someone breaks one of our laws, the goal of the legal system should be to rehabilitate the person and return the person as a productive participant in society as quickly as possible. Punishment is inappropriate. Some individuals may need to be removed from society to protect society from them. Society should only be protected as long as necessary to rehabilitate the person.

What can we do?
1. Practice loving everyone and speak out against prejudice.
2. Lobby for equality for everyone regardless of gender, sexual orientation, race, religion, or any other human group.
3. Demand governments provide educational opportunities for everyone to the limit of each person's aspirations.
4. Demand governments provide universal health care for everyone.
5. Demand governments provide each person with enough food for their nutritional requirements.

6. Demand governments provide each person with adequate housing.
7. Demand governments form a one-world government like the United States, but the United Governments of the World.
8. Demand governments operate with openness and transparency and govern based on what is best for all of us, and not for special interests.

As humans, we are evolving. The process is slow. Part of the problem is we can't agree on most things. In practical terms, this means world peace will not happen tomorrow. We are evolving in many areas such as religion, education, politics, knowledge, social customs, and technology. A standstill in one area can impact other areas. Advancement in one area can spur faster developments in other areas. Imagine the impact the discovery of a source of practically free energy would have on all areas of society. Some improvements will occur in the near term, while other improvements will take moderate or long periods of time to reach. In general, the things we want the most will occur the quickest. Some improvements have not even been thought of and therefore will not happen for a very long period of time. Some improvements are even thought of as undesirable now.

We haven't been very observant. We have not noticed what is working and what is not. To rule the world most efficiently we will need to know what works. Do our present systems give us what we want? Do they need to be replaced? What are some new ideas we can use to improve the present systems? As new ideas are applied, they must be evaluated to see if they work. If the new ideas don't work, they will need to be replaced with ideas supplying us with what we want.

Allow all things. This is practicing forgiveness. Forgiveness is an allowance. Forgiveness involves forgiving ourselves too. Trust, embrace, and transcend everything. Allow the world to be as it is. Allow our perceptions to be changed and see things differently. This is the act of letting go and trusting. This is the road to freedom. We're dumping the need to be correct. We'll see the world as a safe place to live with enough for all.

Allowance is seeing all events as neutral, and seeing ourselves as connected to Everything, and the impossibility of anyone being guilty of sin. Allowance transforms. Allowance allows us to be who we truly are, the Christ, the Child of God.

Our world doesn't teach allowance, but it does teach us to strive. We are taught to be makers and doers. We are taught to control and manipulate our environment to make it conform to what we think it should be. Allowance is a way to see life differently. Allowance is built on the truth we are already loved and there is no need to be successful to be loved. Allowance sees obstacles as stepping stones. With allowance, we accept everything we experience. We begin to understand all people and events are brought into our lives to provide exactly what we need to evolve. By allowing we are permitting God, the source of who we are, to dictate and control our lives. Allowance fosters the growth of trust and provides for a fuller utilization of intention and desire in time. With allowance, we perceive the world differently, and we submit, but not naively. We will realize we are living in an illusion. When we allow, we start the development of humility, the control of the ego, and the recognition doing and making are inadequate.

When we allow, we accept everything. We accept all attitudes, beliefs, actions, words, and physical characteristics of people and all environmental conditions. We may not condone everything, but we will accept everything. A refusal to accept is to judge. Judgment is an attempt to murder the unacceptable. Judgment is the reverse of forgiveness and is based on fear.

In the spirit realm, no one is judged or condemned, and forgiveness is unnecessary. We who are perfect, exquisite children of God, and have our being in Love, are loved unconditionally. There is nothing to do to earn this love. Forgiveness is important in the Physical World where things are thought to be good and bad. In the Spirit World where there's no judgment, pardon is unnecessary. All our creative energy and everything we do is necessary to produce the infinite magnificent Whole. Everything is necessary.

When we are being, rather than doing, we are living in a state of allowing. This means not judging who or what we are. What we do flows from our feelings and emotions while staying focused on the present. Our actions flow from our passion and zest for life, not from fear.

If we are in a state of pure allowing, we are where positive change easily happens. We will allow ourselves to be who we are, and welcome anything we feel passionate about.

Allowing also allows negative emotions to flow. Fully experiencing negative emotions is better than restricting them. Allowing negative emotions to flow without judgment is self-love in action and helps create a happy life.

We should abandon any thoughts of changing the world or even changing one person because this comes from a judgement of the world or the person. When we judge, we have decided something is wrong and needs correction. This just reinforces the judgmental energy creating the problem originally. Allowing others to believe or think as they will, produces more expansion and synchronicity in our lives. Like attracts like, and if we are kind to ourselves, kindness will flow into our lives.

If we desire something, allow it to come to us instead of pursuing it. Pursuing is fear based and allowing is trust based. Allowing requires no energy. Pursuing requires lots of energy. The more energy required, the greater the indication something is wrong. Allowing is realizing what we desire is already ours and requires no effort. Everything desired is on the nonphysical plane and all we must do is expand to receive it since everything already exists. Expanding our consciousness to allow is all that's needed.

If all of us had a spiritual transformation and realized our nature of perfection, the world would also have a spiritual transformation. We would be self-empowered, and tolerant, with less fear and less strife. There would be less crime and greed, and we would be healthier. Our children would grow up in a loving environment with better health and more trust. The whole planet would support this way of life. Our job is not to change the world, but to be the change, to be love.

Life is a spiritual event we all participate in, and we're constantly changing and evolving. God requires nothing, so we will function best if we have no rules. We only need to follow what feels good. Doctrine, dogma, ritual, or other rules and regulations are unnecessary. Being unique and a part of God, no one is in a better position to dictate how we should live our lives than we are. Typically, religions dictate rules and regulations. After a religion establishes its doctrines, all the members are expected follow these rules and regulations, and if we don't, we're judged negatively. Instead of unity, rules and regulations produce strife and divisiveness. Even if we follow a religious path, we're not guaranteed a life free of fear. If we follow our own spiritual path we can develop a friendship with God.

Each unit of time is unique, and we only get one chance to live each unit. This is a good reason to live in the present. It's a good practice to leave the past behind and face each new unit with a clean slate and new possibilities. Aim for the most joy and pleasure in each moment. This will vary from meditation to eating ice cream depending on our feelings.

Enjoy life. Don't take it too seriously. Laugh often each day. Problems lose their import when we're looking through love and humor.

We have created all our problems, and we are the ones who must undo them. We are not alone, and if we allow it, God will direct our efforts. The problems are in our consciousness. All we need do is closely examine our problems, dis-identify from them, and be the presence of love in dealing with them. We are all equal to the task for none of us is less capable than Moses, Buddha, Jesus, or Muhammad.

We don't need to "fix" the world or anyone in it. Only love heals. If we are wise we will love ourselves and allow the unimpeded flow of the love of God.

We all create our experiences and choose the value we place on anything from thoughts and beliefs to objects and things. Because we do this, it's impossible for us to be a victim or to find fault in another. There is no one to blame except ourselves.

All events are neutral. Up to now, we have placed a high degree of value on judgement. We consider it important to judge. When we choose to judge and impress on another they wronged us, and we are justified being angry with them, and attack them, we instantly create the energy of conflict, war, disease, unhappiness, separation, and death within ourselves. The solution is to forgive.

It is impossible to be a victim. Anything taking place in an illusion, and everything in this world is an illusion, is powerless to have any effect on us.

So then, how do we rule the world? First, respect and honor all of life and everything is alive. When it comes to our food, in general, something must die so we can live. A plant or animal must die to provide food for us. Now nothing actually "dies," but it can change form. We should respect all the plants and animals supplying us with food. We could carry things to extremes in any situation, and when it comes to food we could refuse to "kill" any plant or animal and all of us would starve to "death" and change form. Or we could destroy an acre of lettuce when we only needed one head. Both are extremes with the middle ground of consuming only what we need to maintain healthy bodies being the best. We should be conservative and use our resources wisely.

One simple thing we can do to use our resources wisely is to plant hemp to provide fiber for paper, rope, and clothing. It's easy to grow because it grows almost anywhere, and cost little to plant, grow, and harvest. Hemp's medicinal properties are outstanding. There is just one problem. A huge lobby is working against it.

When dealing with pests, such as termites, again we should respect them. We could decide to let them live, but then our houses would eventually collapse. Or we could declare war on them and try to totally eradicate them from the face of the Earth, a costly and destructive decision. A better course, for now, would be to eliminate the problem in our houses and allow them to practice their wonderful service of recycling dead trees in our forests. Eventually, we will develop technology and the means to live peacefully with them where they will avoid eating our houses.

So, stop resisting life, stop whining about life, stop lamenting life, and stop worrying about life. Get on with life because we'll live forever.

World Peace

When it comes to ruling our world, world peace is very important. Unfortunately, we squander billions of dollars each year blowing ourselves to kingdom come. The process of peace starts with each of us. Peace is a state of being, and it comes from within. When we are all at peace with ourselves, the whole world will be at peace. Honesty is the basis for peace. The way to peace is to accept everything, choose the best, and refuse to make anything wrong. Love and work for peace, but don't hate and work against war. Living in a state of abundance, needing nothing, produces peace. From a practical perspective, it will take centuries or a millennium or more for all of us to reach this state. But we can start now on this journey.

Inner peace is reached by going within through meditation. Meditation is a personal thing and we will experiment to find a form of meditation ideal for each of us. We can develop a friendship with God and see the face of God in the face of everyone we meet. By knowing we are all One, we can reach out and touch the face of God in everything around us. We will work on ourselves to eliminate prejudice. Racial prejudice will eventually cease to exist because over time all the races will interbreed to produce just one race. Now, we can learn to respect and love the members of all races. Everyone is basically the same, Love.

We will start a movement now to change from an exterior orientation to an interior orientation, by becoming more spiritual. Spiritual solutions to our problems will favor our welfare and our unity. Bless, respect, tolerate, and forgive if necessary.

One very practical thing we will start to do now is teach our young violence is not an acceptable way to settle any dispute. The depiction of violence in our movies, TV programs, comic books, and video games must stop. Religions will remove their blessing for the use of violence. They will have to rethink their beliefs in a God of violence and will develop tolerance of other religions. The realization of the equality of the sexes, races, religions, and nations will be a major step forward for peace.

Our young will also be taught to love everyone, and they will be made aware of our unity and our world citizenship. The Golden Rule will be taught as a beneficial way to live. Universal education will be provided for all with an auxiliary language learned by all to facilitate communication. Initially, where funds are limited, women and girls will be educated first to speed up the process.

Extremes of wealth and poverty will be eliminated, and the basic needs of the poor will be provided. Philanthropy is part of the solution to this problem. Economic barriers will be eliminated. Advances in technology in the future supplying unlimited energy to the world will foster peace. God is the ultimate source of everything, including harmony.

Unbridled nationalism will be tempered because first and foremost, we are all citizens of the Universe and of the Earth.

In a few centuries, we will finally have the wisdom to establish a world government. This is one of the most important things we can do besides changing our beliefs. This government will use courts to enforce peace till our hearts enforce it. Except for a world peacekeeping force and local police departments, the world will disarm. This world government will finally limit the sales of armaments allowing the shift of money from tanks and guns to food, education, and the wellbeing of all of us. It will guarantee each of us the ability to be all we can be. Imagine a world where all of us will have the potential to create tremendous and wonderful things to improve our world. If we have done wonderful things down through history to the present, and we have, think of the exponential explosion of our evolution when we are all guaranteed the possibility to develop to our full potential. Changing our government and social structures to reflect our unity will transform the world for the better.

The act of creating a world government is pivotal to our future development. Not only is it a giant step toward world peace, it is important to the freeing up of tremendous amounts of money to improve the lives of all of us. As living conditions improve for all of us, there will be less incentive for war, strife, theft, drug addictions, and murder. We will be more peaceful, and content. Much more than just content, we will be joyous, and excited about life.

There are so many advantages to be joined together with the major benefit being peace. We are now joined globally in many ways, and our perception of union will only increase in the future. But we will have peace, glorious peace.

Sex, Marriage, and Nudity

Sex is great. Marriage is a commitment. Nudity is natural.

God made us naked and it is natural for us to walk around naked, except in cold climates. But most of us feel uncomfortable exposing our naked bodies to others. It is inappropriate to feel ashamed of our naked bodies. Nakedness along with sex carries a lot of emotional baggage because we have been taught and we continue to teach our children to be ashamed of their bodies and the physical act of sex. Marriage as we have constructed it is a commitment lasting till a marriage partner dies. But time passes, and we evolve and change, and the marriage partners can change their minds about the commitment.

All this will change as we evolve. It will require a lot of effort and take a long time to reach the point where we are no longer ashamed of our naked bodies or sex and reform the concept of marriage to allow total freedom. All relationships will be seen as life sharing creative opportunities.

Sex will be used to lovingly experience pure joy and ecstasy. We will see sex as a glorious expression of Godliness. Moral codes, religious restrictions, social taboos, and emotional norms are used to prevent us from freely expressing our love for one another. God gave us intense desires to embrace each other. This is natural and preventing what is natural produces all kinds of problems. Giving ourselves joy, pleasure, and ecstasy leads to Heaven. Self-denial is limiting and self-destructive. These regulations will be removed, and sex will be perceived as being normal, and natural, and unlimited. Shame and guilt will disappear.

We teach our children sex and our sexual body parts are shameful by the way we act. Children will be allowed to fully experience their sexuality, and the sexuality of the parents will not be hidden from their children. Hiding our shameless naked bodies from our children is not necessary. We will candidly tell our children about the wonders of sex. We as parents transfer our attitudes about everything to our children, including sex, by the way, we act and speak. We are so traumatized by the attitudes we inherited from our parents about sex, it will take many generations before we can openly enjoy intercourse in the presence of our children. We can start by openly kissing, hugging, touching, and fondling our children and ourselves to illustrate our love in physical form, and how natural, wonderful and desirable it can be. Sexual feelings will be equated with joy and celebration. Children will see their parents as the loving sexual creatures they are. It's helpful if we understand our own sexuality so we can talk to our children about sex. Answer any question about sex truthfully and as fully as necessary. Simple and incrementally is best.

Sex provides the experiences of abundant life and Oneness. Sex is noble and holy - Wholly. It is best experienced on all three of our levels, soul, mind, and body. Love is honesty and when we find ourselves loving someone new, the loving thing to do is to inform any and all partners of our new love. Loving unconditionally, honestly, unlimitedly and without need, allows us to grant total freedom to the subject of our love, a radical change from our current paradigm. This allows the loving of many and the experiencing of sex with many and with all accepting parties.

In enlightened societies, all are completely free. Each person is free to love others in any manner that is true, authentic, and appropriate at the time. Laws, social taboos, religious restrictions, psychological barriers, tribal customs, or other unspoken rules and regulations relating to who, when, where, or how people may love one another do not exist. This works because each person decides what love would do now, and each person is an adult, mature, and capable of making such decisions for themselves. In a three-way relationship, each person speaks their truth, and they each can decide how they will proceed from their knowing their loving another does not mean loving themselves less. There is no sacrifice and no abuse. Loving another does mean allowing them full freedom. We will eventually accept our sexuality and openly and lovingly practice it.

We would be wise to abstain from sexual activities with others who do not wish to engage in sex with us, and those who would be negatively impacted because they are too young, or those who are mentally or emotionally unstable. Rape is an assault and not sexual expression. Sex crimes and dysfunctional sex result from repressed sex. Laws limiting sexual expression are not beneficial. They produce anger, shame, and guilt, causing us to hide our sexual activities from others. There are laws regulating human sexual activity where there is no civil damage. We will rescind such laws in the future.

Many people have defined homosexuality as being wrong, but this is like saying it's wrong to be left-handed. It's just what they are. Homosexuals should be accepted as they are. If homosexuals choose to marry, they should be free to do so.

The marriage vows of the future will reflect our unity and unlimited freedom, and the truth of who we are. We will be free to express our love for anyone, anywhere, anytime, and physically when among consenting adults. None of this will be hidden from anyone. We will be open and honest, about our decisions, choices, and preferences, and will accept the resulting outcomes and consequences. Honesty is the only sacred promise we can make in any marriage. It is appropriate to love everyone to the maximum, and it is the most joyful way to live. Special, restrictive relationships are inappropriate. We are change, and we are constantly changing. So, we can't promise to stay the same, and the time may come when we choose to leave a marriage because of changes. We are love, and love is unlimited, eternal, and free. The marriage laws as we have constructed them impinge on our unlimited and free nature. Such marriages exclude. Any marriage vows less than unlimited, and unconditional are a sacrilege and are limiting and stifling for our evolution. Marriages based on love would be unlimited, eternal, and free, and therefore inclusive, including everyone.

Marriage should provide opportunities, not obligations. Life in marriage should be a metaphor for life as One with Everything, the union of those in a marriage as the union of the All with the All. Marriage will be a partnership where everything is shared equally and will be an institution where there is unity, and a joining. We may decide to define marriage any way we wish, and we have chosen many variations in the past. Marriage like other parts of society will be continually evolving. No rules and regulations will be placed on it. Everyone gets to choose what they say, do, and be. If there is a conflict, everyone gets to decide how they will react to the conflict. If all involved will take responsibility for their actions, then the possibility of there being a villain or victim is eliminated.

Marriage will only be entered into only after careful consideration and will be based on love and a genuine commitment. The joining in marriage will not be seen as filling a void in anyone, and each will see themselves complete unto themselves. A free, unlimited, honest, and loving marriage would never provide ownership of one person over another. There can be times in a marriage, even a good one, when to allow for greater growth, each must go in different directions. A marriage will not be continued just to provide stability or to provide the appearance of solidarity. But if a marriage is dead, it's time to lovingly part ways and move on. A marriage will not be dissolved without careful thought, and not because of temporary pressures.

The economics of the present tying women to a marriage must change to allow freedom of choice. Of course, in most countries, a woman may leave a marriage, but in certain circumstances, it would be economic suicide. No one will be forced to stay in a relationship they don't choose to. Health insurance, a stable income, shelter, and education should be provided as needed for everyone. Each person will be allowed to walk their own path. Love attaches no strings.

All laws, rules, regulations, and vows relating to marriage will change to allow all marriages to be unlimited, and unconditional. Legal and religious requirements will be divorced from marriage. Entering and leaving a marriage will be as simple as saying hello and goodbye. Marriage will be totally unregulated.

Marriage is a choice, and we may choose never to marry during a lifetime, or we may marry many successive or simultaneous partners. In each moment of the marriage, all involved will be free to continue the marriage, leave the marriage, change the marriage, or add to the marriage if they so choose. Free, unlimited, and loving will define every marriage.

The requirement of the raising of children by their parents will be removed from marriage, and no single unmarried woman will be forced to raise her children alone. In the past grandparents have helped fill the void, but in the future, community elders will raise our children. It will take a long time for this transition to take place.

We as humans, tend to stay in romantic relationships for a period of time before moving on to another. Emotional attachments tend to hold the relationship together over time. Most romantic relationships don't last a lifetime, so when a person chooses to leave the relationship, this person should be able to leave being loved. The relationship can be called a marriage or nothing at all. In the future, everyone will freely and lovingly come and go from romantic relationships as they wish.

Over time, we will evolve to where we believe the naked body is the pinnacle of beauty. Shame and modesty will fade as we realize naked is natural. We will move from thinking our bodies need improvement to acceptance of the natural beauty of our bodies. When we are naked, we are transparent, and so we will be transparent.

It will take time to develop control of our weather to the point we can all walk around all the time naked, and likewise, it will take time to overcome the shame and guilt we feel when we expose our naked bodies. We can start by being naked in our homes in front of our family members and work up to being naked on nude beaches. Laws will have to change, but when enough of us feel comfortable being naked, they will.

Religion and Spirituality

Religion has the potential to do great things. In the past, most religions have been subverted by power and wealth. In the future, their destiny will be fulfilled in uniting us all with God. Of course, we are united now, and can never be ununited, but we have forgotten who we are. We are not our bodies. We are unified immortal spirits, pure energy. What a wonderful future we will have when we realize each one we meet is a magnificent creature, holy, wholly, loving, immortal, and God. To get to this future in our illusional world, religions will evolve and fulfill their scriptures by teaching us we are all One. They will comb their sacred scriptures for the nuggets of golden truth hiding in plain sight.

In the future, religions will put more emphases on the experience and thinking abilities of individuals, allowing everyone to find the truth we each hold in our hearts, from the ultimate source, God. Each person will decide what is true and correct for themselves rather than rely on what they are told, relying on their own experiences. There is no need for an intermediary between God and us. There never has been and never can there be. Each will develop a personal relationship with God, and each will spend time daily, in meditation communing with God. Religions of the future will encourage and facilitate all of this. The intimate relationship between God and us will be all important.

Religions of the future will see us as what we are, the Christ, the Messiah, the Buddha, the Son of God. We are all, perfect, pure, holy, divine, worthy, sinless, lovable, loving, loved, and in truth, Love. Each person we meet is an angel. We are unlimited, all-powerful, and immortal. We are evolving beings, and ever shall it be. In the future, religions will encourage and facilitate this evolution.

Fighting and intolerance between religions will eventually be a thing of the past. Religions will build bridges connecting cultures, races, nations, and other religions. Separation will be eliminated. There will be mutual respect among the various religions. The idea there is just one true religion will be abandoned allowing a more unified vision.

We as humans will enlarge our concept of God and Life, and religions will stop quarreling and condemning each other. They will realize some of the information they don't know could change everything they thought they knew about God. The religions of the world will get together in conferences to build mutual respect and cooperation. They will not try to eliminate differences, but they will then realize the importance of each religion's uniqueness and explore ways to honor their differences. The religions of the world will seek to meld their different perspectives into a new larger view of God not available through just one religion. Theologians of all faiths will deeply explore the contradictions among the various religions to find a Larger Truth in the midst of apparently conflicting truths. Many times, Great Harmony will be found in these contradictions, proving the Divine Dichotomy where two ostensibly contradictory truths can both be true.

The illusional world where we live is not an **either/or** reality, but a **both/and** reality. Religions will see the truth in this statement and embrace **both/and**. They will see there is nothing outside God, and God is Everything. They will fully embrace the omnipotence and omnipresence of God and abandon the belief God is everything positive and the Devil is everything negative. Religions will realize Satan does not exist and is a state of mind. They will see everything in life is perfect and valuable just as it is. To deny this is to deny God since God is Everything.

Religions of the future will be evolving constantly. God speaks to us all the time, and religions will have their ears open to hear. Religions will become humble and say they don't know everything about God, hoping to find a new truth that could change everything. The leaders of the religions will be open to new ideas from all sources, not just their chosen sacred scripture. To the best of the old beliefs will be added an expanded view of other old ideas, plus totally new ideas to produce a better overall package. It all starts with us changing ourselves by changing our beliefs.

God will be viewed as being all-inclusive, joyful, unconditionally loving, accepting, blessing, kind, gentle, and grateful, and He will be viewed as a God who shares all power with us. It will be understood, God is a being, energy in motion, and God loves us just as we are, regardless of what we have done in the past, or will do in the future. God will be seen as more than just a "he," with an included "she." Religions will teach we have free will in fact, with God having no preferences for how we live our lives and requiring nothing from us.

Guilt, fear, shame, superiority of any kind, sin, judgment, and punishment will fade from religion. With fear gone, we will live fearlessly, and we will abandon our civilizations' protective structures, such as morals, justice, ownership, armies, locks, passwords, and the idea of needing salvation from sins. It will generally be understood God has given us a tremendous opportunity to demonstrate our highest ideals in the lives we live. We may demonstrate this by living a life of pure unconditional love. Religions will eventually use awareness of how life works, honesty in expressing the truth as it is known, and taking responsibility for actions as the basis of their beliefs. They will allow our basic beliefs to change, leading to the solutions to all our problems. The idea we are all One with God will be accepted. We will then live in love, harmony, and unity with each other. Religions will finally be tolerant, integrated, united, accepting, joyful, unlimited, eternal, and free, and these new spiritual values will change our politics, economics, educational systems, relationships, sexuality, and parenting.

Religions will support science and science will support religion as both come to understand they are each looking at the same Thing but from different directions. This realization will then foster the rapid evolution of humans. The greater the unity and communication among humans, the greater our accomplishments will be. Religions and science will coexist harmoniously.

Soon, Earth changes will force massive changes on us. Millions will be displaced by wars, economic conditions, rising oceans, and earthquakes. We will be faced with unprecedented opportunities to demonstrate compassion and love for our fellow humans. Universal, world, and personal relationships will change forcing us to reexamine our beliefs. This reexamination of beliefs will revitalize religions by their emphases on personal relationships with God. This will lead us to develop our inner abilities. We will treat each other as equals, as different aspects of ourselves. God has only compassion and unconditional love for us and never judges us. Being a part of God, it is natural for us to act the same way. The best possible way to live life is to nurture ourselves, creating an unlimited life to allow us to see our true magnificence. Failure is not an option. We can only succeed.

In the next fifty years, religions will start the process of rewriting their doctrines by searching their sacred scriptures for new ideas. They will become more tolerant and respectful of other religions. Over the next thousand years or two, they will slowly merge into one religion as they accept the various views of God from the various religions as being a more complete picture of God when combined. As we evolve, we will change our rules and regulations with a trend toward fewer and fewer. Our beliefs will change, and this is evolution.

THE MOST IMPORTANT CHANGE WE CAN MAKE IS TO CHANGE OUR BELIEFS, SO THEY'RE BASED ON THE TRUTH, AND ESTABLISH A PERSONAL RELATIONSHIP WITH GOD. THE TWO MOST IMPORTANT TRUE IDEAS TO BASE OUR BELIEFS ON ARE **WE ARE ALL ONE WITH EACH OTHER AND GOD,** and **GOD NEEDS NOTHING.**

Science, Technology, Health, and Medicine

If we believe something is impossible, then it is. If on the other hand, we believe the same something is possible, then it is. What we believe is fundamental to how we experience life. We are unlimited beings with the potential to do anything. Any limitation we experience is self-imposed.

Science and religions will eventually support one another. It may take a thousand years or more, but scientists will study things both spiritually and scientifically. Science will not try to prove a certain doctrine of a certain religion, but will with honesty, search for the truth, and eventually arrive at the truth of God. There are two truths, one involves our illusional world, and the other involves the Spirit or Real World. Both truths must be known to know the whole truth, and God is involved with both. Learning the truth only leads to God, because God cannot be separated from reality.

We will have visitors from other planets and sooner rather than later. We are not alone in the Universe. Even now they are showing themselves to us around the world, and eventually, they will speak with us appearing in front of our TV cameras. It won't be the first visit for they have visited us down through history. They are not here to harm us, and in fact, are even now protecting us. Their technology is far superior to our own.

We will visit other life forms on other planets. To gear up for our travels through the Universe, we will first explore our solar system. It all started with the Moon. Along the way, we will develop fantastic technologies. To do this we must all work together, unlike our first visit to the Moon.

The gold standard for truth is whatever works. Science and religion will lead the way in the search for truth. Honesty is the key principle in science for this search. The unification of everyone in science, freely and honestly sharing information, will escalate the increase in technology. Think of the implications of all the world's scientists freely sharing information with no military secrets. Today this is unthinkable, but with a world government and trust, it will be a fact.

Improvements in technology will be based on new ideas, different from past ideas. In recorded history, all our energy sources have been based on force. We are soon to transition to attraction as the basis of energy sources, a totally different idea. The toxicity of past energy sources will pass into history, as non-toxic attraction eventually supplies all our energy, and supplies it very cheaply.

Love, or God, is the source of energy to power everything. In our Physical World, we experience this as magnetism. Love joins things, and people. Energy is produced in a magnetic vortex through compression and expansion around a zero point. Each successive compression produces new energy with the energy being released with each expansion. All primary particles and energies work this way. In the Universe, there is a fixed and stable amount of energy available including magnetism. Through Love, there is an additional unlimited amount of energy available. To tap into this energy, scientist must understand the properties and completeness of infinity. Understanding energy as a potential, mathematically expressed as a quantity, a constant, and a quality, we will be able to understand conditions of infinity. $E=MC^2$ is an example of such an expression. Magnetism is accessed through the paradigm shift to attraction from our current force-based technology and using attractor fields and alignments of infinity. This will be better understood when scientists understand primary particles (particles of infinity), and unity of infinity.

The idea of limitation, especially the perceived scarcity of resources, has produced a competition for these resources. There is no scarcity. We have access to unlimited amounts of energy, and energy can be compressed into matter to produce anything we want. In the near future, an overlooked technology will be coming into use to allow the cost-free production of electricity except for the cost of the machine to produce it. This is a resonance machine requiring an initial input of energy to start the machine, and then it uses a little of the energy it produces to power a resonance core and an electric motor to keep it running to produce more electricity than it uses. And in the next fifty years, other types of technology will be developed to produce other sources of free energy. This technology will be initially opposed by big corporations, but this new technology will solve our current energy problems. As time passes there will be other solutions for other energy problems of the future. Problems will be fixed at the place they were created with more advanced thinking. The answers are right in front of us for us to find. We will think outside the box using unlimited ideas about Life.

Presently we don't have the technology to travel to the nearest star, and travel in our own solar system is difficult. We will slowly explore our own solar system, and when we develop the technology, we will explore our galaxy, and eventually the Universe. We will develop the technology to use "folds" in the framework of space to travel great distances in very little time. New forms of energy will be developed to propel us throughout the Universe. Becoming peaceful will facilitate our travels.

These other sources of energy will be cheaper, less polluting, and less damaging to the Earth, and they will solve a lot of our problems. But if we don't change our beliefs based on fallacies, our domination mindset including conquering the Earth, belief consumption is beneficial, and population growth is desirable, we will continue to court disaster.

As we master our inner world, we will find we are better able to master our outer world. We will see the correlation between our ideas and the manifestation of objects and events in our lives. This will demonstrate our creative powers to ourselves. New technologies will force us to make what we term moral and ethical decisions. Based on past beliefs some of us will denounce these technologies as wrong and immoral even if the new technologies will work wonders. These wonderful new technologies may be ignored initially, but over time they will eventually be adopted, just because they work. This will be a major evolutionary step for humanity.

As we decide to work for Life, we will base decisions on the long term. Short term decisions may work over a short period of time but are less productive than long-term solutions. Indeed, many of these short-term solutions are now shortening our lives. Anything detrimental to the human body should be avoided. Poisons are poisons, even if it takes fifty years to cause death. We will eventually learn this, but we would do well to learn it now. Life is a choice. Eating poisons is a choice for death.

Now, we can do a lot to improve our health by just eating properly and exercising our bodies regularly. This is a choice for Life. These two simple steps will radically improve our health and save billions of dollars in health care costs each year if everyone did them. Also, no thinking person would eat or do anything harmful to the body. This means no smoking or drug use. These are choices for death. Eventually, we will come to know eating organic foods and living on vegetarian diets are the healthiest way to live while eating foods tainted with pesticides, genetically modified foods, and food from dead animals are less healthy. When we take care of our bodies we will live longer. This transition will take hundreds of years and will really accelerate when we develop substitutes tasting just like the various meats we consume today, but with more nutrition, according to Tom Moore's October 18, 2014 *Gentle Way News*.

In the future, our agricultural practices will change to reflect our desire for organic foods. Plants will be used as the basis of new better tasting meals. The use of pesticides and inorganic fertilizers will eventually cease. Genetic breeding will continue, but with more care so as not to produce undesirable plants such as Johnson grass. Mother Nature will be the yardstick used to determine how to farm. In the long run, we will learn how to live in a symbiotic relationship with the insect and disease pests of our crops, and with Earth itself.

The future for antibiotics is not good. Bacteria can always outsmart us. Instead of waging war on bacteria, learning to live in a symbiotic relationship with them is the ultimate solution. Instead of fearing and hating them, we should love and care for them. We will discover stimulants in the future to create this mutually beneficial partnership. We are One with Everything including bacteria and loving all life forms leads to eternal life.

Sickness is encouraged by large corporations for financial gain. Any illness is produced by our own creative selves. We can selfheal if we so choose, and we may believe in any therapy to achieve health. We may also use the illness as a vehicle to leave the Physical World. Our therapies have changed in the past and will continue to change into the future. Presently, we are transitioning from pills to homeopathic remedies, and will eventually use DNA therapies. Eventually, we will learn to use our innate abilities to selfheal and our beliefs will prevent all diseases.

In the long run, self-sufficient communities will replace cities. This will return us to the awe and wonder of life and the wonder of the Earth. We will live kinder, gentler lives with the end of wars on ourselves or other organisms. Psychologically, there will be an end to worry, hate, rage, jealousy, panic, shame, and guilt, all detrimental to our bodies. The definition of the self will be enlarged to include everyone. This will facilitate humans living longer.

Just as we have health campuses now with a concentration of health services, there will be health communities providing health services in the future. These communities will have beautiful and peaceful landscaping integrating nature throughout. These places will be sanctuaries for the ill of mind, body, and spirit. By applying the correct frequencies of sound and light the body can be balanced and healed. Healing sounds and lights, physical exercise, nutrition, emotional strengthening, and joy of expression will be some of the modalities used for healing. Joy and laughter will be very important healing treatments. We will be able to monitor the energy distribution of the body, and by adjusting, health can be restored. Health will be maintained by exercising the mind and body, eating nutritional meals, and meditating each day. Good health involves caring for our minds, our bodies, and our spirits, and in the future, our goal will be to keep our bodies healthy so there is no need to heal them.

If we could see the technological advances two hundred years from now, we would be blown away, and we will continue to develop for another 7,000 years as Tom Moore says in his October 18, 2014 *Gentle Way News*.

Politics

Governments should be inclusive, unlimited, eternal, and free, so they can support all citizens as they evolve. They function best when they are separate from religions and are not influenced by money from businesses or other sources.

However, the totality of the citizens' sacred beliefs should form the basis of any government's rules and regulations. This is the way it is. As the citizens' beliefs evolve, so should the government with elected representatives truly representing the wishes of the public. In the future the people of the world will hold more similar beliefs in common, producing similar political systems.

All our present problems come from having beliefs based on fallacies. As time passes, our beliefs will change, more quickly than in the past, and eventually, they will be based on the truth. We will eventually believe we are omnipotent, creator of everything, omnipresent, unlimited, totally free, omniscient, inclusive, peaceful, lacking vengeance, and equal, and then define our politics this way.

Over time, our beliefs will evolve to the point where we all will hold similar fundamental beliefs. As we unite in our beliefs, we will see ourselves as citizens of the world, uniting us further. Uniting our efforts in all fields will increase our evolution in all fields exponentially. Our destiny is political unity, religious unity, the unity of nations, the unity of races, the unity of language, and our unity as humans to produce lasting peace and prosperity.

As time passes, nations will join as the European Union has for economic reasons. Eventually, the countries on a continent will be joined together. In a few hundred years we should be ready to form a government of the whole world, making of our governments what we are as humans, united. By then, governments will be more transparent and will be working for the welfare of the citizens, and not special interests.

A peace treaty will be signed by all countries forming a federation of nations with three branches of government, legislative, judicial, and executive. The legislative branch will be composed of representatives from the various nations to enact the laws. The judicial branch will settle disputes eliminating the need for war. The executive branch will run the government. The best-qualified people will serve in the various positions of government. The various nations will disarm except for local police forces to keep the peace. The federal government will maintain security forces to protect worldwide commerce. If any nation breaks the peace, all nations of the world will confront the offending country. The tremendous savings from not having to arm the nations of the world will be diverted to improving the living conditions of all humans, to end starvation, to clothe the needy, to provide housing for the poor, to care for the elderly, and to provide health care for everyone. The united-world government will allow the sharing of the world's resources. This will be a gigantic step to produce world peace. As time passes, this government will evolve as we evolve. The government will shrink, and our freedom will increase as we individually take responsibility for our lives. The form of government may change from a representative democracy to rule by a small committee.

The final, complete, and sustainable solution is spiritual where world peace is created by the internal peace of all the citizens of the world. This will take more time, but it will happen.

Governments of the future will work for the independence of all citizens, allowing them to exercise their personal power, creativity, and ingenuity, granting them dignity. Each person will know they can provide for themselves. Governments will assist those in need while moving them toward self-sufficiency. They will write accurate histories, so corrections can be made to correct past mistakes. Decisions will be made to provide a win-win solution best for all involved. Laws will reflect our unity and divinity. As time passes and as we evolve, fewer and fewer laws will be needed. We will eventually, each, be self-governing. In the future, we will love and care for everyone, not just our family and friends, allowing us to govern our individual selves and making laws unnecessary. When we live as One, awareness, honesty, and responsibility will guide the actions and activities of our governmental bureaucracy.

Governments will shrink, and taxes will be reduced. Eventually, taxes will be eliminated and replaced with donations. The citizens of the world will gladly donate 10% of their incomes to support these enlightened governments, with no tax forms to complete, just a simple donation. There will be major changes in how we govern ourselves. For example, the copyright and patent laws will be rewritten to reflect our unity and be based on sharing, and the wars over these rules and regulations will end because they're non-productive.

Procreation is important, but we've gone overboard producing the highest peak in world population ever in recorded history. Soon, the population will drop because of a drop in our birthrate, and because of calamities and war. Earth's population will eventually stabilize much smaller than today.

Living in communities is the way to live. Communities will eventually replace large cities, and will be more efficient with a moderate population, and will vary from place to place dependent on resources and other factors. The population should be diverse in ages, sexes, interests, and abilities to make each community self-sufficient. They will operate with respect for the Earth. Renewable resources will be used when possible instead of non-renewable types.

Practicing the concept of community is a demonstration of oneness. We and God are all One. And we are all One with Mother Earth. This unity is important to building communities on the land.

The practice of community doesn't require a location on Earth. Community is the communion of the souls regardless of location. Each person we meet can be a reunion with ourselves. Community is the reconnection with "others."

In the future, we will be part of many different types of communities with apparently different goals of service, but all in communion leading to the evolution of the soul. We need not wait till these communities are built to experience community. Each person we meet provides an opportunity for communion and community. We only need let prejudice and all artificial boundaries evaporate.

Communities will be developed to replace large cities in local areas populated by people with similar interests. They will share the food supply, the energy sources, and living space while working to ensure an adequate supply of all these things. These communities will provide for survival, safety, and human communion.

The first step in constructing a community is to build a nurturing, safe, functional structure. The ideal structure is decentralized, generally small, providing equality for all, and giving a voice to all in the operation of the community. Good quality leaders, who are humble, who nurture others, who follow what works, and who give without expecting anything in return, are important. These leaders, who in general are elders with much wisdom, experience, and expertise, are the essential members of the community and will be utilized instead of removing them from participation as is done presently with the older members of our world. These communities will recognize and utilize the abilities of these elders.

Leadership positions in these communities are not positions of power, but positions of responsibility. The leaders will be caring and effective, present, accessible, noncritical, non-abusive, and thus providing for the success of the community. Communities set up to sell members something, or control them, or to exploit them will fail. The successful ones will be independent, and self-sufficient. They will have the best chance of surviving boom-and-bust economic cycles, as well as major catastrophes because of the sharing and union of the members.

The biggest difficulty in establishing a community is the corporate job market where workers come home after a day's work too exhausted to do much except watch TV. The key to establishing a community is having the people involved interdependently with one another for survival, friendship, and/or livelihood. They could be living and working together, just working together, or living in proximity to each other and providing goods and services among themselves. This last method was the way life was a hundred or more years ago in small-town America where a small town was the hub of a community with farmers selling their produce to the members of the town and the town providing their goods and services to the farmers.

Just living close to each other is not enough. Rural land is not required. It can be done with no land. The community can be a virtual community with the members widely separated with communication taking place on the internet. Communion among the members of the community is important.

It is good for us to associate with people who share similar beliefs and intentions with us. Sharing a group consciousness with associates produces joy and comfort and provides support for one another. This association could be a church, temple, ashram, or another positive group. It could also mean associating with family members, or friends who have similar beliefs. A trend of the future will be the formation of new spiritual communities centered on common beliefs, meditation, and group expression.

The evolution of communities will occur over a long period of time. As with all things, communities should be based on freedom, should be unlimited, and should be based on love. They will take on a wide variety of shapes, no two being the same.

Tremendous changes are about to take place causing the shifting and elimination of large populations. To survive, we will favor life, love, personal integrity, and community. All relationships will be open and honest, and we will live our lives as a reflection of who we are. We will face the future unafraid.

When it comes to the type of government we choose for ourselves, we will choose a government providing individual freedom where we each take responsibility for our actions, and a government recognizing the worthiness of each person. It will combine freedom with caring for all, and will be unlike anything used today, and will be based on love, sharing, and freedom. Christ Consciousness will be fully developed in all citizens in the future. Governments will be simpler with advisory bodies guiding them, and there will be no laws. This will require thousands of years to evolve.

We are all powerful. No despot can retain power over us without our consent. We will decide how to rule the world.

Law and the Penal System

Daniel Okrent in his book, *Last Call: The Rise and Fall of Prohibition,* said the attempt to stop the use of alcohol by legislation only produced more crime, corruption, hypocrisy, pain, suffering, and murder, and eliminated an income for governments from taxes on alcohol. Morality cannot be legislated, and prohibition in the United States is an example of this failure.

The current drug laws in many countries are likewise failing. Being the free spirits with free will we are, anything limiting our freedom will be met with opposition. The drug laws will be repealed, the sale of drugs will be regulated and taxed, and drug use will be treated as the health issue it is. This will reduce the prison population and associated costs, generate more income from taxes, and divert income from drug cartels. There will be a spike in the use of drugs once decriminalized, but drug use will slowly fall over time as the novelty wears off.

When life becomes unbearable for anyone, many turn to alcohol or drugs to make it more endurable. When, not if, we change the world to make life the joyous, exciting, exhilarating experience it can be for everyone, alcohol or drugs will no longer be needed as a crutch. A thoughtful person would never take anything into their body causing damage to it, something both drugs and alcohol do. As we evolve we will eventually refuse to put anything harmful into our bodies.

Victimless crimes will be abolished granting us all the right to fully exercise our free will. If free will is freely used by all involved in the event, it need not be considered a crime.

Although this world and everything in it are all illusions and no one can be harmed, any abuse such as murder, rape, terrorism, and family abuse, must be stopped and not allowed to continue. Both the abuser and the abused are both abused by allowing the abuse to continue. Since we are all One, what someone does to another, they do to themselves. Once the abuse is stopped, those involved can be healed. When we finally realize we hurt ourselves when we hurt someone, the hurting of others will cease.

Our penal system will cease to be for punishment. The goal will be the reformation of the person if possible. There are some who will need to be separated from society because they will continue to harm people and property. But even so, punishment will not be a part of the treatment of people in the system.

Rehabilitation of the lawbreaker will start with an overview of the process and include motivation for change. But no one will be forced to change or be rehabilitated. This all involves a change of beliefs and understandings of how life works.

Providing plants and pets to residents of mental hospitals and minimum-security prisons are important therapeutic aids. To help offenders to heal, they must be engaged in a non-judgmental manner that allows them to share their emotions freely. They must be willing to take responsibility for the offense to heal, but they must be allowed to do this freely. Then they must be lead past self-hatred by discovering the why of the event. People who commit unspeakable acts against another, are really confused, frustrated, and experiencing pain and self-hatred. They are emotionally diseased. Unfortunately, criminals and terrorists are treated with disrespect with little or no opportunity to receive help for their condition. This allows criminals and terrorists to multiply and continue to be a problem. Our world is not dealing with the root cause of the problem. The solution is to develop within each of us an understanding we are all magnificent creatures who are loved, respected, appreciated, and unified with the Whole, and to develop as joyful and happy people. Then we will know if we injure another person, we are injuring ourselves. By changing from a mindset of fear to trust, anyone can be changed from a villain to a loving person.

Finally, when someone is ready for release from prison, the system will not just throw them out the door and leave them on their own. Job training will be part of the rehabilitation process, and each person will have a job, transportation to the job, and a place to live when they leave the system. Anything less will set the lawbreaker up for failure and a return to lawbreaking.

In the future, we will base our laws on what works to get us to our goals, and not on morals. First, we will have to define our goals, the hard part. We will eliminate the death penalty because it doesn't work. It cost more and doesn't deter murder. In a strange way, we have laws saying we should not kill, and then we kill the murderer. This vengeful justice will end, and we will work to rehabilitate criminals because it's cheaper than locking them up in prison. Transgressing a law is not a moral failure, but an incorrect choice. We will end our system of rewards and punishments. Jail will only be used to prevent continued transgressions of the law. Everyone will be allowed to experience the consequences of their actions, allowing all of us to realize the necessity of adjusting in our lives when we make an incorrect decision. Transgressors will be given the opportunity to become aware of all the outcomes of what they did, honestly assess their role in the events, and take responsibility for the outcomes. Then they can correct, change, or heal as necessary. Offenders who commit acts of violence such as rape should be held accountable. This makes a positive statement about how individuals in our society should treat one another. Judgment is never appropriate, and eventually, we will evolve to the place where we do not judge.

In the future, all "deaths" will be seen as choices because we all have free will and it is impossible for any of us to "die" without our permission. None of us actually "dies" because we are immortal. We just change shapes. This puts a different perspective on suicide, assisted suicide, and murder, and we will change our laws to reflect this truth.

Laws relating to crime will be simple. Crime destroys unity and must be addressed, but endless lists of right and wrong don't work. We will learn forgiveness is more important. When we live in Love, laws will be unnecessary. This is exemplified by loving God with all our heart, and our neighbors as ourselves. As we treat everyone fairly, crime will be reduced. Everyone should be treated with unconditional love regardless of past offenses, restoring offenders to full brotherhood. There is a need for trust, and we will develop this attribute. With us being One, it is impossible to have victims and villains. Any condemnation or punishment is done by us to ourselves.

Crimes are the result of conditions we have created. Correct the conditions, and the crimes will cease. Treat everyone fairly, with loving respect and attention, and provide all with the essentials to live a full and productive life, with equal opportunity for all. End starvation and prejudice. End sexual taboos and restrictions and allow everyone to enjoy the wonder of sexual energy properly channeled. Each should be given the freedom to be themselves. Raising our children correctly will greatly reduce crime. Our young delinquents are not delinquents by nature. They are neglected, and they know it, and so they take their anger out on society. The solution is to provide them with loving attention.

Those who have mental illnesses, drug addiction, or alcoholism will be treated for their health problems, and not committed to prison. This is dealing with the root cause of the problem and not the symptom.

Civil law will evolve too. No one will be forced to keep a promise. We change, our beliefs change, and we don't know the future, so we can't make a promise in good conscious. Written agreements will become a thing of the past. Forcing people to keep promises against their will inflects damage both ways. Force solves nothing, and revenge injures the one seeking revenge. Granting others freedom grants us freedom. Legal documents, agreements, and loyalty should not be used to maintain conformity. Such restrictions restrict creation. There are consequences for our actions, and we will take responsibility for our actions. The place of least restriction is love. All of us are innocent.

For now, we will need police, prisons, courts, and lawyers. We can change the function of our penal system to a rehabilitation system. We can reduce the number of prison offenses. We can restructure the court system to eliminate the advantage the wealthy enjoy. We can work to eliminate the root causes of crime. And as time passes, the need for police, prisons, courts, and lawyers can be reduced. Eventually, we will live peacefully without any laws. But for now, and for a long time to come, we will need laws and prisons to protect us from ourselves.

Economics and World Hunger

Our current economic system exchanges ownership of something or some service provided for some form of money. It could be coins, paper, or an electric transfer of the ownership of money for some goods or services. Credit is built into the system where we can spend money we don't have by borrowing the money from some person, or business in exchange for the payment of interest on the borrowed money. This system is built on the fallacy we are separate. There have been other systems in the past, and we will have still others in the future.

In the distant future, when we evolve to the point we can share the whole world with everyone, and trust each other, we will no longer need money. Then, hoarding will not exist, and we all will take an interest in the wellbeing of everyone in the world. Our present desire to collect things of the world will cease when we find spiritual things more interesting and satisfying. Eventually, we will only buy what we love, and never to simply acquire. We will find spiritual truth, spiritual reality, and spiritual experience the focus of our lives. Our desire will be to experience the greatest feeling of love we can imagine through expressing love. We will be absorbed in knowing God, self-discovery, growth, fulfilling ourselves, and expressing the Truth. Economic systems will have zero interest for us. All this will happen after we go through other systems.

We will provide equal opportunity to everyone, although we won't guarantee each will achieve equality of positions, possessions, or fame. Each will be ensured of having the basic essentials of food, clothing, shelter, education, healthcare, with equal opportunity for advancement. No one will starve to death! We will nurture all humans by supplying not only economic and biological needs, but also with thought, emotion, play, work, celebration, and worship.

Living as One, and living as one big world community, means we will increase our quality of life, ensure our survivability, and accelerate our evolution as we share the Earth's resources, share our technology, share our beliefs, and share ourselves. We will share information, truth, liberty, honor, and the right to exercise free will.

Compensation will be different soon. Those tasks needed for a community to exist will be the most highly rewarded. Words such as drudgery, overtime, pressure, and phrases such as getting ahead, rising to the top, and being successful will disappear for lack of use. Fame and fortune as goals will be replaced with producing benefits for all. We will be compensated based on the value of what we produce. What is the value of producing a financial report, or the value of educating one student, or the value of producing one pair of shoes? Robots will do all the repetitive, boring jobs, freeing many of us for more creative work. Initiative, imagination, and creativity will skyrocket. Inflation will become a thing of the past when we use organizational efficiencies to increase production by doing such things as learning new skills and attracting and utilizing the help of others. The economies of the future will be based on producing value and perceiving value. Leisure time will increase.

Compensation and payments for goods and services will be fair. Too little or too much are both inappropriate. By giving fairly, we will receive fairly. In all exchanges, we are all really exchanging love, even though it may appear we are exchanging money for goods or services. What's really happening is we are exchanging friendship, trust, and values to build justice. Without justice, there is no trust. Without trust, there is no civilization.

In the future, businesses will try for win-win solutions. Even competing businesses will have more success by sharing knowledge and technology. All businesses who share will expand. Expansion is the name of the game in life. Opposing the expansion of anyone or any business opposes life and opposes the opposer. Our economies will not be based on supply and demand because a win-win solution is not provided with this system but will be based on sharing. Ownership as a word will be erased from our vocabulary for we will freely share all things in our possession with everyone because everyone is us. The law of the Universe is the more we share, the more we will receive. We are the stewards of everything in our possession.

Respecting the rights of others naturally facilitates sharing when needed. We will respect, and trust others, and share the whole world.

In the world of business, true profits benefit everyone. False profits are just the moving of money around to ensure power.

We have periods of expansion and compression, and so will it ever be. All things are cyclical. If the expansion and compression cycles are out of balance, failure will occur. As we implement spiritual solutions for the economy, these cycles will continue with only minor disruptions if we go with the flow and don't try to eliminate the compressions.

Living moderately will be the accepted way to live in the future. All things will be done in moderation including the accumulation of wealth and physical comforts, the amount of food eaten, mental activities, work, and play. Even our institutions, corporations, and governments will be moderate.

We will develop spiritualistic capitalism where we will develop a belief in abundance, and we will do what we love to do while serving the world and earning money and trying to produce the highest benefits for everyone. We will eliminate all systems and beliefs based on scarcity, such as acquisition, hoarding, and greed. Goods and services will be freely, fluidly and copiously exchanged. This will prevent hunger, and unemployment, and provide for the utilization of workable ideas. Our idea money is bad will change to money is a useful tool being neither good nor bad. We will love our fellow humans instead of loving money. Our socioeconomic systems will be changed to end the discrimination of any group of people. The two greatest changes in the field of economics will be our change in beliefs to "We are all One," and "there is enough." We will greet each person we meet as another version of us having a different experience, and we will act like and believe there is an abundance of everything we need. In addition, we will not destroy or waste our natural resources. It all starts with knowing God.

Our charity and benevolent actions will be aimed at helping others to become independent of any help as soon as possible. Whether it's personal or through governments, the aim is the same - to produce independence. All we do is for ourselves because there is only us. We are all One.

The hardest thing to deal with in dealing with poverty is poverty consciousness. For those who believe they are poor, to become independent and self-sufficient, they must develop a deep sense of empowerment and self-esteem. We may start with giving food to the poor to prevent malnutrition or starvation, but we will then have to change their beliefs, so they now believe they can rise above poverty. They will be taught they are worthy of abundance. We are all deserving, and we will remind them they are inherently worthy and all of us are inherently equal. All of us are by nature kind, pure, worthy, innocent, and beautiful just as we are. We are light and love, and we are Divine with incomparable value. We are all powerful spiritual beings capable of doing anything. At the same time, we would empower them by giving them training or some form of education to allow them to provide for themselves. We will all move from the idea we don't have enough intelligence, enough education, enough beauty, enough money, or enough of anything thus making us inferior. We will empower ourselves by accepting ourselves just as we are. Once one-person escapes poverty, this person can then be used as an example for others to follow. Changing beliefs and emotional habits take time. As these change, the world will change. We must walk our own path, believing in ourselves, and contribute to the transformation of the world in our own unique way.

Poverty is an inner state of mind. If we can experience our own Divinity, gratitude, and fulfillment, then we will experience abundance no matter how poor we are. We will have our emotional and physical needs provided for and surround ourselves with beauty. We will create our soul's desires, providing us with more than any material thing can.

The first big step to producing a world where the basic needs of everyone would be provided for and opportunities for advancement would be available to all will occur in a few hundred years when a one-world government will be established. The second step will occur about a thousand years later when a spiritual change takes place where we live as One and live in abundance. These shifts would produce a peaceful resolution to all disputes, end poverty, starvation, and mass exploitation of people and resources, stop the destruction of the Earth, end the need for bigger, better, and more, provide an equal opportunity for all to reach their highest expression of themselves, and end limitation and discrimination. The redistribution of wealth would not be required, but the free access to the Earth's resources would voluntarily occur. Basic needs such as adequate shelter, clothing, and food would be provided guaranteeing basic dignities.

As is today, some will amass more wealth than others, but all will be richer because of the joy of doing what each one loves to do. An arbitrary upper limit on income would be agreed to by everyone. Anything earned above this figure would be donated to the world charitable trust in the donor's name. Everyone would know who the donors are. Donors would have a say in how sixty percent of the money is used. The other forty percent would be used in legislated programs by the world federation. The concentration of wealth in the hands of a few is the largest single factor producing the most persistent social, and political problems in the world.

The money saved through the elimination of the mass production of weapons of war would be enough to supply the basic needs of the world. The ten percent donation would elevate the entire world's population to new levels of dignity and abundance. The contributions from earnings above the established ceiling on earnings would end jealousy and social anger because of unheard of opportunities, and the resulting satisfaction of the world's population.

In the future, all our money transactions will be transparent. This will transform the world, producing fairness, honesty, and the best for all of us. Our compensation will be published for all to know. Everyone will know how much each person, business, corporation, government, and religion have, and how the money is used. When this happens there will be a revolution in the world's population demanding and getting fairness. Transparency produces appropriate behavior.

A totally transparent monetary system will replace the system in use today. All transactions would be visible, traceable, and accountable. The new system would give credits for goods and services produced, and debits for goods and services used. All transactions would be covered including interest earned, wages and salaries, tips, lottery winnings, inheritances, and gifts. Credits would be needed to buy anything. This would be the only currency. All records would be open to everyone. Each would know more about everyone and everything then at any time in the past. Consumers would know the costs of production to corporations for products for sale, in addition to their price.

We will be transparent about everything. All records for each person, government or business would be open to inspection at any time. There would be no secrets or private matters. Being One, it's impossible to hide anything forever anyway.

Today we try to hide our information, and such transparency would be vehemently opposed. But the day is coming when we will let the light of day in and become totally transparent. This may take a thousand years.

Education and Raising Our Youth

"Except ye be converted, and become as little children, ye shall not enter into the kingdom of heaven. Whosoever therefore shall humble himself as this little child, the same is greatest in the kingdom of heaven" (Matthew 18:3-4).

Our children are clean slates waiting for us to write upon them with our beliefs, taboos, customs, and cultural stories. We pass all these ideas on to them because we believe them to be true. After all, our parents and culture passed all this information to us. But what if these "facts" contain errors? They do. To make matters worse, we don't teach our children to think for themselves, because we want them to believe like us. And if they end up believing something else, we excommunicate them.

As time passes, we will come to understand the education of our children is not about passing on "facts," but about instilling in our children a sensitivity, awareness, understanding, compassion, acceptance, a celebration of, and appreciation for Life. They will be totally awed by the wonder of Life.

In the future, ownership will cease to exist, and parents will no longer "own" their children. They never did anyway, but then it will be official. Now parents are responsible for raising their children. In the future, the community will take responsibility for raising our children. The elders of the community will oversee the raising and education of children. The accumulated wisdom of many years makes older people uniquely qualified to raise children. The elders will pass on to our children our wisdom, teachings, and traditions with the understanding this is the best information we have now, and it is subject to change. In the future, producing offspring at a young age will be allowed because the elders will raise the babies, resulting in the elimination of sexual repression, rape, deviance, and dysfunction. Even now, many grandparents end up raising their grandchildren. Childbearing is best done by those with young strong bodies. Child raising is best done by those with well-developed and strong minds based on the experience of many years. The parents may be involved as much as they wish but will not be burdened with the responsibility. Today many young children who become parents are forced into raising their own children, a job they are unprepared and unqualified to do. And they and their children suffer for it. A major cause of juvenile delinquency is lack of love and attention for our young, but this won't happen in the future because each child will feel wanted, appreciated, valued, and loved. All children will be taught each is unique, each has a wonderful body, and each has unlimited potential to do great things in their chosen field of endeavor. All children will experience unconditional love and be taught they are love and are spiritual beings using bodies to navigate this world. Being spiritual beings, they have unlimited potential and abilities. Shame and guilt will be removed from their experience, and love will not be withheld. They will be taught to love everyone, eliminating prejudices. The elders would provide the education and values for the children, in addition to overseeing the housing, feeding, and care for them. The entire community would provide the physical, social, and spiritual needs of the children. This is a major paradigm shift for our societies, so it will take centuries for this change to take place.

For this system to be implemented, first, we must realize our present system has problems. And then we must learn to recognize what is so and learn to recognize the truth when we see it. Next, we must build communities and extended families. Finally, we must honor our elders and put them to work.

Tom Moore in his December 13, 2014 newsletter, *The Gentle Way News,* said our use of computers and the internet, would drastically change the way we educate our youth, making our school systems obsolete. Computers will be used at earlier ages than presently. In time skull caps will download information into the students' brains the way information is downloaded into a computer in a relatively short period of time.

This will allow more time to be spent on working with this information and analyzing it. The students will be taught how to think and reason, and how to arrive at their own truth. The major emphasis will be on critical thinking, problem-solving and logic, and on developing abilities and skills. Children will be allowed to make as many decisions as possible, based on the complete information provided to allow them to make an intelligent decision. The freedom we grant them will be tempered by our knowledge of what is safe for them. Education will be more individualized with each student studying what they are interested in at the moment when learning will be the greatest. At the appropriate time, each student will be evaluated to determine their interests, and their education will be customized to focus on developing these interests. Much of the student's time will be spent alone studying their current interest, but there will be times when the students will assemble to work together on projects. Schools as we now know them will be a thing of the past. Learning centers for various subjects will spring up on the internet and elsewhere, for students of all ages, genders, races, and cultures to use, producing a synergy of diversity stimulating learning at unbelievable rates. This will result in great savings in the costs for transportation and buildings.

Education will involve creativity and fun, instilling an interest and joy in learning. The joy of dance, music, and art will be taught. The mysteries of fairy tales and the wonders of life will be covered. An important skill for teachers will be imagination. Education will be a shared experience with a teacher and student learning from each other. Each child will learn how to experience everything as One, and themselves as Creator, and Authority of their lives. No one will be graded, but feedback on each student's progress will be collected and used to motivate and guide future learning. There will be no competition for best student. Violence in any form will be absent from the raising and education of our children. We will eventually be able to raise children without our scaring them or hurting them, or having violence depicted with our lives, in movies, on TV's, or in games. Children will be taught to be unashamed or unembarrassed of their bodies and bodily functions, and they will be allowed to explore and pleasure their bodies. They will be allowed to progress in their education at their own rates.

Education will be available to everyone, and as much as they want. Now, this is not possible because the money to support schools is lacking. In the poorest of nations, women and girls will be educated first to allow for the transfer of information the fastest. Everyone will be taught they are citizens of the world, not just citizens of one country, and will learn a universal language in addition to their native language, facilitating communication with everyone. This will be important until we learn to communicate through our thoughts with our minds.

The early years of the students' education will cover core concepts. Learning to read, write, and compute with mathematics are important for allowing the students to learn more important concepts. Learning unorthodox abilities not taught in today's schools such as psychic abilities, and manifestation abilities, and meditation will occur just as learning physical abilities for sports. Students will be taught the relevance of what they are learning and will be awed by life by increasing their sensitivity, awareness, understanding, compassion, acceptance, celebration, and appreciation of life. Each generation of students will then be able to foster the higher and higher evolution of civilization.

Core concepts to be taught include:
1. Transparency
2. Sharing
3. Freedom
4. Unlimited Self-expression
5. Joyful Celebration of Sex
6. The Bonding of Humans
7. Our Diversity While Being One
8. Reconciliation, Re-creation, and Reunification
9. Unity with Everything
10. Making Mistakes or Failure is Impossible
11. All creations are Perfect as Created
12. Creating is the Purpose of Life
13. All Actions have Consequences
14. Help and Love Others without Harming Them
15. There is Enough to Make Everyone Happy
16. Life is Eternal without Judgement, Condemnation, or Punishment
17. Creating Through Thinking, Speaking, and Doing

Courses we could teach our young are:
1. The Nature of Power
2. Resolving Conflicts Peacefully
3. Components of Loving Relationships
4. Creation of the Ego and the Person
5. How the Body, Mind and Spirit Function
6. Being Creative
7. Appreciating Ourselves and Others
8. Joyfully Manifesting Sexuality
9. Fairness
10. Tolerance
11. Our Differences and Similarities
12. Ethical Economics

13. Developing the Power of the Mind and Consciousness
14. Life Awareness
15. Honesty and Responsibility
16. Openness and Transparency
17. Spirituality and Science

These would be semester-long courses. The curriculum would change from a facts-based curriculum to a values-based curriculum. Concepts for living would be taught at a very early age. The focus is on understanding the core concepts.

Teachers of the future will ask questions instead of giving answers. Information about past discoveries, observations, decisions, and choices will be presented as information, and not as correct information. Students should be allowed to decide for themselves what is true and correct. Everything from the past will be questioned. Students from earliest ages will be encouraged to examine, to explore, to apply, to functionalize, and to question past values.

Awareness, honesty, and responsibility will be modeled by all adults and easily acquired by children. Children, as at any time, will absorb their culture by watching adults, and in the future, future adults will model enlightened behavior.

Here are some principles for educating our children:

1. We need nothing exterior to ourselves to be happy. No person, place, or thing is needed. Happiness is found within and we are sufficient unto ourselves.
2. God blesses everyone alike. No one needs to compete with anyone to have anything or to have a dignified and satisfied life.
3. Consequences and punishment are two different things. We will experience the consequences of our actions but will never be punished for anything we do. There is no death. God condemns no one.
4. The greatest gift anyone can give is unconditional love. Love has no conditions. All children will be told they will never lose our love or God's love for them.
5. All children are special, but none are superior to another.

6. Children can do anything. Ignorance is an illusion and the illusion can be eliminated. The only need anyone has is to be shown Who They Are.

We will restore respect for life by teaching our children the Universe is a Living System, our Earth is alive, and we are all part of this System. Children taught this will, as adults, revere life, holding it as the most important value. They will see life everywhere from one end of the Universe to the other.

We have a sacred duty to caringly and lovingly raise and educate our children properly, and in the future, we will.

Earth and the Environment

We have abused the Earth even though the Earth supplies everything we need to live. Worldwide we are eroding more topsoil than is being regenerated each year. Guess what happens when we run out of topsoil? Even now people starve to death and most people are malnourished. The biggest producers of oxygen in the world, trees, and phytoplankton, are producing less oxygen over time because of us. The amount of oxygen in the atmosphere is dropping. Guess what happens when we run out of oxygen? Millions of people have poorer health because of toxic chemicals produced by us and put into the air we breathe, the water we drink, and the food we eat. Why would we want to cause our early deaths?

As destructive as we have been to the Earth, we will learn to love, appreciate, respect, and care for the Earth, and everything on it and in it. We will stop destroying rainforests, stop destroying the ozone layer, and stop destroying our ecosystem. We will learn to work with nature, will stop the extreme rates of soil erosion, restore the practice of alternating the crops grown in fields, and abandon the practice of using chemicals to attempt to restore fertility to the infertile soil. We will change our mantra from "more and more", to "enough is enough", and we will share the Earth's resources with everyone, we will cease squandering these resources, and we will use them wisely. Pollution of our air, water, and land will be a thing of the past. Fossil fuels will be replaced with free energy from the Universe.

We will learn to live as if we are all One, One with each other, and One with the Earth, the actual truth of our being.

Advanced thinking will be used to carefully evaluate the development of new technologies, so we don't end up destroying ourselves and the Earth. This involves appreciation and respect for everything. Before we alter the DNA of any organism, we will know the impact it will have on our ecosystem and us. Before we implement technology to control the weather, we will know how the changes will affect the Earth and everything on it.

We will finally understand the Earth by studying the ecology of the Earth, seeing everything as part of One Whole, and learn every organism is important to the whole. This knowledge will empower us. Animals have wisdom and knowledge and are made of the same stuff as us. They are worthy of our respect, and in the future, we will treat them as our equals. Our perspective of the world will change from us and them to only us. Trees, plants, microorganism, and rocks, soil, and water are all part of us. We can communicate with trees. In the future, we will honor and respect every part of the Earth and every organism living on it. Destroying the Earth, or the birds, flowers, grain, or animals on the Earth only destroys us.

Ownership is a construction we have created to ensure we have what we need to survive. It is a defensive mechanism based on a fallacy we have constructed for our own protection. It is based on the fallacy there is not enough of what we need to supply everyone. But there is enough. We will eventually realize we are only stewards of what we have in our possession and learn to share the whole world.

In the far distant future, we won't live in houses or buildings, because we will be able to control the Earth's weather. We will live in the natural environment, just as wild animals do here, and create, control, and maintain the environment. We won't damage or destroy our environment because it supports us.

Now there is enough of everything for all of us to be happy, but for us to be good stewards of the Earth's resources, we must manage them as if they are limited. Up to now, we have been managing our resources as if they were unlimited, wasting them, and have been hoarding these resources for our exclusive use. We will honor the Earth, be good stewards of the Earth's resources, protect the environment, and renew and share the Earth's resources. Cooperation with the Earth and everything on it is our destiny. All of life and everything is life, is sacred. Competition at times is necessary, and killing at times is necessary, such as when we eat. When we eat, we will appreciate the source of our food.

There will be a slow change from eating animals to eating only vegetation over the next several hundred years. Along with this change will be a change to eating only organically grown food. We will learn not to poison ourselves by applying poisons to grow our foods. Farmland will be cared for and erosion will be greatly reduced. Conservation, a way of living for self-preservation, will be practiced in the future. It does not waste resources and is an efficient way to live. Conservation is the wise use of our resources and ensures the sustainability of our resources. The guiding principles for the future for managing the resources of our planet are We are all One, and Everything is interrelated.

We will pay attention to our surroundings, by being alert, alive, aware, and conscious of what is going on, and by seeing what is so, including the divinity in Everything. This will teach us what works and what does not work. The richest and most powerful will lose their control of the Earth's resources because this is not working.

In the near term, we will start accepting new ideas about how life works, and slowly change the way we live and view life. Natural events will force us to make major changes in the way we live. We humans will start living simpler lives, moving away from the image of wealth and status, projecting honestly who we are, and engaging in activities we love to do. Following this will be the recognition of our divine nature and our unity with all living things, including the Earth.

The Next 50 Years

We will still have terrorists, but their impact on the world will lessen over time. The world will become more peaceful. There will be a major shift in power. First, dictators will become extinct. Then China will replace the United States as the number one superpower. By then, the nations will be more benevolent. The people will take back their power, and governments will be more responsive to the wishes of the citizens.

The revolution of the acceptance of gay marriages, and the acceptance of homosexuals and transgender individuals have started, but just as with race, prejudice and discrimination will be with us for a while, although over time it will lessen. Women will obtain true equality with men in most of the world.

Because of major revelations by the Vatican through the release of ancient documents, and the visitation of extraterrestrials, who will inform us of our history, religions will start a major transformation with a major reevaluation of their doctrines and beliefs. There will be those who will resist these changes, but the change will start and gain momentum over time.

Science and technology will develop at a rapid rate with major developments producing non-polluting forms of energy. We will make it to Mars and discover people lived there in the past. We will make major advances in medicine with DNA therapy and the use of a holistic approach to healing, including the use of light, sound, nature, herbs, and self-expression through the arts. As stated in Tom Moore's September 19, 2015 newsletter, *The Gentle Way News*, cures for mental illness will be discovered using DNA therapy. People will start taking better care of their bodies, reducing health care costs, and allowing people to live longer.

More and more healthcare communities will spring up to care for the sick. While we have some communities now, there will be a lot more in the future. Most will be somewhat self-sufficient, and some will be for specific purposes, like assisting people as they transition from the Physical World to the Spiritual (Real) World.

Drugs will be legalized, and drug addicts will be treated as health patients instead of criminals. The use of drugs will be regulated as cigarettes are regulated today. Prostitution will be legalized and regulated in more parts of the world. Capital punishment will be all but abolished. Following these changes, the prison populations will plummet.

Although there will be much suffering from natural calamities, there will be the start of a trend for a smaller Earth population, and the general economic future for most people will be improved. The implementation of free energy machines will spur the development of the poorer countries as stated in Tom Moore's February 7, 2015 newsletter, *The Gentle Way News*. We will make great strides in eradicating starvation.

Education will be much more computer-centric with education being tailored for each student. Logic and critical thinking will be major topics for students.

With new forms of non-polluting energy, air pollution will be almost eliminated, and other forms of pollution will be much reduced. We will make great strides in accepting organic farming.

The Following 400 Years

As time goes by, nations on the various continents will form economic and political alliances like the European Union. This will culminate with the formation of one government for the entire world. These unions and the ultimate one-world government will be major stimulants for economic growth because of the ending of trade restrictions. Peace will be ensured by handling disputes in the court system, and the disarming of the world's nations. This disarming will free tremendous amounts of money the nations will use for the betterment of conditions for their citizens, by ending starvation and providing universal education for all. Transparency will be common in governments, businesses, and religions. These changes will be a major turning point in our evolution.

During this period, prejudice and discrimination will end, as the beliefs of the fathers and mothers being passed down to the children will not contain prejudice. Also, the mixing of the races, especially in the United States, will be well on its way to melding all the races into just one. Women will obtain true equality in the entire world.

Nudity will be more accepted, and shame about our bodies will be reduced. Guilt about sex will be eased. Marriage will continue its transformation with expectations of a lifelong union eliminated.

Religions will finally be tolerant of each other's beliefs and will be actively working with each other to find common ground to work with each other.

By now, we will be well on our way to exploring our solar system. This will lay important groundwork for the exploration of the Universe. Medicine will have extended life expectancy to unimaginable lengths. Initially, decisions will have to be made about who lives and who dies because of limited availability.

The transition to legalizing drugs will be passed, with the number of drug addicts almost eliminated. Because people will take better care of their bodies, and have a better outlook on life, using drugs is not something people will want to do. Prison inmates will be truly rehabilitated and released into society with a great chance of never being returned to prison for a crime. Prison populations will be small. Prostitution, while regulated, will slowly diminish as the economic situation for everyone, especially women, improves and as the world's treatment of sex becomes transparent.

An economic safety net will slowly be implemented where everyone who can work will be guaranteed a job supplying them with a sustainable income. Those unable to work will be guaranteed a sustainable income, as stated in Tom Moore's February 7, 2015 newsletter, *The Gentle Way News*. This will start in the Western nations and spread to the rest of the world. A maximum income will also be set.

Education will incorporate values training as well as training in reasoning, allowing students to think for themselves and decide what works and what doesn't. Students will develop their psychic abilities and become directors of their education.

Education will be creative, and indoctrination will be eliminated. Skull caps will be used to infuse information into students to save time for other more interesting subjects. Coercion and punishment will be phased out of the educational process.

Pollution will be at an all-time low, compared to present conditions. People will become vegetarians, and organic farming will have replaced today's chemical laden farming practices.

The Following 1000 Years

We will have evolved by now to where we will live the peace we feel in our hearts. Our hearts will now ensure the peace the one-world government enforced earlier. We will truly love each other as we love ourselves, and we will truly love ourselves. Our goal in life will be to serve others as we serve ourselves.

We will have total transparency. We will know everything about everything, and this will be OK with everyone. Being One, this is the way to live.

Nudity will be normal. There will be no shame associated with our bodies or our bodily functions. Sex of all kinds will be normal among consenting individuals. Marriages will continue as long as those involved agree to continue the marriage, and if it is decided to end a marriage, those involved will part lovingly. There will be total honesty and transparency in marriages. There will be no guilt associated with any of this.

Religions will be Spirit-filled, and each religion will look more and more like all the others. The joy of a Spirit-filled life will be a characteristic of the citizens of the world.

Science will confirm what religions have said all along, there is a God. Toward the end of this time period, we will be gearing up for a trip to the stars. We will have unimaginable technology.

Medicine will be needed less because of changes in our nutrition, and lifestyles. Everyone will meditate. And if someone becomes sick, doctors will help the patient cure themselves rather easily.

Governments, businesses, and religions will be much simpler in structure. Governments will no longer impose taxes because people will donate ten percent of their income to support governments and their programs. The world population will stabilize at a much smaller number than today.

Laws will be simpler granting us maximum freedom. Eventually, we will be a law unto ourselves. There will be no prisons by the end of this period.

Our economic system will be totally transparent and localized. We will know where all the money goes, what the costs are, and how much each of us gets paid. This will produce fairness like never before. Sharing and availability will the hallmarks of this economy, and it will be based on local communities. The elders will raise our young, and all will receive a customized education. Each person will have an equal opportunity for advancement in life.

We will love the Earth, our home, and do all we can to protect and support it. We will know what we do to the Earth, we do to ourselves.

The Far Future

Evolution is a long drawn out process. We can't jump from the bottom of the ladder to the top in one leap. In fact, there is no top to the ladder, because evolution will never end.

The far future will astound and amaze us. The future will be so different; it will be difficult for us to understand. Eventually, the Earth will be vacated by us and eventually, the Universe will collapse in on itself. Everything created in time will end in time. But we will live on in other dimensions because we were before time.

How to Rule Now

Tom Moore in his May 15 and August 7, 2014 newsletters, *The Gentle Way News*, said the most important thing we can do at present, is to respect and accept people regardless of their race, religion, or sexual orientation. Allow people to be whom or what they are. Allow people to be different. Doing this will produce a more loving world. This is our starting point. We must learn to tolerate other people just as they are.

To change the world, we must first change ourselves. Becoming tolerant is one change. The process starts with reevaluating our current beliefs and eliminating those that are not based on truth. Then, we must be open to new ideas, and they too must be examined for truth. We can start with the ideas listed in this book. Those passing the test are added to our collection of beliefs, and those failing the test are ignored. One person changing has little impact on the world. Groups of people changing their beliefs have a bigger impact of an exponential magnitude. We can start with groups of at least 12 or13 all with the same positive intention to reach a common goal. Starting small, we can develop our skills and then transfer these skills to larger groups where the real power lies to maximize our manifesting power. With any change, when critical mass, i.e., enough people believing the same thing, is achieved, a dramatic transformation of the world will take place. It all starts with us, one at a time. One by one we will break with current society limitations and express our heartfelt longings and visions. To be true to ourselves, we must each fearlessly walk our own path, believing in ourselves, and contributing to the transformation of the world in our own unique way. All this involves going within to find our own truth through meditation.

Meditation is very important for our future. Our inner guidance will lead us to the meditation method best for us. We will be drawn to the books or other sources of information necessary to guide the way we meditate. There is a style for each one of us.

We are all powerful, and we may do things faster or slower than suggested above if we wish. Or we could do things differently. However, it happens, we will rule the world based on our ideas of the truth. Humanity is destined for great things, and great things we will do.

We will always succeed. Failure is an illusion. What we think of as a failure is an aspect of success. Since we are all part of God, "failures" are just aspects of God manifesting.

We have done the seemingly impossible. We know we are conscious, and we have built extraordinary civilizations, with highly developed arts, sciences, philosophy, and spirituality. We will discover as we check out the rest of the Universe, only a small minority of all the life forms in existence have been able to do this. We are loving, dynamic, productive, compassionate, caring beings. We care about the feelings of others and desire the betterment of everyone, and we courageously push the boundaries of our knowledge to create a brighter future. As great as our progress has been, the future will be even greater.

Our evolution will eventually produce a heaven on Earth. Life will be free of fear, judgment, misery, guilt, or blame. We will finally overcome our fear of offending anyone and live our own truth. We will live in total freedom. We will live in a world where there are no rules and regulations, no borders or boundaries, and where anything is possible.

God is infinite and complete freedom, and God's only desire is to expand Love, exactly what God is. When we decide to make our will the same as God's, then we will produce only Love, only what is beneficial, only what is holy, and only what is beautiful.

In our world of illusions, we get to play God. We are unlimited beings who have limited ourselves resulting in the world we see today. We can live our lives in an unlimited fashion where all institutions are based on freedom. This is a new way of living and we will require courage and the desire to do this.

We are always loved, are never alone, can never die, can never lose anything of true worth, can never be separated, are always connected to our creator, always succeed, can never harm anyone or anything, and we are always innocent, lacking the ability to sin.

There is an infinite number of ways to live life. The ways we live our lives now are based on fallacies. This produces difficult and unsatisfying lives. If we lived our lives based on the truth, and eventually we will, we will have the most wealth, the most productive society, the happiest lives, the greatest technology, the best education, the healthiest lives and psyches, the greatest governments and laws, the most spiritual religions, a totally peaceful world, the most fantastic sex, and the healthiest Earthly environment. We will rule the world based on our unity, and to do this we need do nothing, just be love, joy, peace, and freedom (exactly who and what we are), and everything will literally fall into place. All there is, is Us. ALL THERE IS, is LOVE. Let us, therefore, go forth and rule the world in LOVE and UNITY.

References

Abdu'l-Bahá, *Some Answered Questions*, Bahá'í Publishing Trust, Wilmette, Illinois, (1981 ed.)

Andrews, Synthia and Colin Andrews, *The Complete Idiot's Guide to 2012: An Ancient Look at a Critical Time*, Alpha Books, New York, NY

Anonymous, *The Way of Mastery: The Way of the Heart, The Way of Transformation, The Way of Knowing*, Shanti Christo Foundation, Sacramento, CA, 2013

Anonymous, *Christ in You*, DeVorss & Company, Camarillo, CA, 2005

Anonymous, *A Course in Miracles: Combined Volume*, Third Edition, Foundation for Inner Peace, Mill Valley, CA, 2007

Bahá'í International Community, *A Compilation on Women*

Baha'u'llah, *Gleanings from the Writings of Baha'u'llah*, Baha'i Publishing Trust, Wilmette, IL 1994

Baha'u'llah, *Tablets of Bahá'u'lláh Revealed After the Kitáb-i-Aqdas*, Bahá'í International Community

Benner, Joseph, *The Impersonal Life*, Filiquarian Publishing, LLC

Brinkley, Dannion, and Kathryn Brinkley, *Secrets of the Light: Lessons from Heaven*, Harper One, New York, NY, 2008

Coates, Judith, *Jeshua The Personal Christ: Messages from Jeshua ben Joseph (Jesus), Volume 1*, Oakbridge University Press, Tacoma, WA 1995

Coates, Judith, *Jeshua The Personal Christ: Messages from Jeshua ben Joseph (Jesus)*, Volume 2, Oakbridge University Press, Tacoma, WA, 2002

Dwoskin, Hale, *The Sedona Method: Your Key to Lasting Happiness, Success, Peace, and Emotional Well-being*, Sedona Press, Sedona, AZ, 2003

Eckhart Tolle, *A New Earth*, Dutton, a member of the Penguin Group, New York, NY 2006

Green, Glenda, *Love Without End: Jesus Speaks*, Third Edition, Spiritis Publishing, Sedona, AZ 2006

Green, Glenda, *The Keys of Jeshua*, Spiritis Publishing, Sedona, AZ, 2007

Gyatso, Tenzin the 14th Dalai Lama, Spiritual leader of Tibetan Buddhism, Facebook, May 28, 2010

Hardman, Allen, *The Everything Toltec Wisdom Book: A Complete Guide to the Ancient Wisdoms*, Adams Media, and F+W Publications Co., Avon, MA, 2007

Hartmann, Thom, *The Last Hours of Ancient Sunlight: Waking Up to Personal & Global Transformation*, Harmony Books, New York, New York, 1999

Hicks, Ester and Jerry, *Ask and It Is Given: Learning to Manifest Your Desires*, Hay House, Inc., Carlsbad, California, 2004

Moorjani, Anita, *Dying To Be Me: My Journey from Cancer, to Near Death to True Healing*, Hay House, Inc., New York, NY, 2012

Morgan, James Coyle *Jesus and Mastership: The Gospel According to Jesus of Nazareth*, Oakbridge University Press, Tacoma, IL 1989

Newton, Ph.D., Michael, *Destiny of Souls: New Case Studies of Life Between Lives*, Llewellyn Publications, Woodbury, Minnesota, 2000

Peace: More Than an End to War, Selections from the writings of Baha'u'llah, the Bab, Abdu'l-Baha, Shoghi

Effendi, and the Universal House of Justice, Baha'i Publishing Trust, Wilmette, IL, Second Edition 2007

Priwer, Shanna, and Cynthia Phillips, *The Everything Einstein Book: From matter and energy to space and time, all you need to understand the man and his theories*, Adams Media Corporation, Avon, MA, 2003

Roberts, Jane and Robert F. Butts, *Seth Speaks: The Eternal Validity of the Soul*, Prentice-Hall, Inc., Englewood Cliffs, NJ, 1972

Schwartz, Robert, *Your Soul's Gift: The Healing Power of the Life You Planned Before You Were Born*, Whispering Winds Press, U.S.A., 2012

Spalding, Baird T., *Life and Teaching of the Masters of the Far East, Vol. I*, DeVorss Publications, Camarillo, CA 1964

Spalding, Baird T., *Life and Teaching of the Masters of the Far East*, Vol. 2, DeVorss Publications, Camarillo, CA 1972

Status of Global Missions, The Center for the Study of Global Christianity at Gordon-Conwell Theological Seminary, Mid 2015, p 29

The Christ, *New Teachings for an Awakening Humanity,* S.E.E. Publishing Co., Santa Clara, CA, 1994

The Promise of World Peace: to the Peoples of the World, The Universal House of Justice, Baha'i Publishing Trust Wilmette, IL 1985

Walsch, Neale Donald, *Conversations with God: An Uncommon Dialogue, Book 1*, G. P. Putman's Sons, New York, New York, 1996

Walsch, Neale Donald, *Conversations with God: An Uncommon Dialogue, Book 2*, Hampton Roads Publishing Company, Inc., Charlottesville, VA, 1997

Walsch, Neale Donald, *Conversations with God: An Uncommon Dialogue - Living in the World with Honesty, Courage, and Love*, Hampton Roads Publishing Company, Inc., Charlottesville, VA, 1997

Walsch, Neale Donald, *Conversations with God: An Uncommon Dialogue, Book 3*, Hampton Roads Publishing Company, Inc., Charlottesville, VA, 1998

Walsch, Neale Donald, *Friendship with God: An Uncommon Dialogue*, G. P. Putnam's Sons, New York, NY, 1999

Walsch, Neale Donald, *Communion with God*, G. P. Putnam's Sons, New York, NY, 2000

Walsch, Neale Donald, *The New Revelations: A Conversation with God*, Atria Books, New York, NY, 2002

Walsch, Neale Donald, *Tomorrow's God: Our Greatest Spiritual Challenge*, Atria Books, New York, NY, 2004

Walsch, Neale Donald, *Home with God,* Atria Books, New York, NY, 2006

Walsch, Neale Donald, *Happier Than God: Turn Ordinary Life into an Extraordinary Experience*, Hampton Roads Publishing Company, Inc., Charlottesville, VA, 2008

Weiss, Brian L. M.D., Same Soul, Many Bodies: Discover the Healing Power of Future Lives Through Progression Therapy, Free Press, New York, 2004

Wolf, Fred Alan, Ph.D., *Dr. Quantum's Little Book of Big Ideas: Where Science Meets Spirit*, Moment Point Press, Needham, Massachusetts, 2005

Young, Wm. Paul, *The Shack: Where Tragedy Confronts Eternity*, Windblown Media, Newberry Park, CA, 2007

Acknowledgments

First, thanks to AZ and the gang. Their inspiration, prodding, and guiding made this book possible. Otherwise, there would be no book.

I am deeply indebted to all of the authors of the spiritual writings cited in this book. Without their wisdom, there would be no book.

Then there are Reneé Schuler, Rachael Williams, Lois Wagner, Amy Tu, Dr. Lynn Deibler, Mary Boyer, David Boyer, Marian Dressler, Dr. Richard Dressler, and Betty Kemp for their comments on the written material. There would be a book, but it would certainly be of poorer quality without their assistance.

This is certainly a group effort. I am honored to be the spokesman for the group.

www.ingramcontent.com/pod-product-compliance
Lightning Source LLC
Chambersburg PA
CBHW071259110426
42743CB00042B/1099